IMAGES
of America

PHILADELPHIA'S RIVER WARDS

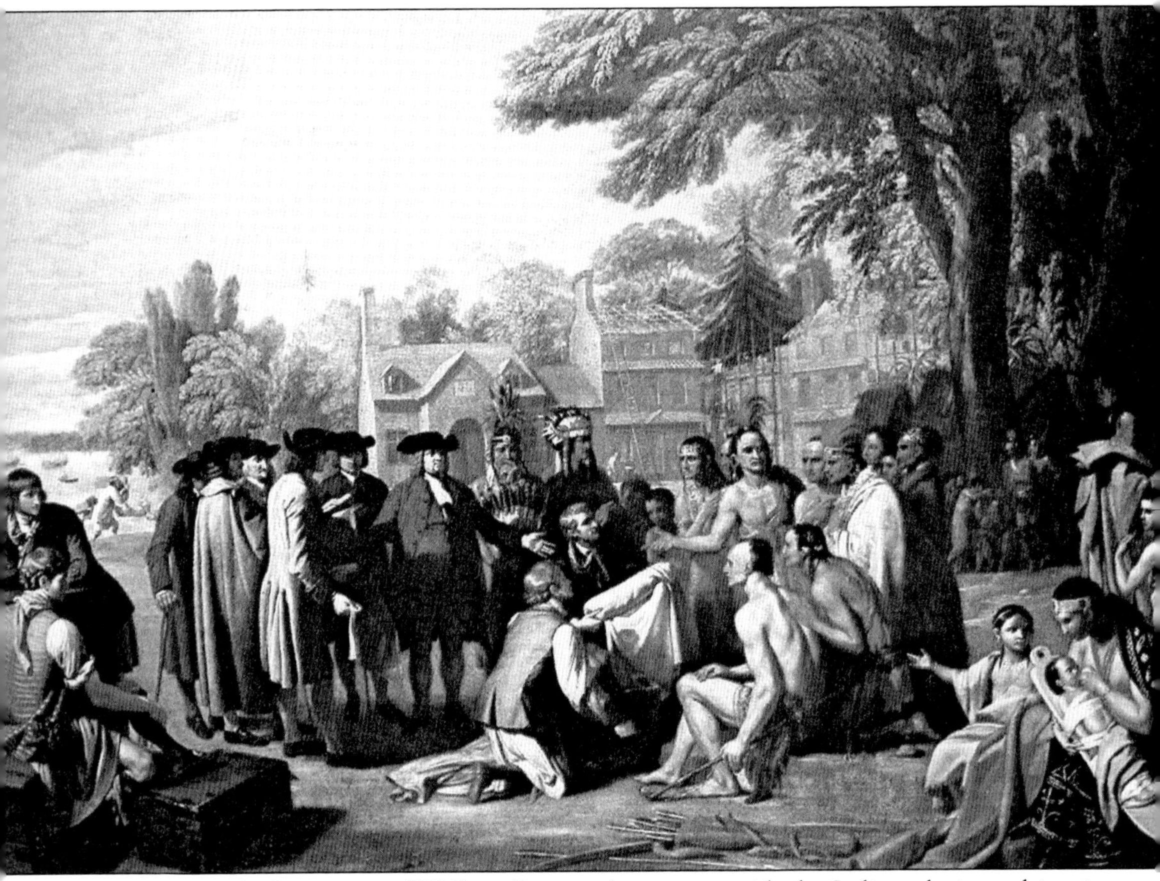

Benjamin West's painting of William Penn making peace with the Indians depicts a historic event of importance to all Americans. It has a more personal meaning for those who grew up and played in the spot where this pact took place. The fact that Philadelphia is the "Cradle of Liberty" makes one who was born and raised in Philadelphia feel special, as well it should. Enjoying the freedoms that were conceived here is a gift for all Americans.

IMAGES
of America

PHILADELPHIA'S RIVER WARDS

George J. Holmes

ARCADIA
PUBLISHING

ISBN 978-0-7385-1212-9

Published by Arcadia Publishing
Charleston, South Caeolina

Printed in the United States of America

Library of Congress Catalog Card Number: 2003103450

For all general information contact Arcadia Publishing at:
Telephone 843-853-2070
Fax 843-853-0044
E-mail sales@arcadiapublishing.com
For customer service and orders:
Toll-Free 1-888-313-2665

Visit us on the Internet at www.arcadiapublishing.com

Author's note: The author welcomes comments at georgeholmes@comcast.net.

*This book is dedicated to the immigrants,
who showed amazing courage by leaving the familiarity of
home to start new lives in a strange, new world. Your determination
was my inspiration. The history of the River Wards is your legacy.*

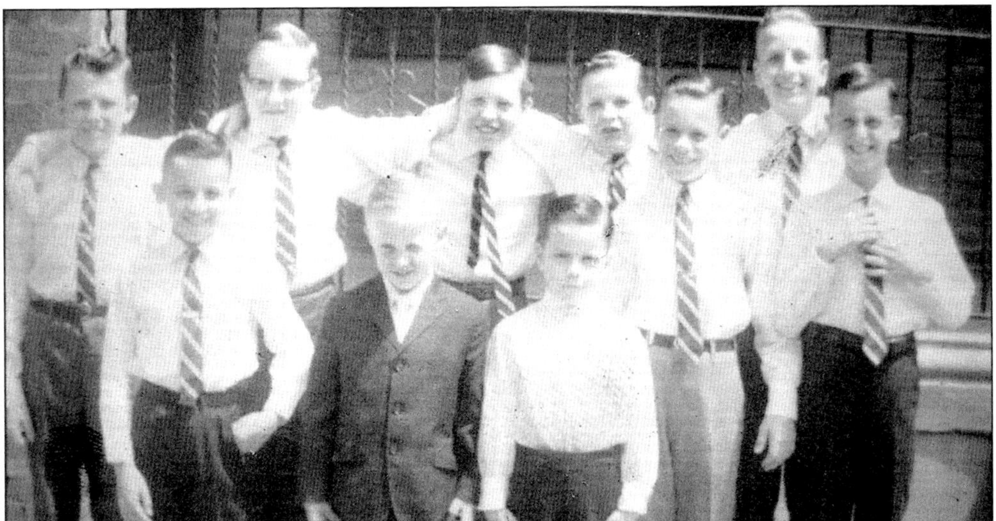

From left to right, Jimmy Johnson, Michael MacIlhenny, Georgie Walsh, Keith Landis, Jimmy Sleva, Michael Sleva, Bobby Landis, Ralphie Thomas, Georgie Holmes, and Franny MacIlhenny pose on the 2100 block of Stella Street before heading off to Nativity Blessed Virgin Mary Church for the yearly boys' May Procession.

CONTENTS

ACKNOWLEDGMENTS

Most of what we accomplish in life could not be accomplished without the help of others. This book definitely lends truth to that statement. First and foremost, I would like to thank my wife, Dot Holmes, for paying attention when the nuns at St. Adalbert's School taught her English and spelling. They taught you well! Thanks, too, for your patience and your belief. Thank you, Allen Hornblum, Ron Avery, and Dr. Steve Davis. Thanks to retired 24th Police District Officer Jim Murphy, Jimmy Tayoun, the crew at the *Philadelphia Public Record*, and Thomas A. Nuxoll, Southeastern Pennsylvania Transportation Authority's (SEPTA) communications manager. To the many neighborhood business owners, past and present; the clergy and staff at the churches and schools; the local amateur historians; the members and employees of the Free Library of Philadelphia; the employees of Temple University Archives; the good folks at Philadelphia City Hall; and certain members of the old K&A gang, thank you all.

Introduction

The northern river area of Philadelphia was the birthplace of an everlasting peace between William Penn and the Lenni Lenape. This region on the banks of the Delaware River, which saw the rise of a new nation, was also the springboard of the American industrial revolution. In the early 1800s, the neighborhoods that made up this area were not yet part of the city but were independent townships.

The 1800s brought a boon to the river townships of Philadelphia. As industry blossomed all along the riverfront, an influx of immigrants found its way to the neighborhoods in search of prosperity. The newcomers found work in Kensington, Port Richmond, Frankford, and Bridesburg in the textile mills and glass industries, and at Stetson Hat Company, Baldwin Locomotive, and Cramp Shipyard, to name a few. But even as industry thrived and more and more immigrants flocked to the area, the "township neighborhoods" became the objects of turf wars as local authorities fought on the street in an attempt to claim the areas. This animosity among the very people who provided public services to the neighborhoods—the volunteer firefighters and constabularies—created a serious danger, as services would not be provided over neighborhood lines. These conflicts caused the dissolution of the townships and their absorption into Philadelphia proper. Although now part of the whole, the neighborhoods retained their individuality and became integral parts of the new Philadelphia, with Kensington at the hub.

As the 20th century began, the neighborhoods, now officially incorporated into the City of Philadelphia, saw even greater growth, as technological advances accelerated the expansion of industry and immigration continued. One of these advances affected the river neighborhoods, as well as the rest of Philadelphia, in a profound way. In 1915, construction began on the Frankford Elevated, a system of elevated and underground rails that ran east and west across the city, connecting the neighborhoods with downtown Philadelphia and the southwestern areas of the city. A modern marvel of transportation, the El forever changed the face of the city. Kensington, in particular, became synonymous with the El as it traveled high above its main avenue, which bustled with activity in the shadow of the great structure.

The ease of access to the neighborhoods, the established industries, and the strips of mom-and-pop stores that lined the streets left the area fairly unscathed by the Great Depression. The Delaware River shoreline grew to become an international marine terminal. Public and parochial schools and places of worship were erected. Theaters, saloons, playgrounds, and other places of recreation rounded out the daily lives of the now-established residents of the neighborhoods. As years passed, the ethnicity that once helped separate the neighborhoods became a blend that connected them, creating a colorful intermingling of cultures.

Today, many descendants of the original immigrants remember the remarkable courage of their forebears as they endured the daily struggle to establish a foundation for future generations. The great river neighborhoods of Philadelphia live on as a monument to those who never gave up on the dream that became a city.

This book takes a unique look at the River Wards. It includes rare and never-before-published photographs, including views of all four corners of the infamous K&A intersection before the construction of the Frankford El and photographs of the El's construction. In addition to providing an interesting look at the history of the neighborhoods, this book captures the lives of residents, past and present. Through these photographs, the richness of life along the river is palpable, almost as real as an actual visit.

One

The First Settlers and Colonials

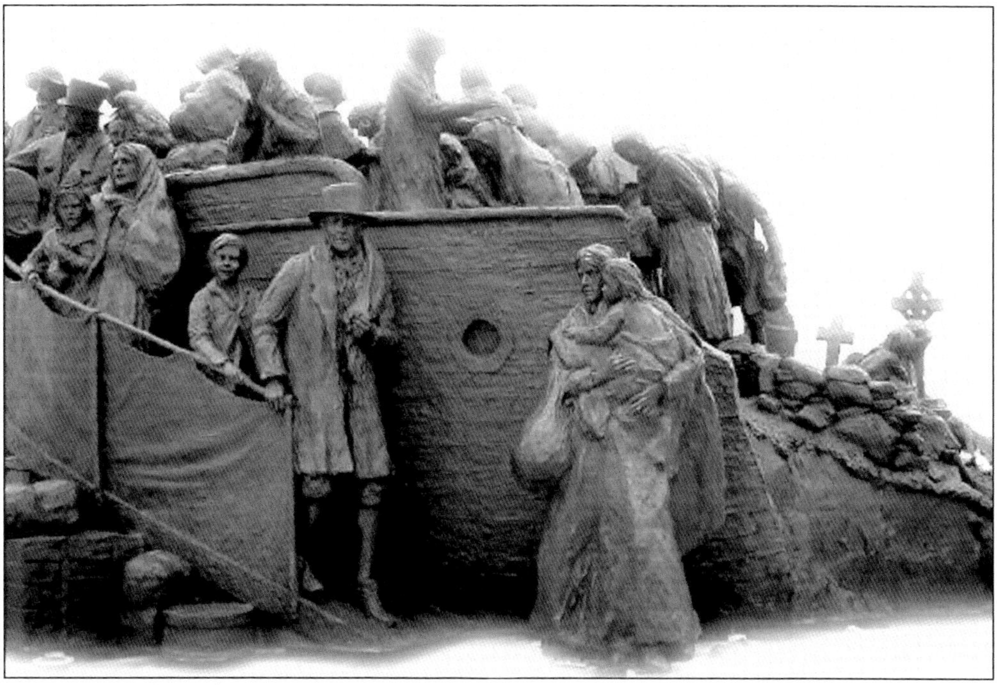

Along the banks of the Delaware River stands a new monument commemorating the immigrants who came from Ireland to Philadelphia in the 1800s. Leaving religious and political persecution, as well as famine, these newcomers came in search of a better life with new opportunities.

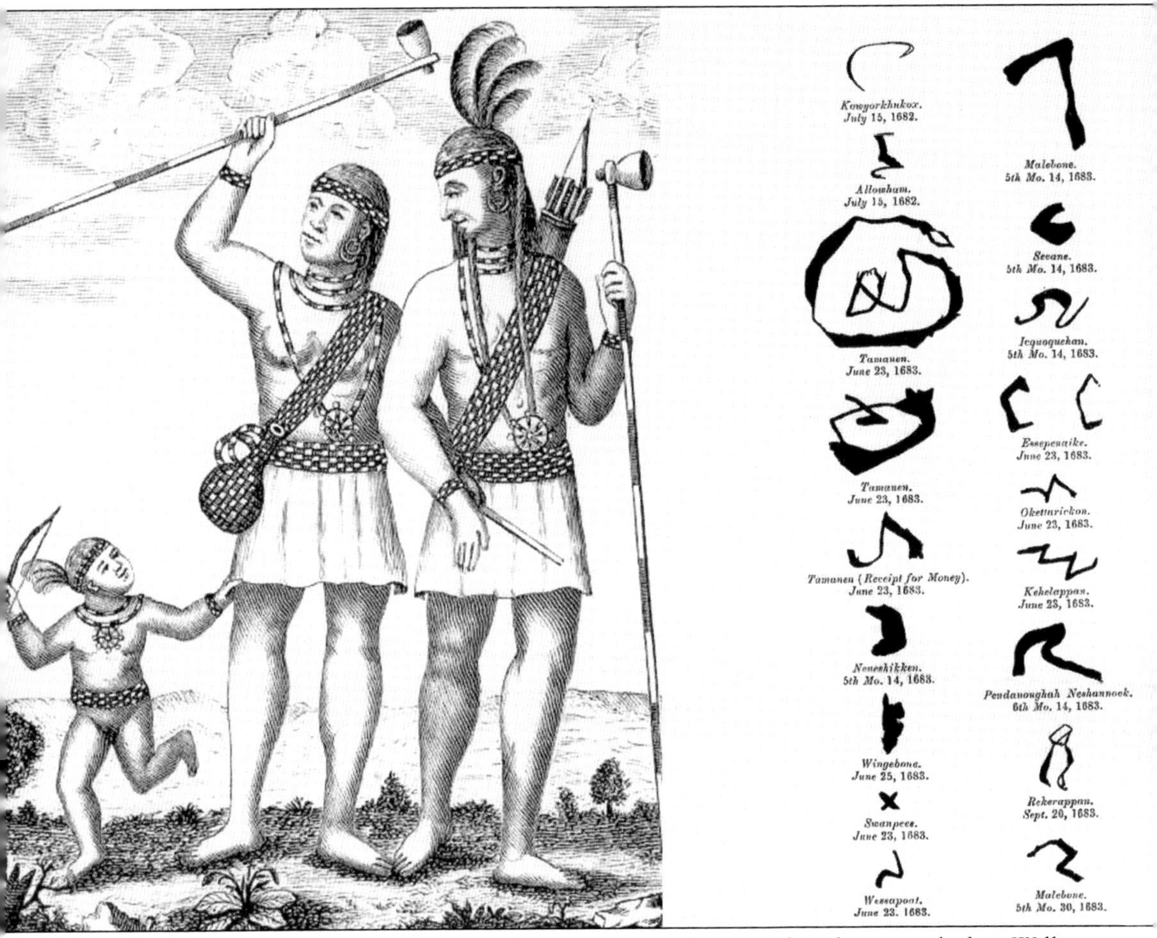

The story of Philadelphia's River Wards begins with a history of settlers even before William Penn and the Swedes. Long before Pennsylvania was born, a tribe of people from America's West known as the Lenni Lenape decided they did not like the area they lived in, so they traveled east across the Namaesi Sipu or River of Fish, later called the Mississippi River. Along the way, they met another tribe called the Mengwe. Sharing the same idea of a better place to live, they traveled east together into a land with very high mountains where a people known as the Alligewi already lived. At first, the Alligewi accepted the new travelers from the West, but were soon threatened by their numbers. After a great war, the travelers from the West defeated the Alligewi and divided the land up between the two tribes. The Lenni Lenape took the eastern end of the Allegheny Mountains, which included the area known today as southeastern Pennsylvania. Here, the Lenni Lenape settled along the Great Salt Water, known today as the Delaware River, with Philadelphia and its River Wards on its banks. Also shown are the signatures of the tribal chiefs.

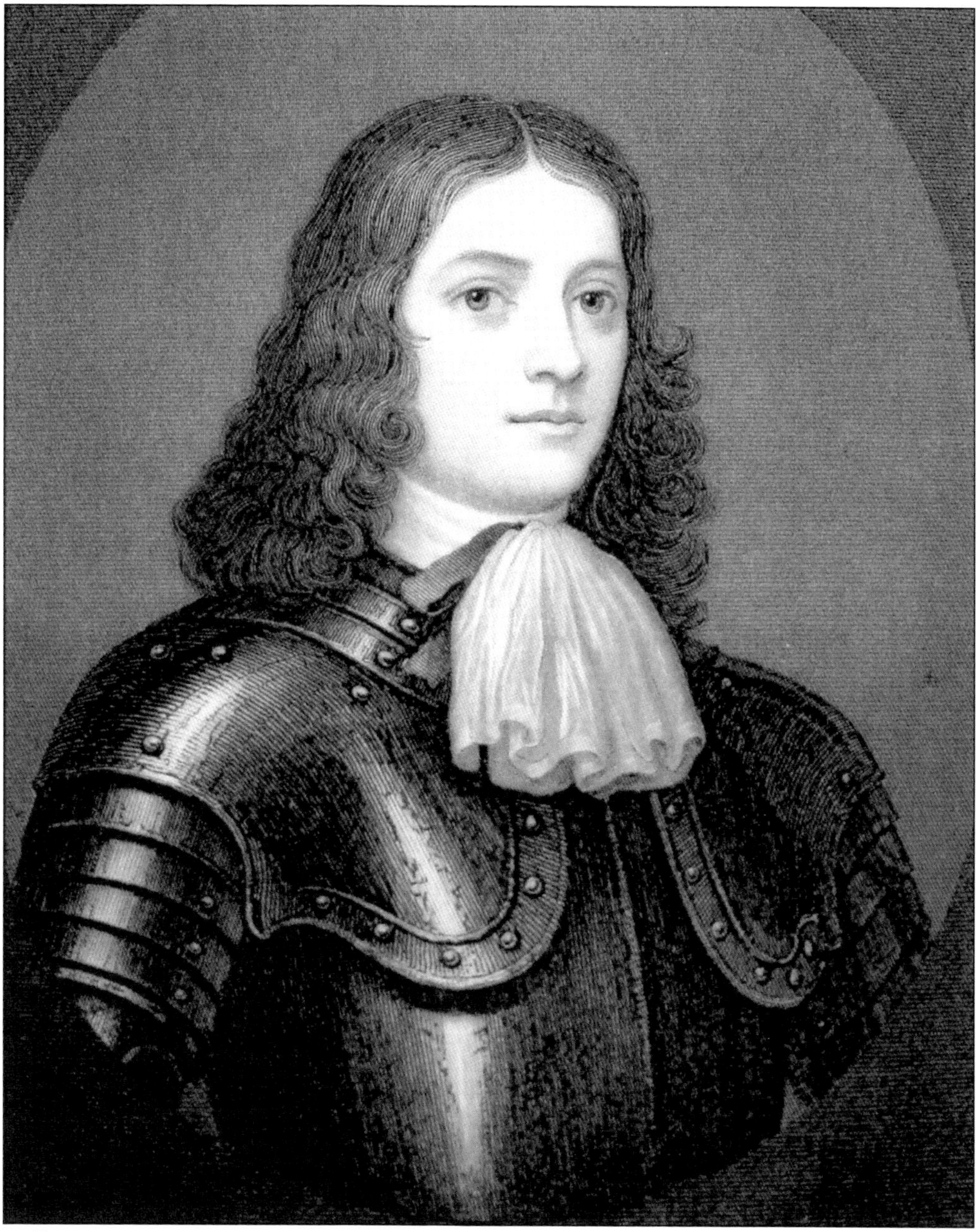

William Penn is portrayed at the age of twenty-two in this 1668 painting by John Sartain. Penn's treaty with the Lenni Lenape is well-known local history. It is a lesser-known fact that he acquired the state of Pennsylvania through a debt owed to his father, Admiral Penn of the Royal Navy, by King Charles. Penn referred to the land as Sylvania, meaning woodlands. When Penn saw that the original charter read "Pennsylvania," he informed the king that he did not wish to be honored in this way. The king replied: "I am not honoring you; I am honoring my friend, your father." Because William Penn had, at an early age, befriended a group of young men in England known as Quakers, King Charles felt that by giving Penn the land instead of repaying the original debt of $80,000, he would be ridding himself of Penn and his troublemaking Quaker friends.

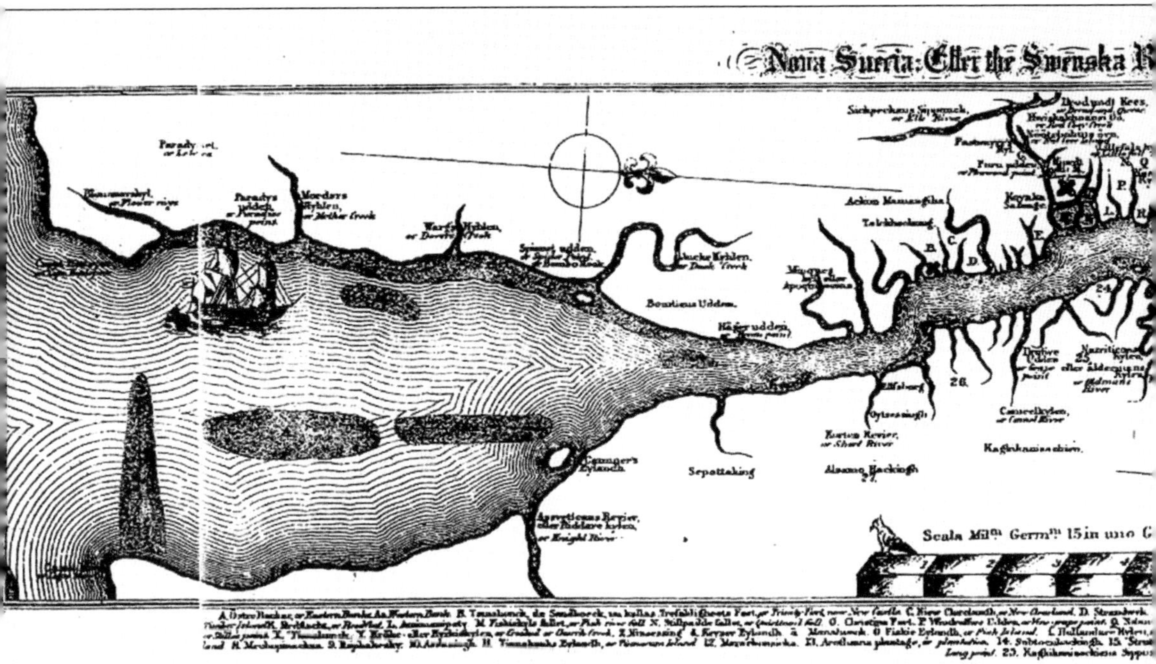

As a cartographer and surveyor for the Royal Swedish Engineers, Peter Lindstrom drew several maps of the banks of the Delaware River. His first known work, dating from 1654–1655, shows a crude drawing of the Delaware River as it flows from the Atlantic Ocean north to Bucks County. The first indication of Philadelphia is Passyunk Village, located to the right of the

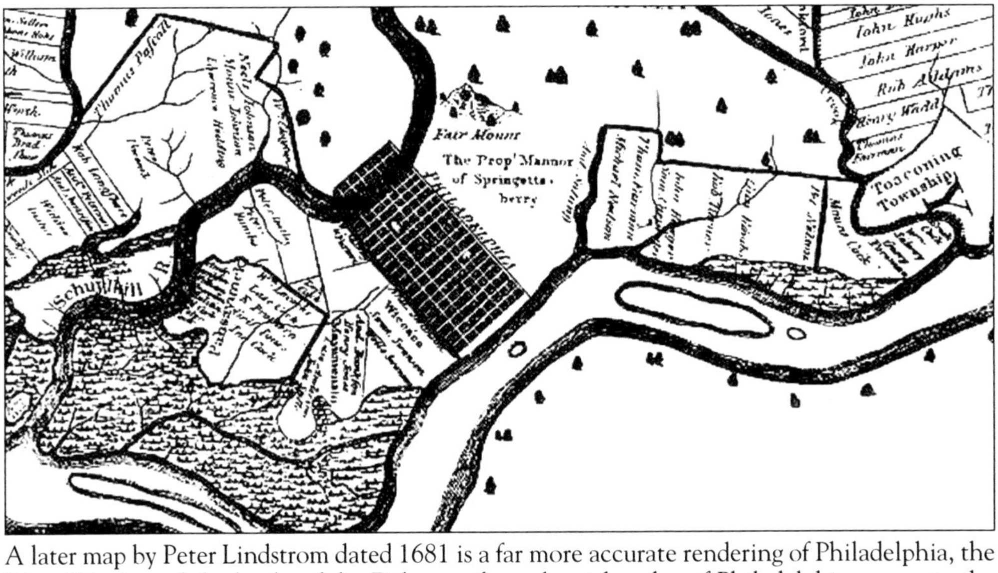

A later map by Peter Lindstrom dated 1681 is a far more accurate rendering of Philadelphia, the River Wards, and the banks of the Delaware from the right edge of Philadelphia proper to the creek not yet named. The property that is labeled as being owned by Thomas Fairman is the section that would become known as Kensington a few years later. Also of note is Toaconing Township just to the right of the creek, which became the Tacony section of the city. Thomas Fairman owned several acres there as well.

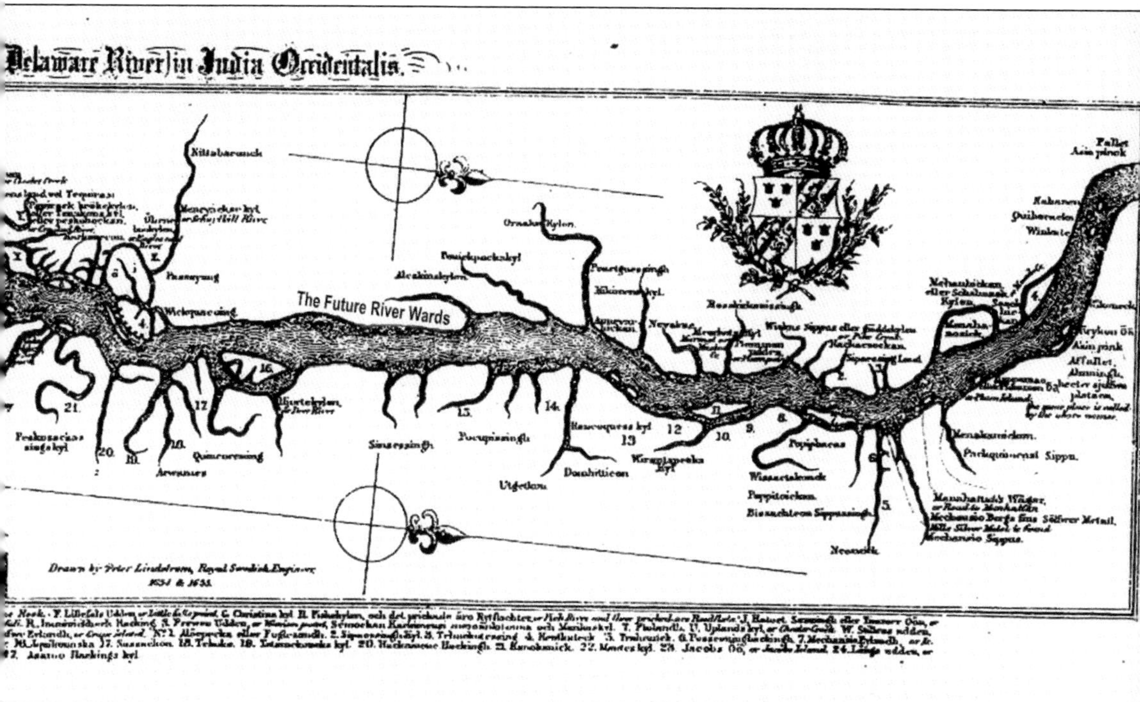

Schuylkill River. Petty's Island, located below the future site of the River Wards, is depicted with uncanny accuracy considering the inaccurate straightness of the river and the overly large widths of the streams and creeks along the banks.

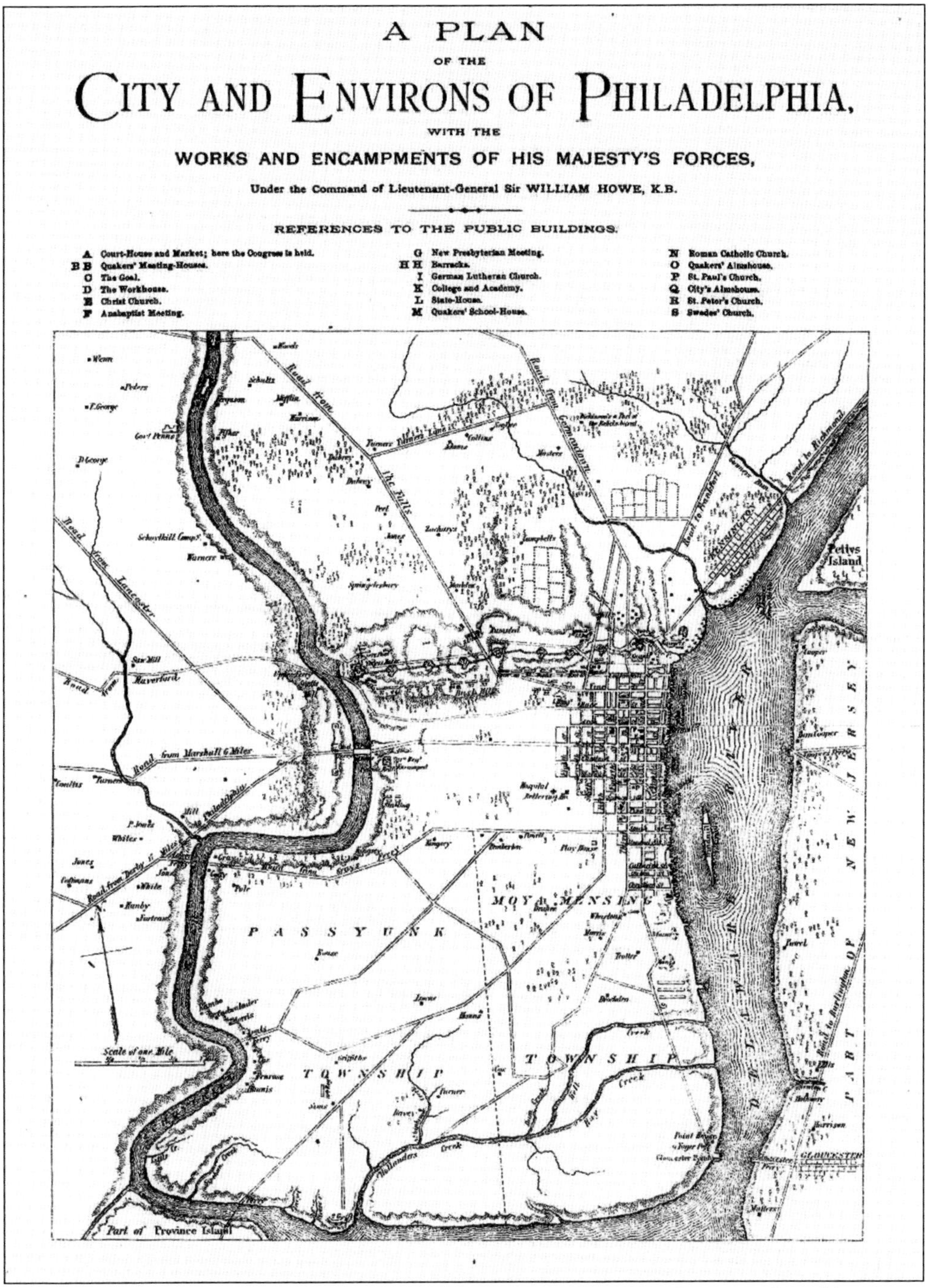

This map, drawn by the British military, shows a different perspective of Gunners Run (Aramingo Avenue) than previous maps. Kensington is shown here with plots of land divided evenly, probably for real estate purposes. Marked are the roads to Frankfort (Frankford) and Richmond. Early city records show these roads were named Kings Road and Queens Road, respectively, but the names only exist in the earliest maps of Philadelphia after the consolidation.

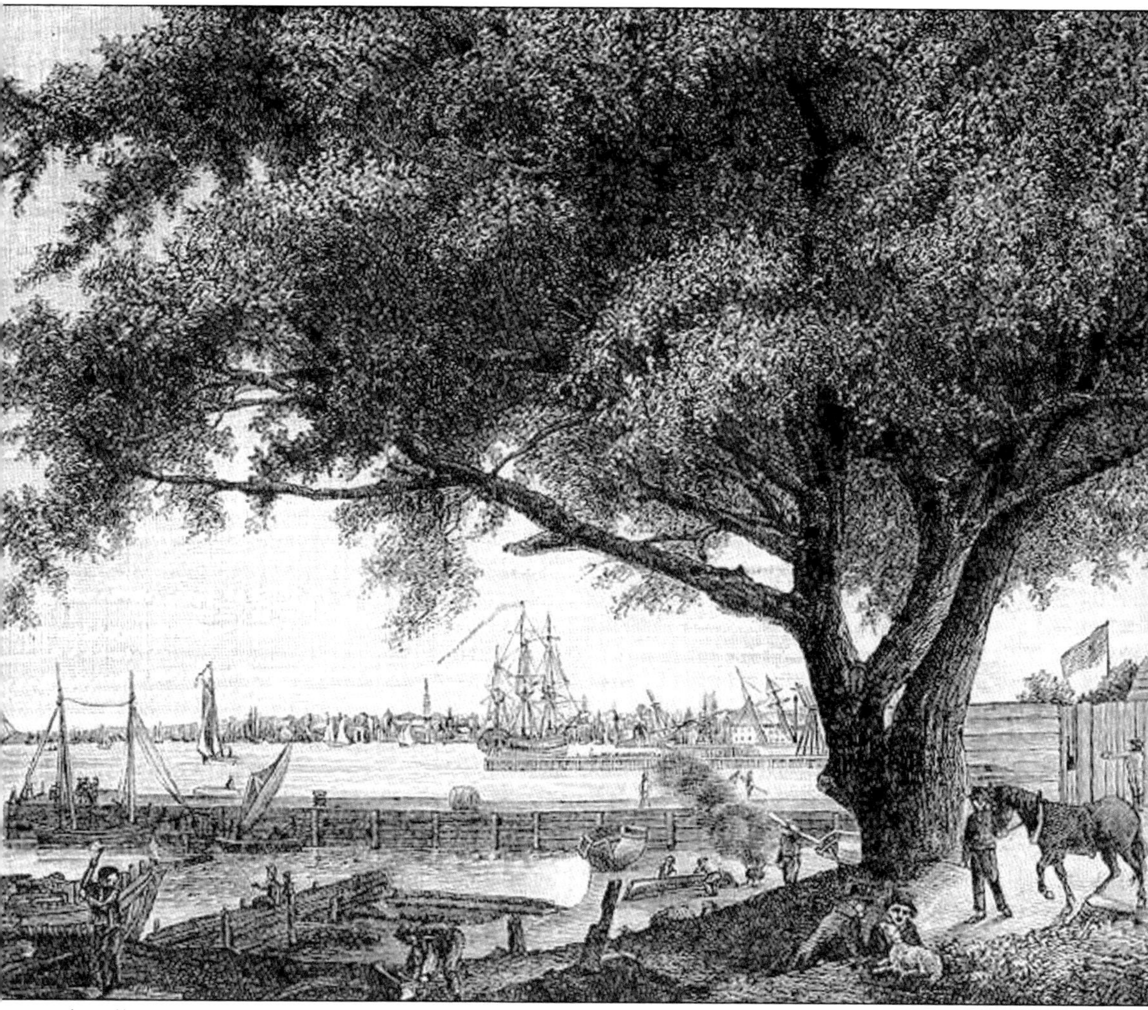

This illustration shows the Delaware River at the foot of Shackamaxon Street. Pictured is the Treaty Tree, where Penn signed the pact between the original settlers and the Lenni Lenape. The land was handed down from Penn to the Fairman family, who built a large mansion near the site of the signing. After the death of Thomas Fairman, his widow sold the property to Anthony Palmer, a Barbados sea captain, *c.* 1733. Palmer named the neighborhood Kensington Township after the district in London, England. Palmer divided the entire property into lots and sold them at a large profit. Small boatyards and fisheries grew along the riverbank, while the inland areas saw the development of knitting mills and rope factories. Small farms lined the dirt roads that made their way through what would become the townships of Richmond, Bridesburg, and Frankford.

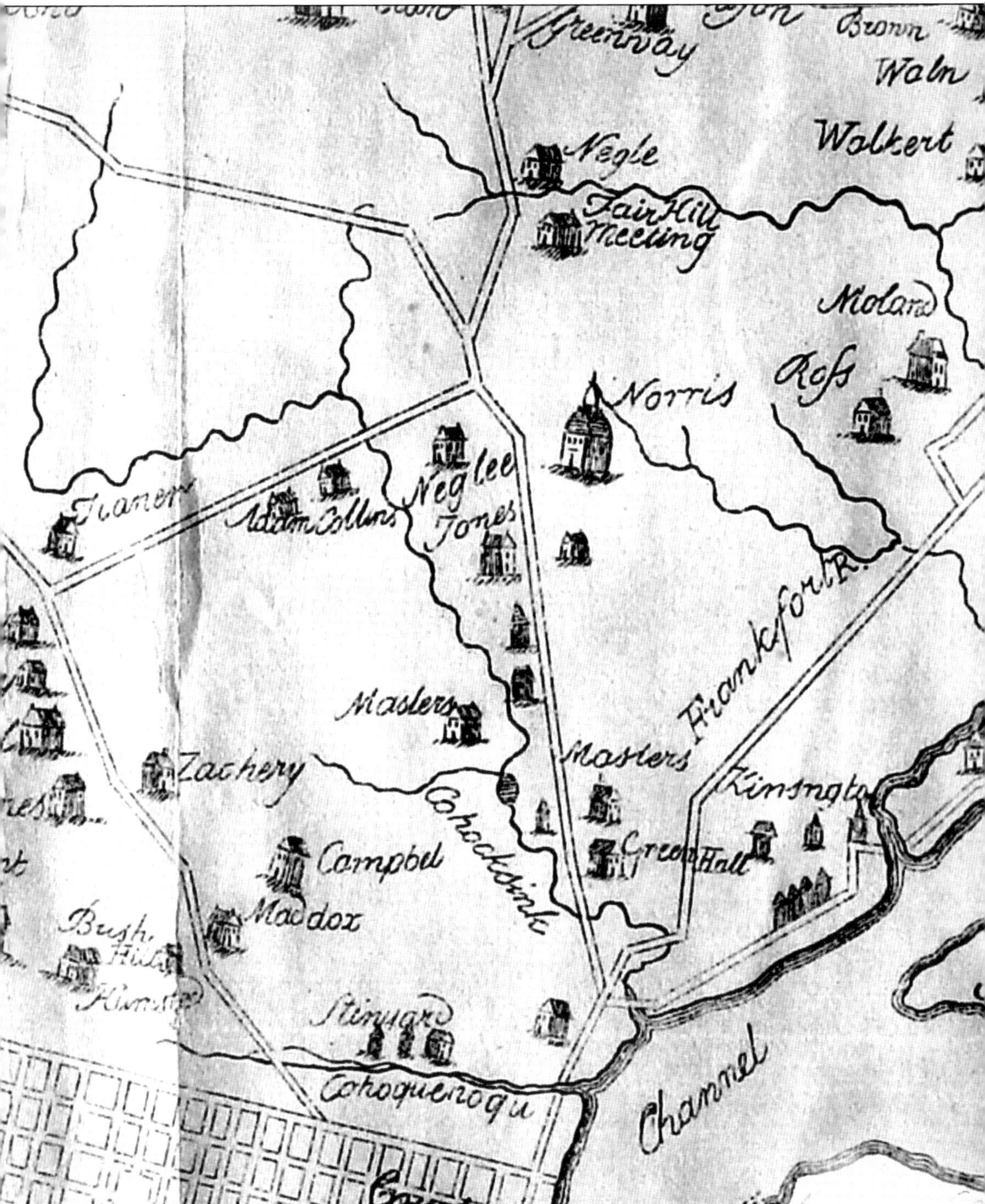

This 1750 map of the River Wards is by far the most significant depiction of the origins of the neighborhoods. Note the misspelling of the name Kensington (Kinsngto). Gunners Run, named after the Swedish settler Gunner Rambo, is clearly marked. Today it is known as Aramingo Avenue. North of Philadelphia proper is Cohocksink Creek. Although the creek

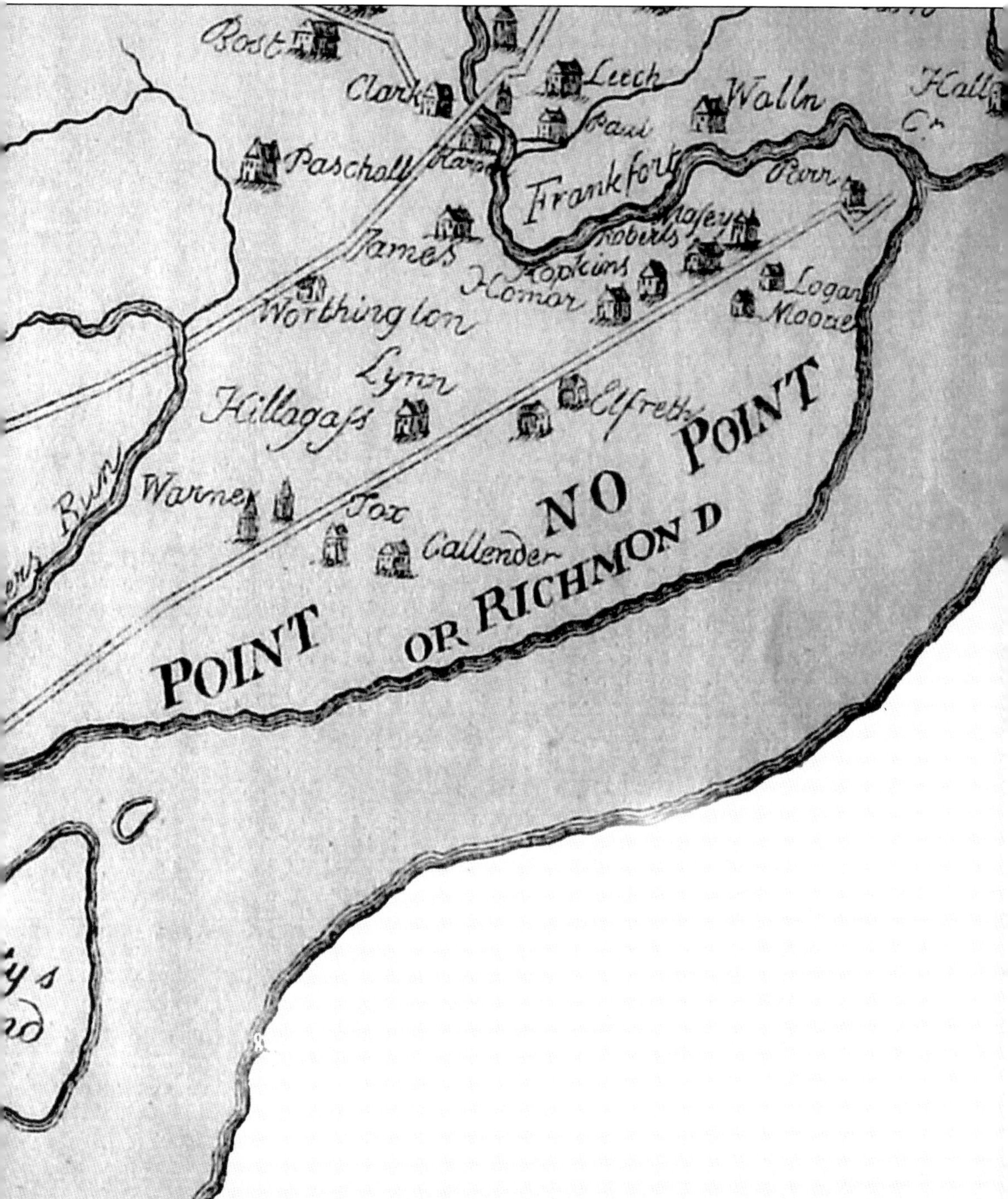

has long since been filled in, its name is still celebrated as the name of a recreation center in Port Richmond. Further north is Frankfort, as it was originally known—the change in spelling came later. Finally, Point No Point is depicted, which was the beginning of the Port Richmond and Bridesburg areas.

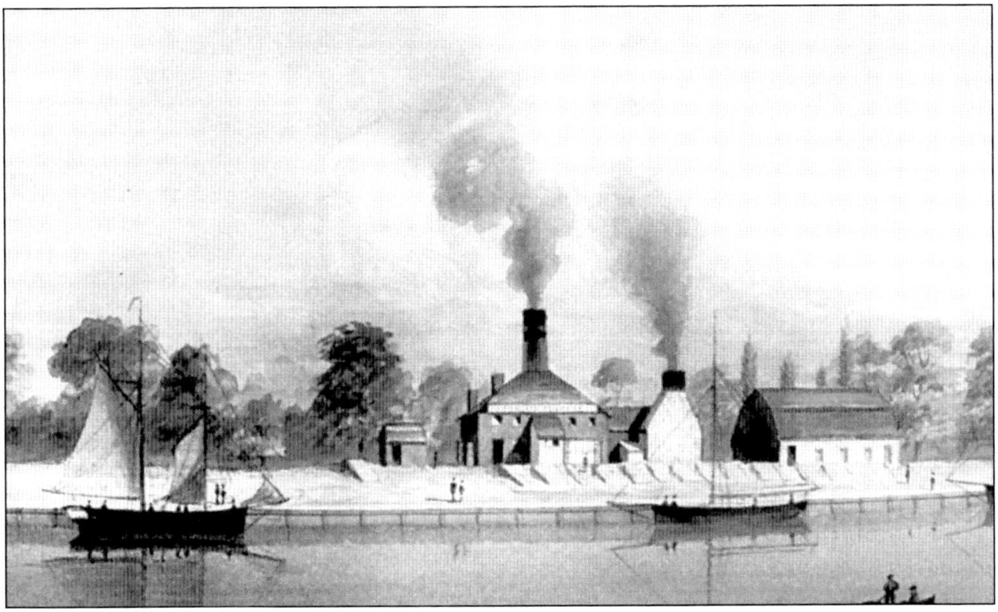

Taken from a turn-of-the-century watercolor print, this photograph shows the blast furnaces used to make glass at Union Glass Works, one of several glass companies established in the Philadelphia area. Another glass company of note was the Flint and Dyott Glass Company. Dr. Dyott, a pharmacist, started making his own bottles for his medicines. Dyott, also known for his benevolence to his employees, built Dyottville, a self-contained community.

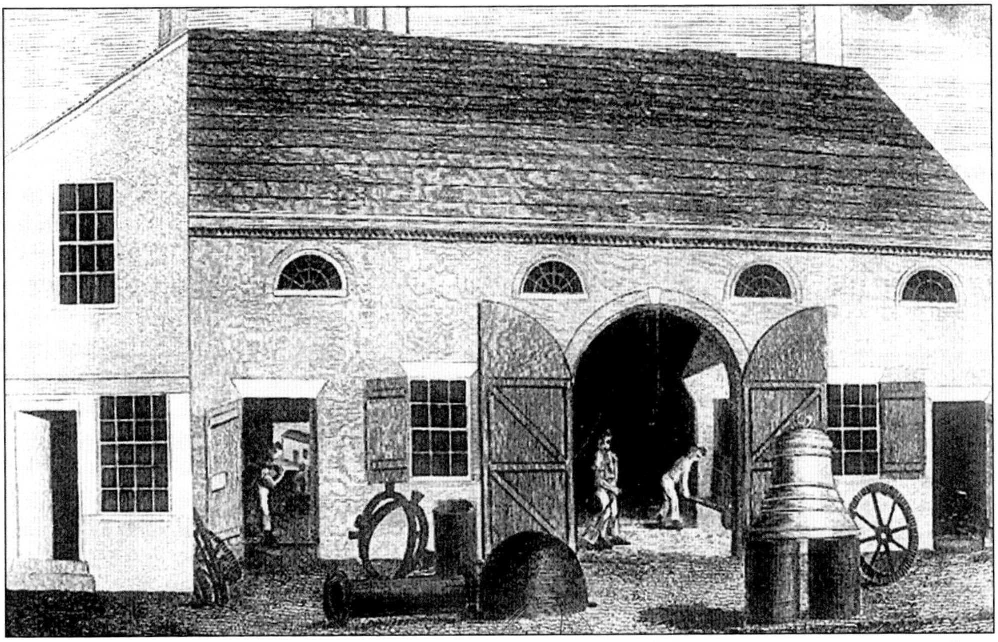

As the city and its surrounding townships grew at the turn of the century, companies such as Parke and Tiers Brass and Iron Company helped support the city and its shipyards. Having one of America's largest naval shipyards nearby also led to federal contracts for Parke and Tiers and other small businesses. Charles B. Parke, senior owner of Parke and Tiers, was also a resident of Kensington, which was true of most owner-operators along the river.

Two

A LAND OF PLENTY

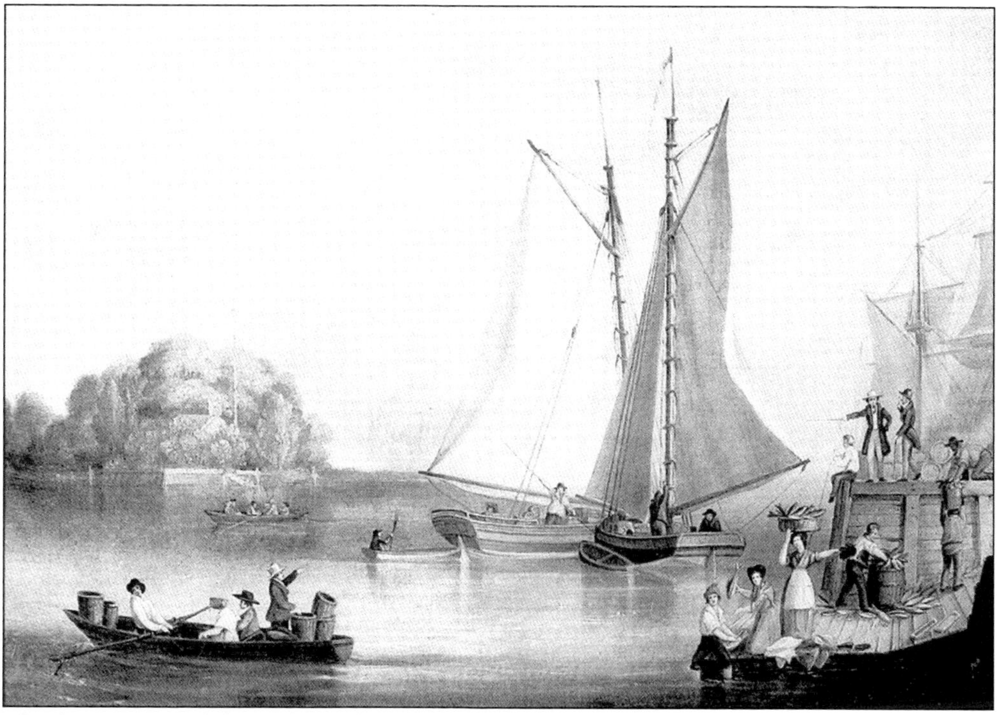

The beginnings of the industrial revolution can be traced to the River Wards. After the American Revolution, business blossomed immediately. The growth of industry and the continuous arrival of new immigrants helped the River Wards grow at an amazing rate. This area along the Delaware made its place in American history, moving quickly from a wooded land where people lived in caves to a richly inhabited commercial center and shipping terminal.

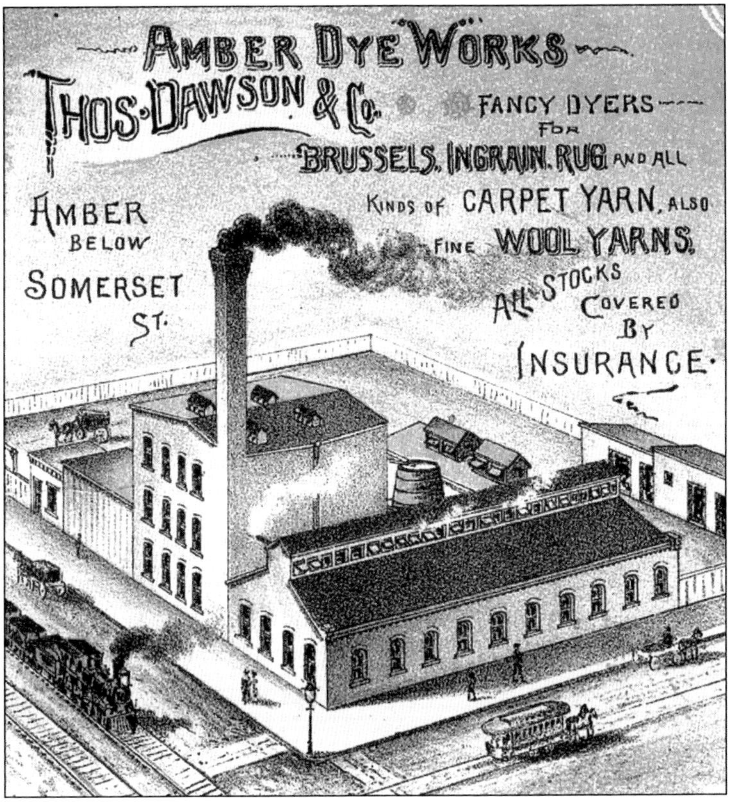

Amber Dye Works was located at Somerset and Amber Streets, one block from Kings Road (Frankford Avenue) in an area that was not distinct in its boundaries. Some maps claim it was part of the Kensington section, others say it was the Port Richmond section. Today this location is a residential area with some light industry. The area's dye industry prospered until the 1950s.

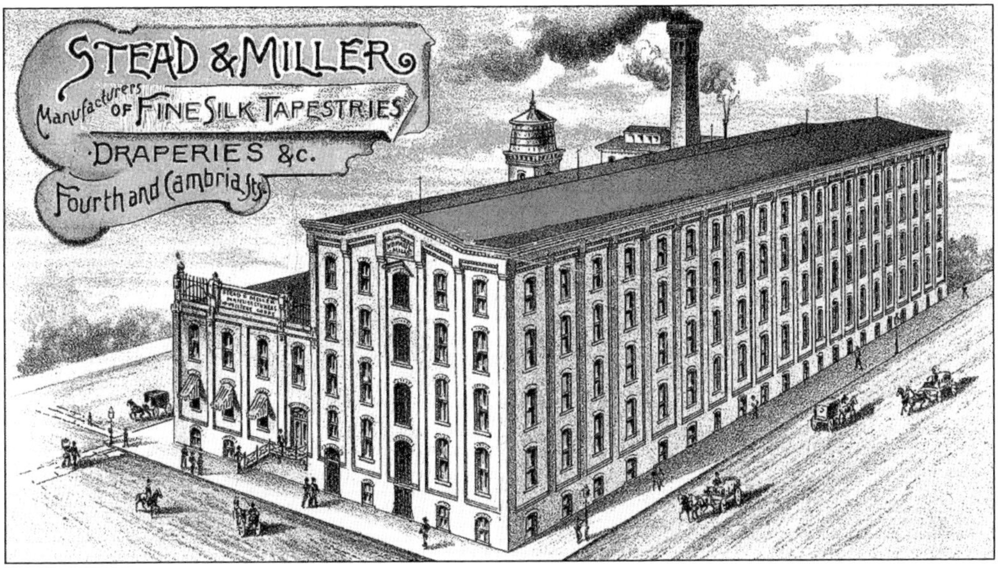

Stead and Miller located at Fourth and Cambria Streets was an internationally known fabric-manufacturing company. Its lucrative federal contracts for army blankets and saddles allowed the company to advance with the times and make improvements in machinery as necessary. The company shared its success with its employees, procuring homes for them in the area.

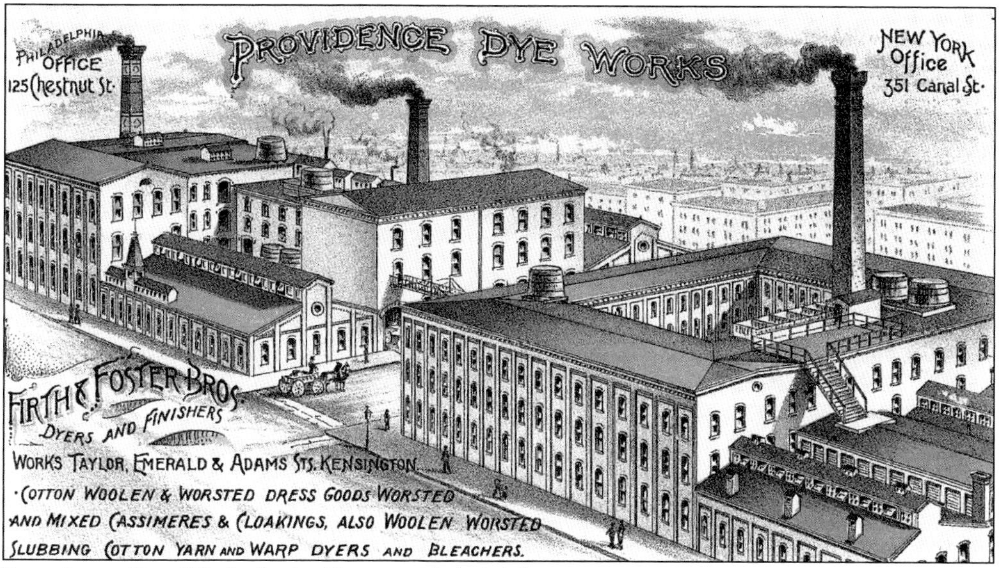

Providence Dye Works had offices in Philadelphia proper and New York City. The mill at Emerald and Adam Streets is shown here in one of the rare illustrations indicating Kensington as an independent township. Adams Street was changed to Haggert Street in the late 1800s.

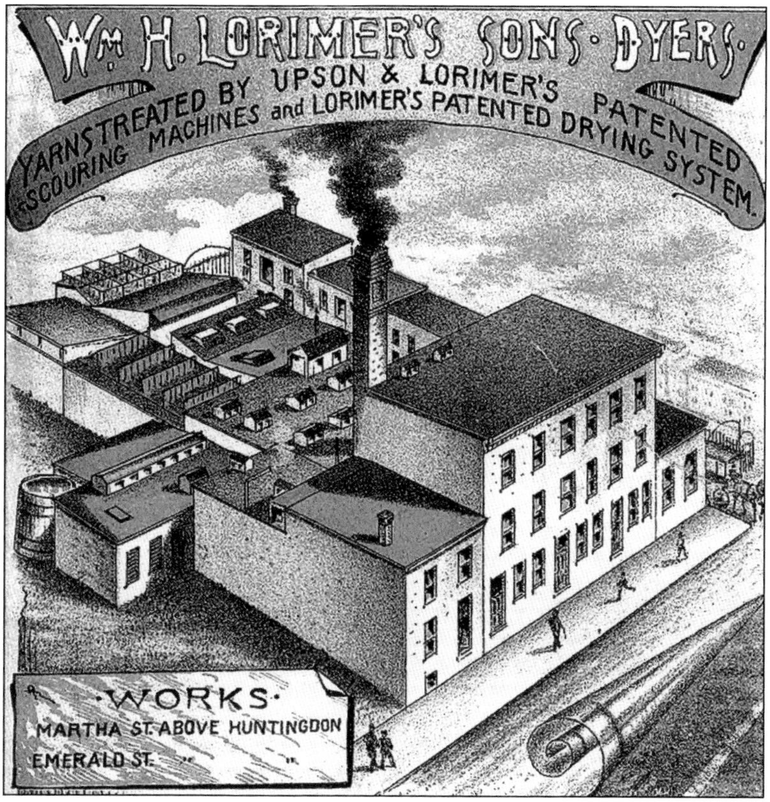

William H. Lorimer's Sons Dyers was located on Martha Street above Huntingdon Street. This illustration is a good depiction of the size of some of these mills, which were two to three blocks long. Through hard work and determination, first-generation immigrants became successful business owners and industry in the River Wards boomed.

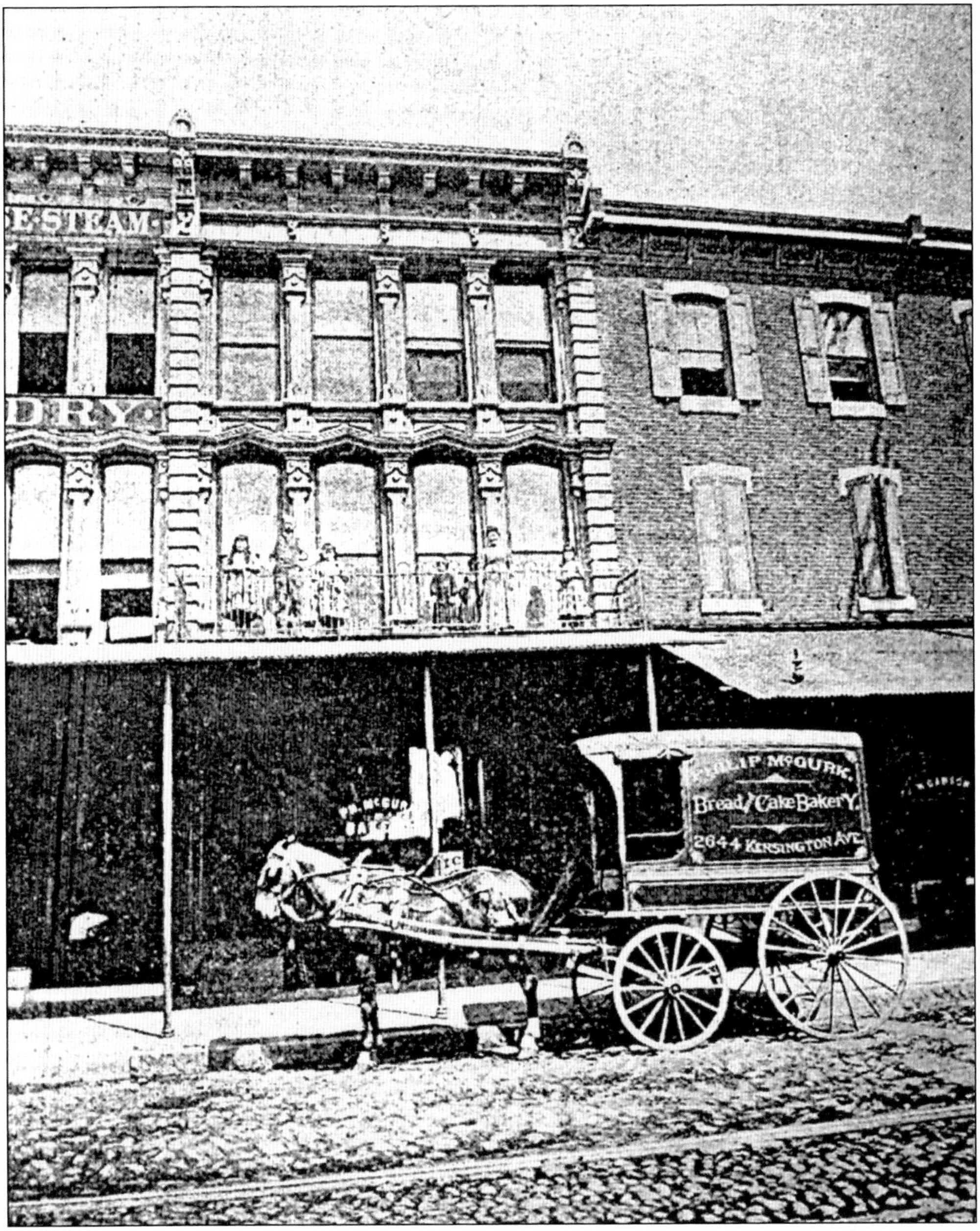

P. McGurk worked as an apprentice baker for six years before he saved enough money to mortgage a storefront property at 2644 Kensington Avenue and open his own bakery. Like most small business owners of the time, the Scottish immigrant and his family resided in his place of business. The store was on the main floor with the bakery in the basement, and the residence was on the upper two floors. The baker's wife and children can be seen on the second-floor balcony. This photograph is believed to have been taken before the Civil War, when photography was still experimental, which may account for its grainy quality.

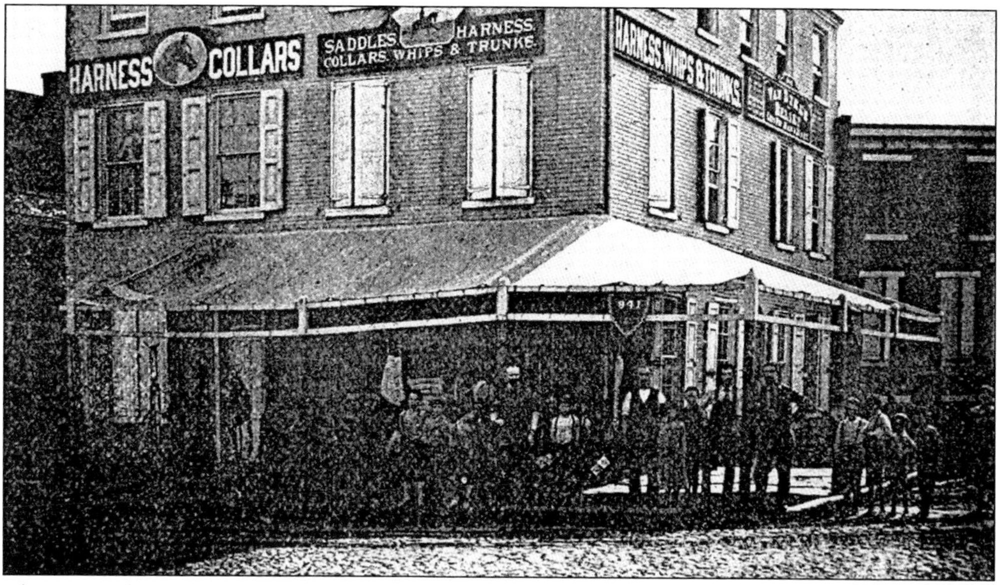

This grainy but still discernible photograph depicts a Fishtown company that outfitted horses in the early 1800s. Fishtown is a nickname that was given to the part of the River Wards around Frankford and Girard Avenues. Legend has it that when Charles Dickens visited the area in the 1800s, the aroma of fish from the shad fisheries in the area inspired him to coin the name. Fishtown has never been officially named or recognized by the Library of Congress but it is, nonetheless, an integral part of the River Wards area.

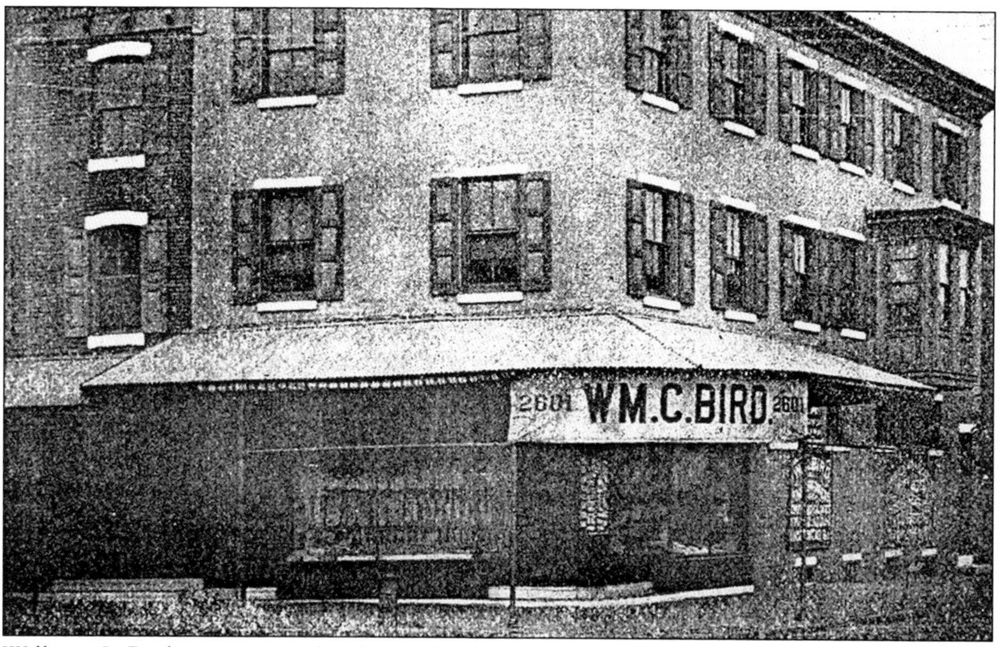

William C. Bird, proprietor of Ladies and Gent's Furnishing Store, at 2601 Frankford Avenue, was also vice president of the business association and the Electric Light Company in the 1800s. Bird, a native of Philadelphia, was very involved with politics in the River Wards; he held a seat on the board that consolidated the neighborhoods into Philadelphia.

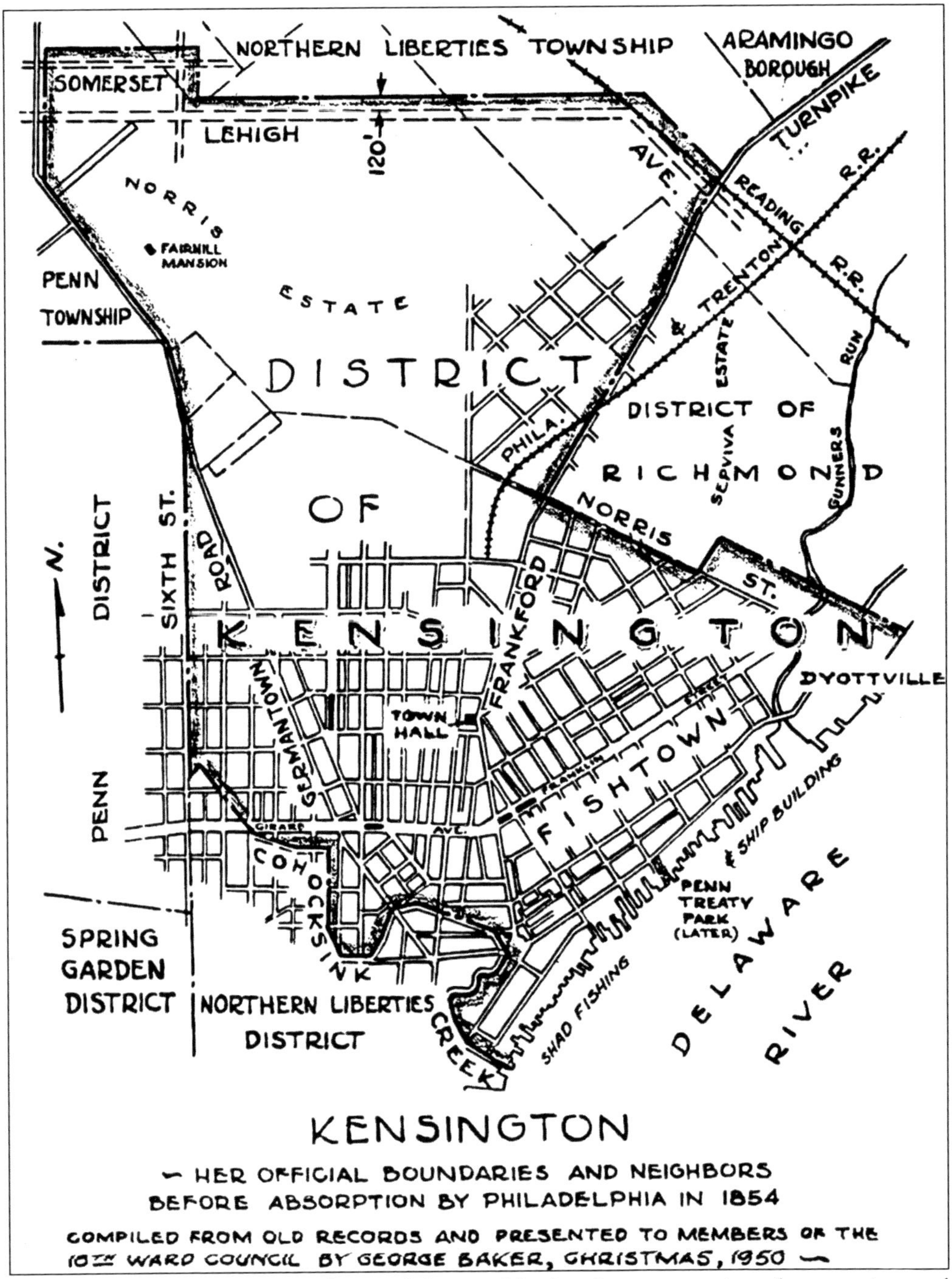

From the beginning, the boundaries of the neighborhoods were a point of contention and remain so today. This unofficial map shows Kensington, the first of the townships of the River Wards, with a boundaries from the Delaware River to 6th Street and from the Cohocksink Creek to Norris Street, with Fishtown east of Frankford Road. This map is one of few that mentions Fishtown, as well as Dyottville, an unrecognized township.

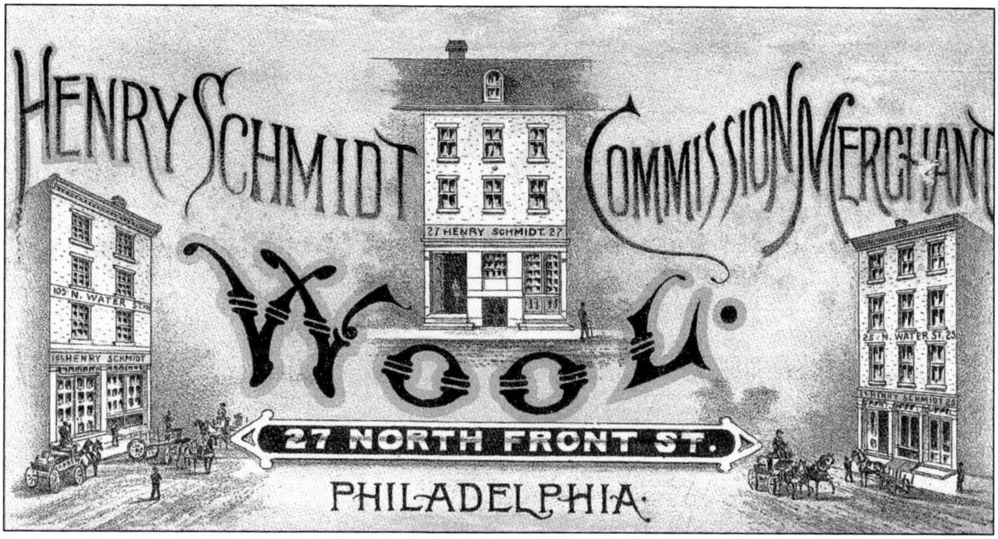

Before photography became common, mid- to large-sized companies paid professional artists to do line art, colored pencil sketches, and paintings of their businesses. These images were quite detailed and adorned the outer boarders of large, extravagant maps used by real estate companies. Today, they are considered choice pieces of art and can be found on display in taverns and restaurants throughout Philadelphia.

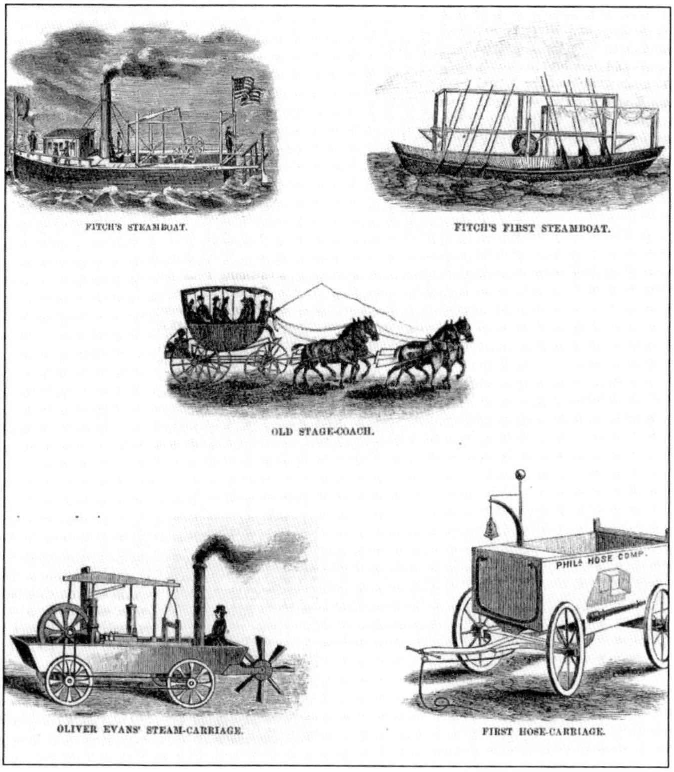

These historical drawings are over 150 years old. The steamboats were built by River Wards residents, such as Oliver Evans, who built many land steam carriages, and a Mr. Fitch, who owned a few wharfs along Richmond Street, where he built a series of steamboats that traveled all along eastern America's rivers. Philadelphia Hose Company, believed to have been originally located on the 300 block of Richmond Street, built the townships' early fire wagons. Finally, Frankford Coach Company made many stagecoaches that found their way out West. The River Wards made many inroads in the creation of the industrial revolution, not least in the area of transportation.

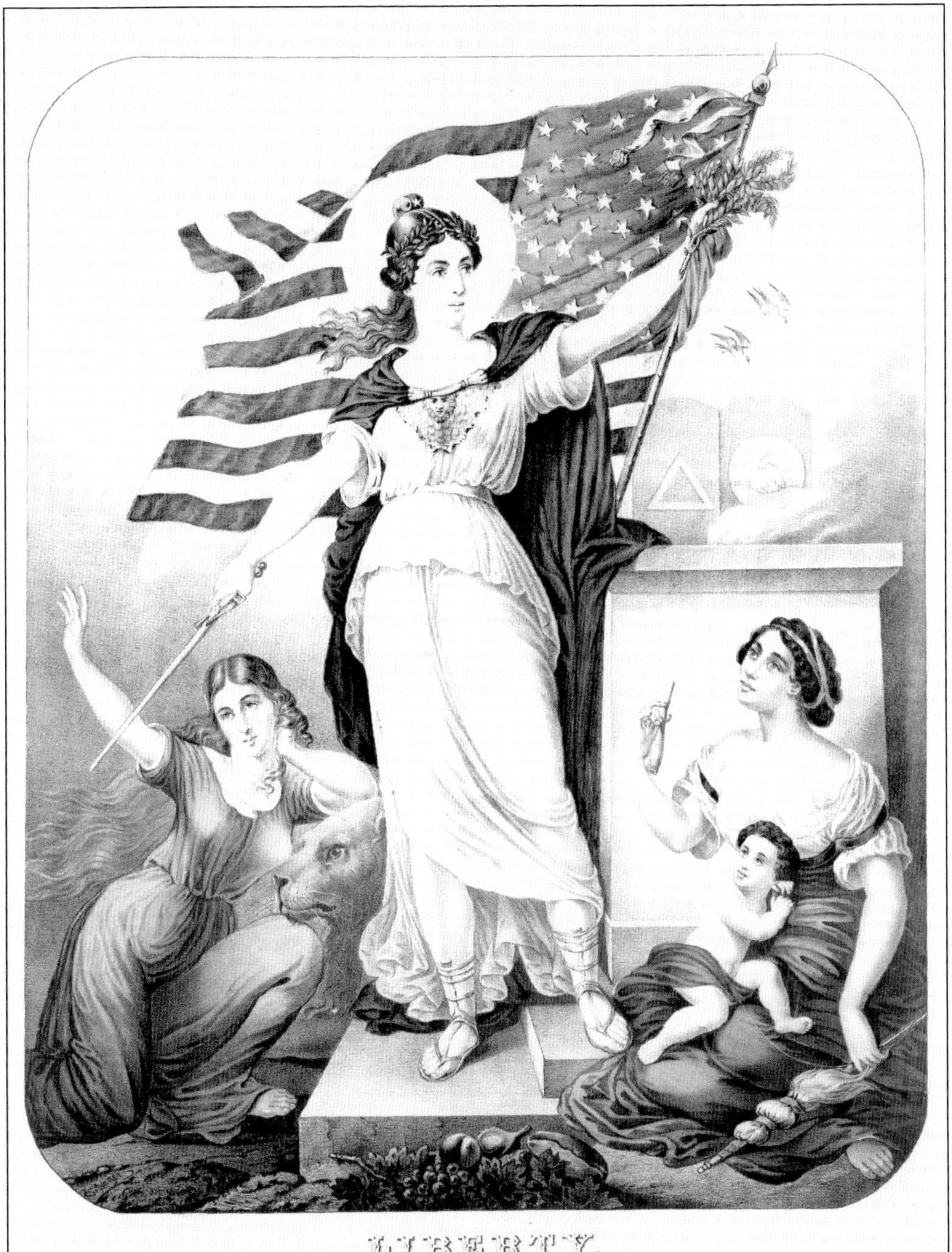

No account of industry in the River Wards would be complete without mention of the printing trade. Benjamin Franklin took on many apprentices from the River Wards area, encouraging them to share in the American dream of starting their own business. They honed their dreams

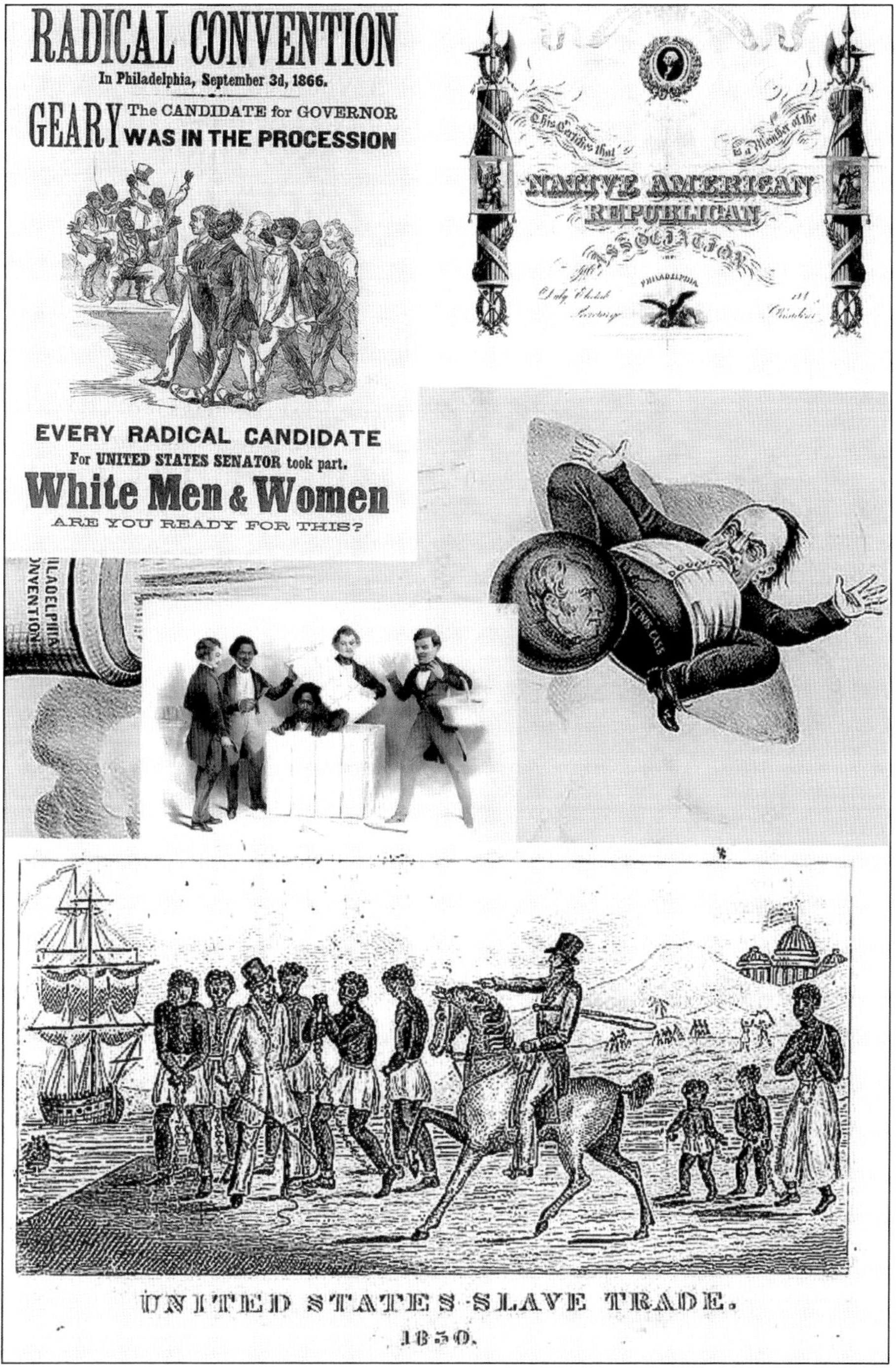

into a fine art. Examples of their craftsmanship are depicted here from prints that are rarely seen today.

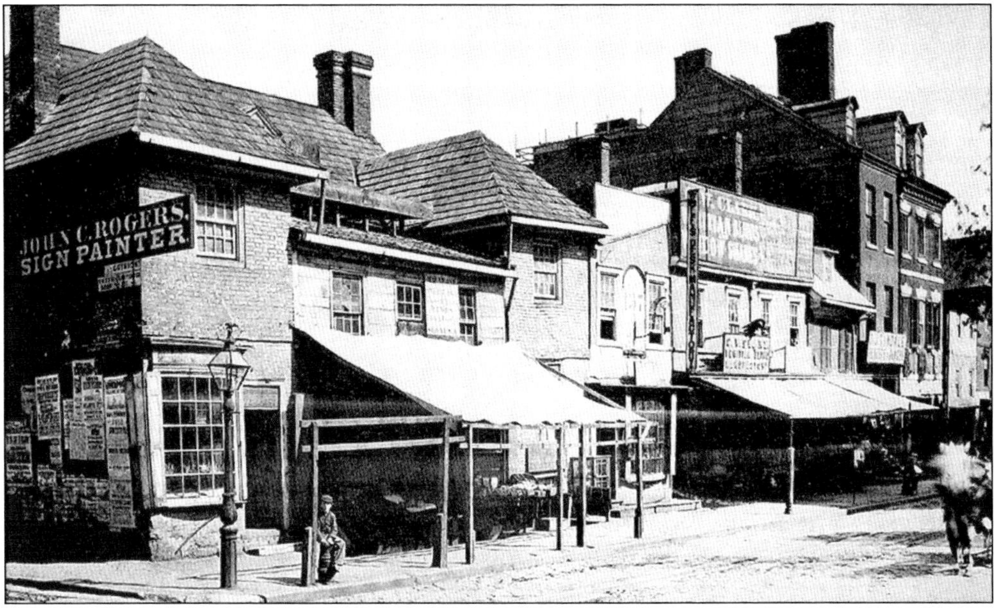

The John C. Rogers Sign Painter Company, located at Second and Norris Streets, was photographed in the mid-1800s. Neighborhood dividing lines locate the business in either Kensington or the unincorporated Northern Liberties. When new owner and resident John Watson did historical research in 1820, he traced ownership of the property back to William Penn, who lived there in the 1700s.

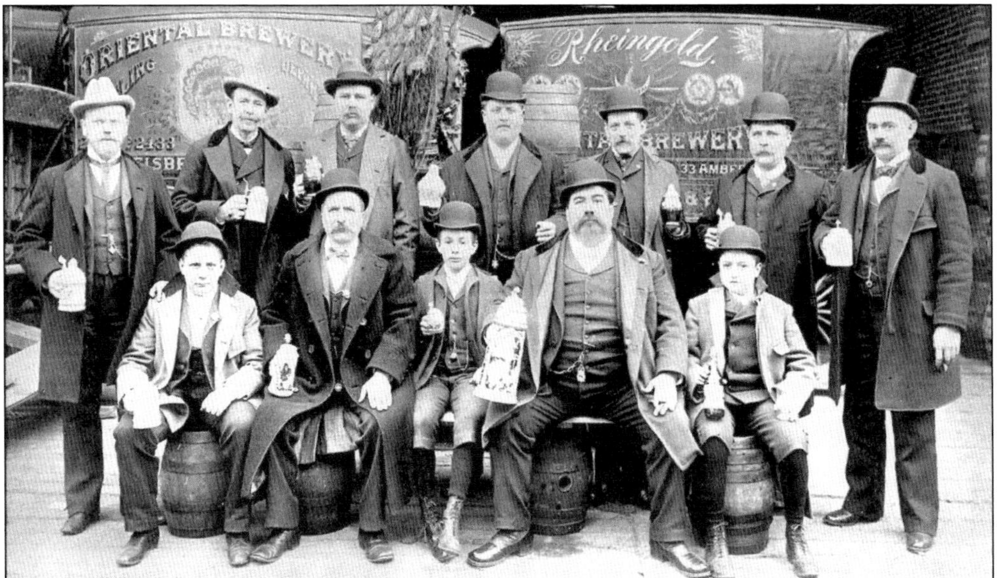

Owners, employees, and family members of Weisbrod and Hess Breweries, located at 2433 Amber Street, pose for a company photograph. In the rear are two delivery wagons, Oriental on the left, Rheingold on the right, with a peacock between them. Over 100 years later, a new microbrewery has taken over the same property. Yards Brewery moved into the building in May of 2000. Owners Bill Barton and his wife, Nancy, brew their golden-brown beer using the same old-fashioned method as their predecessors.

Three

THE FRANKFORD EL

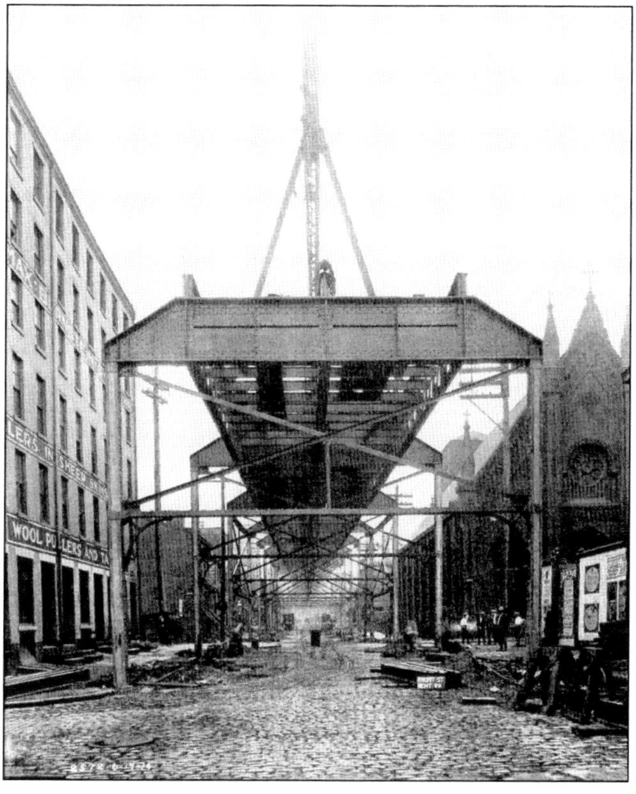

Transportation was an important aspect of the River Wards from the start. Frankfort Road was the main thoroughfare from Philadelphia to New York. As time went on, the need for better travel within the city itself became apparent. The building of the Frankford El, quite an ambitious undertaking for its time, made the River Wards more accessible to each other as well as to the rest of the city. The El transported riders from Philadelphia's northeast section to the River Wards and onward to the downtown area and the city's western end. The El was built to last and just recently has taken on a major restructuring.

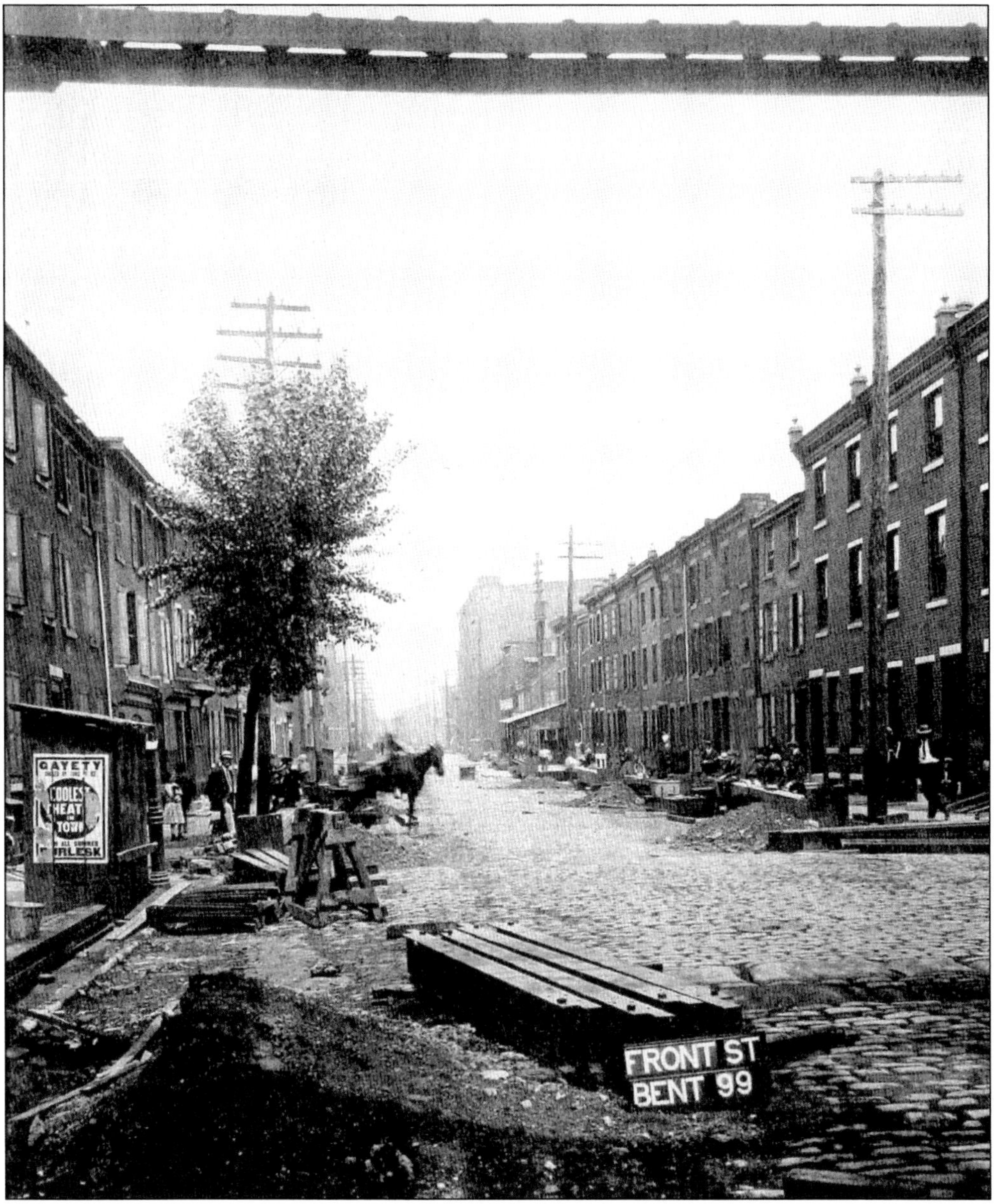

Bent 99 was located at Richmond and Front Streets. (The term "bent" was used to label the uprights and their location.) The steel frame structure, considered state-of-the-art for its time, has long since been replaced by a concrete structure. "Gayety, Coolest Theater in Town, Burlesque" is advertised on the side of what appears to be an old wooden toolshed. Also noteworthy, in the row of houses on the right is a house that seems to be narrower and shorter than the rest. This was characteristic of many Philadelphia residential blocks. Many houses were built moving inward from each end of the street, leaving the last house near the center a little narrower and shorter.

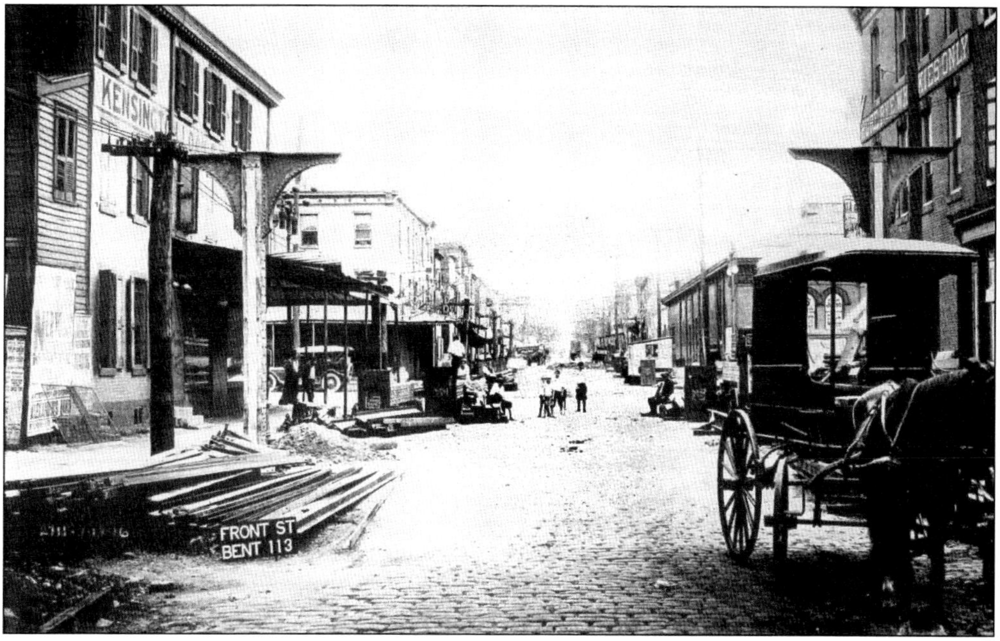

Bent 113 was located at Front and Norris Streets, looking north on Front Street. On the left is the Kensington Loan Company. This photograph, from the SEPTA Archives, shows the very beginnings of the El construction project. Note the uprights on the sidewalks on the left and right; this is apparently phase one of the construction.

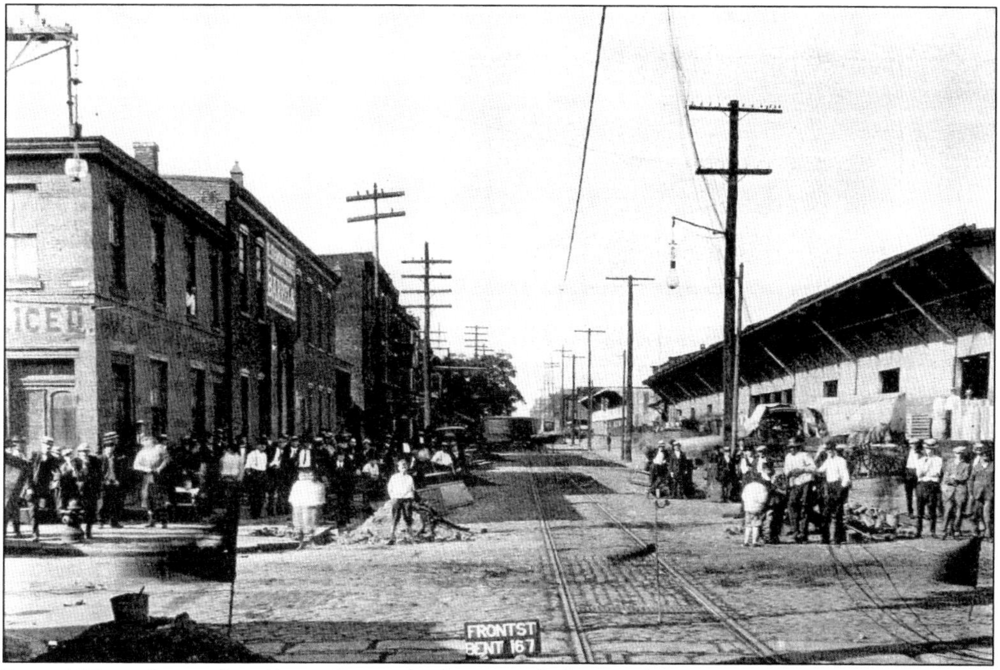

Bent 167 was located on Front Street, looking south from Palmer Street. This rare photograph shows a large crowd gathered for no apparent reason. Some neighborhood historians have concluded that newspaper reports and city notifications of no parking of cars or wagons in preparation for the construction of the El may have created this gathering.

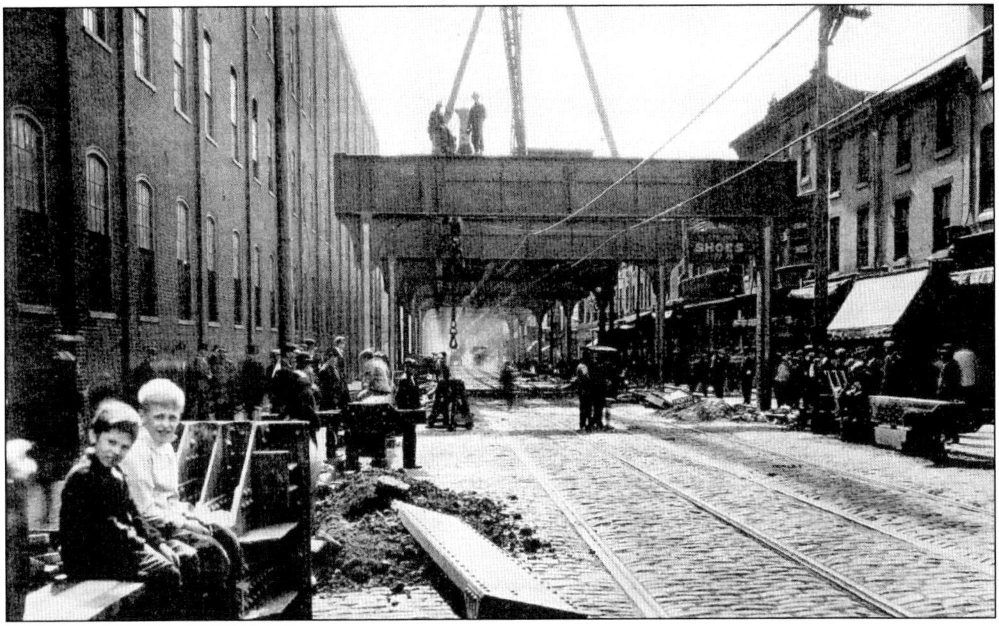

This photograph was taken on September 25, 1916, as the construction of the El continued along Front Street. Two youngsters are seated on the beams that will be used for cross risers, which run across Front Street, perpendicular to the El.

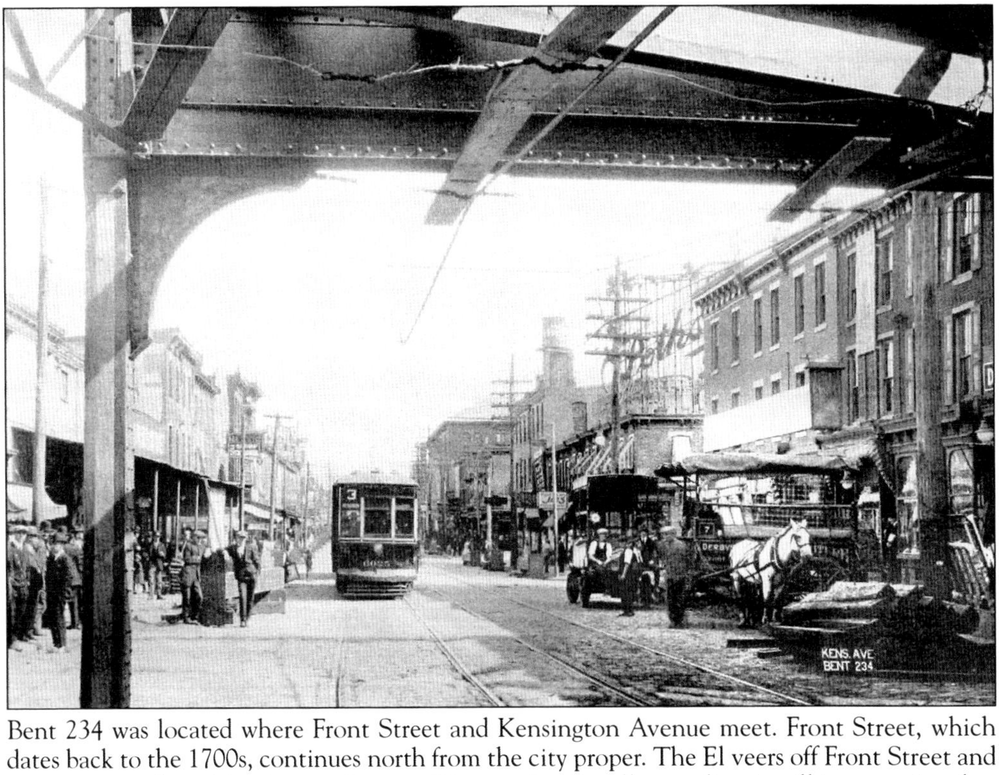

Bent 234 was located where Front Street and Kensington Avenue meet. Front Street, which dates back to the 1700s, continues north from the city proper. The El veers off Front Street and continues north on Kensington Avenue. The number 3 trolley-car line is still in operation, but the trolleys have been replaced by buses.

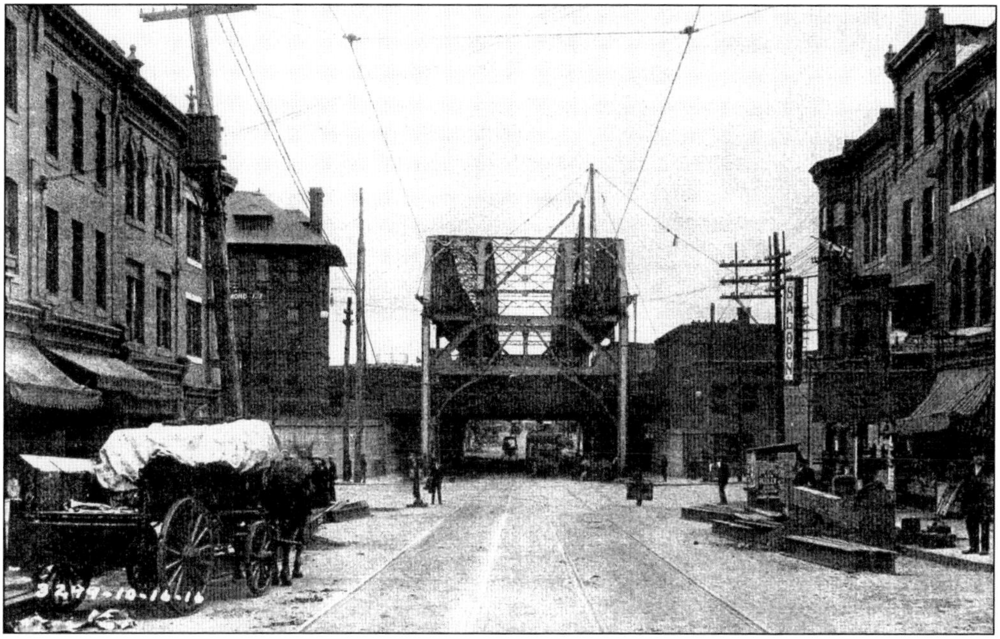

Kensington Avenue is shown here south of Lehigh Avenue looking north. Notice the 10-foot-high retaining wall. A few years prior, the Reading Railroad dug out millions of tons of earth along and around the intersection. Today, this rail system is still used by Conrail to reach the port of the Delaware River.

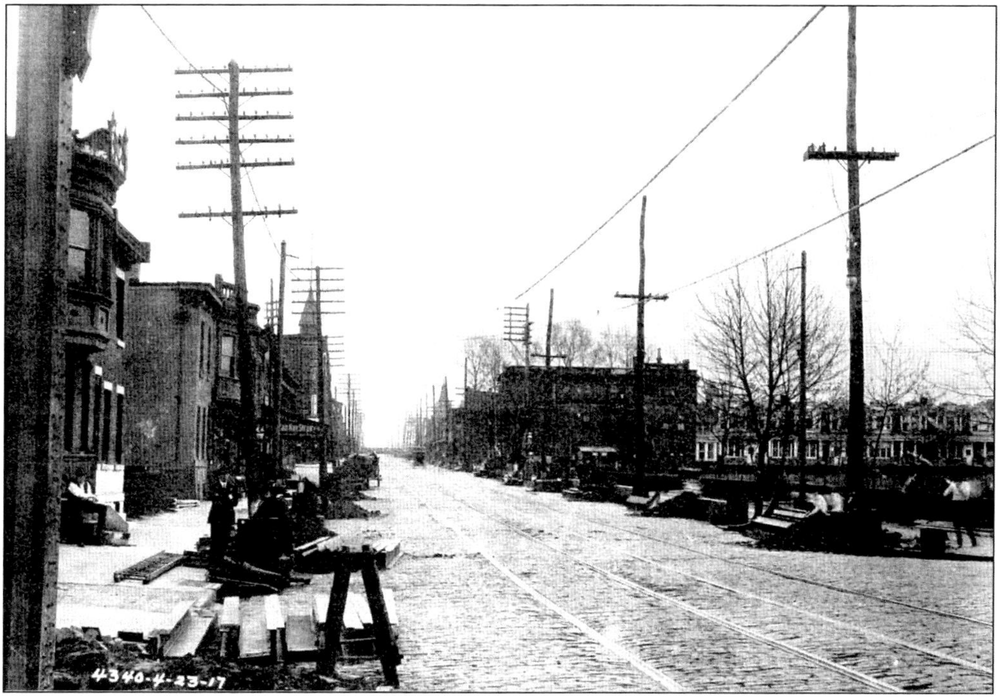

By the spring of 1917, the construction of the El reached as far north as Schiller Street at Kensington Avenue. The two attached homes on the left are still intact today. To the right is Harrowgate Park, and the homes fronting it also remain intact today.

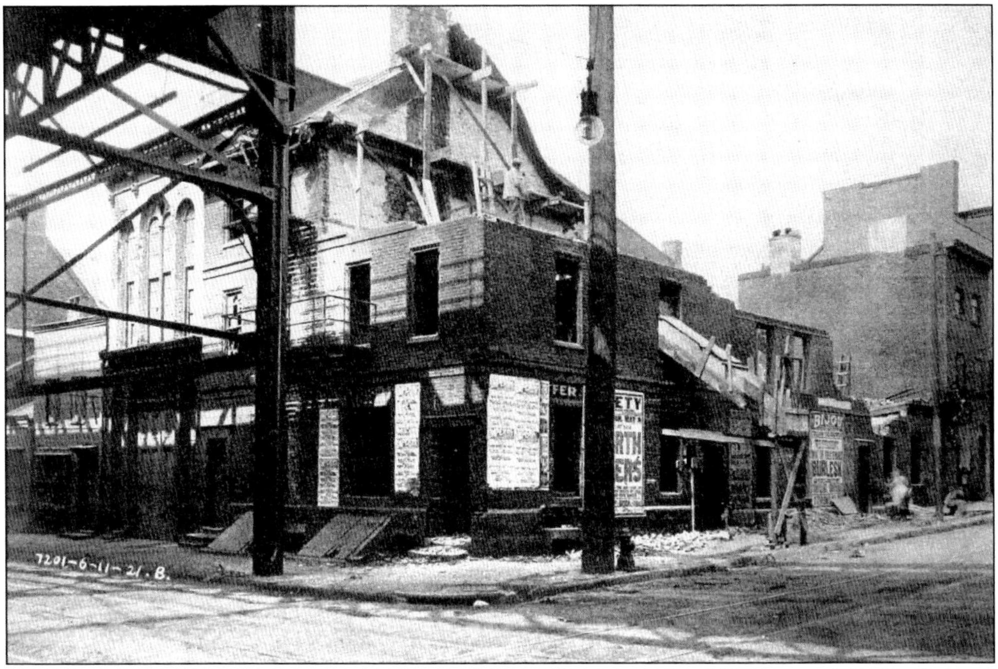

This was the future site of the El stop on the northeast corner of Front and Berks Streets. Note the chute coming from the building on the right. It appears demolition was done quite tediously, by hand. The burlesque advertisements also indicate the heavy foot traffic this intersection saw.

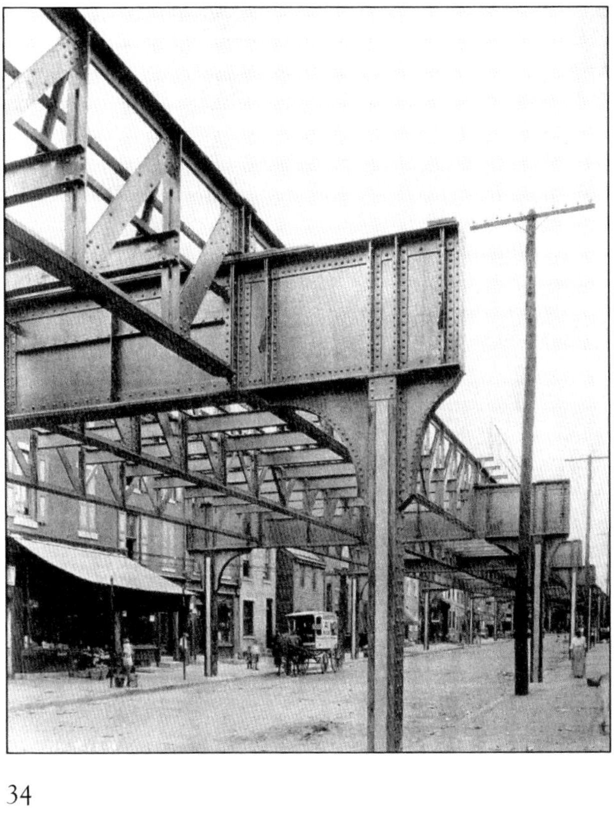

This 1917 vintage photograph shows the upright structure of the El in detail, before the laying of the concrete track bed and tracks. Also notice the two young boys standing next to an Abbott's milk wagon. This may indicate that this part of the El is in the Harrowgate or Frankford sections because Harbison Dairy serviced most of the Kensington and Richmond sections.

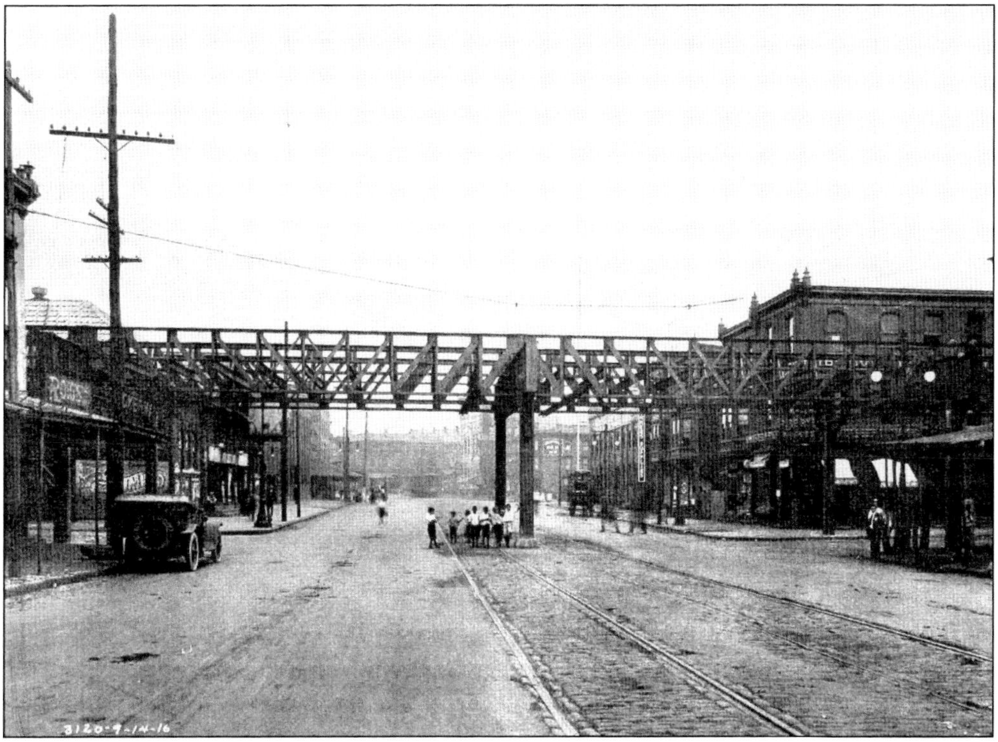

This photograph from July 14, 1916, shows the structure of the El over one of the four major intersections it crosses. Looking west on Girard Avenue, this view shows the bridge structure along Front Street. In the distance note the confusing turn on Girard Avenue that is contrary to the original city plan of straight, directional streets that run true north, south, east, and west.

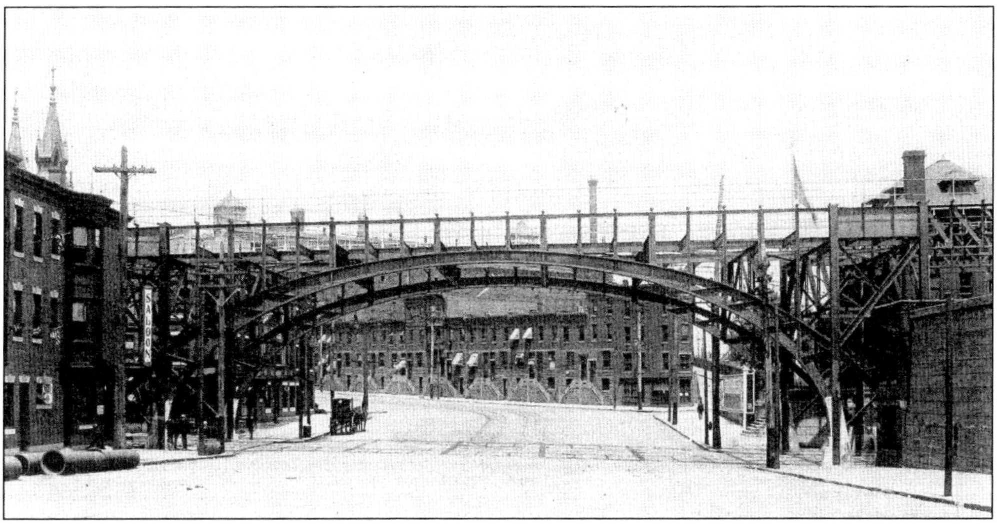

This photograph of Lehigh Avenue at Kensington Avenue again shows the sharp turn that is in contrast to the original plan of straight, directional streets. On the left of the photograph, you see the steeple of Visitation Catholic Church at B Street and Lehigh Avenue.

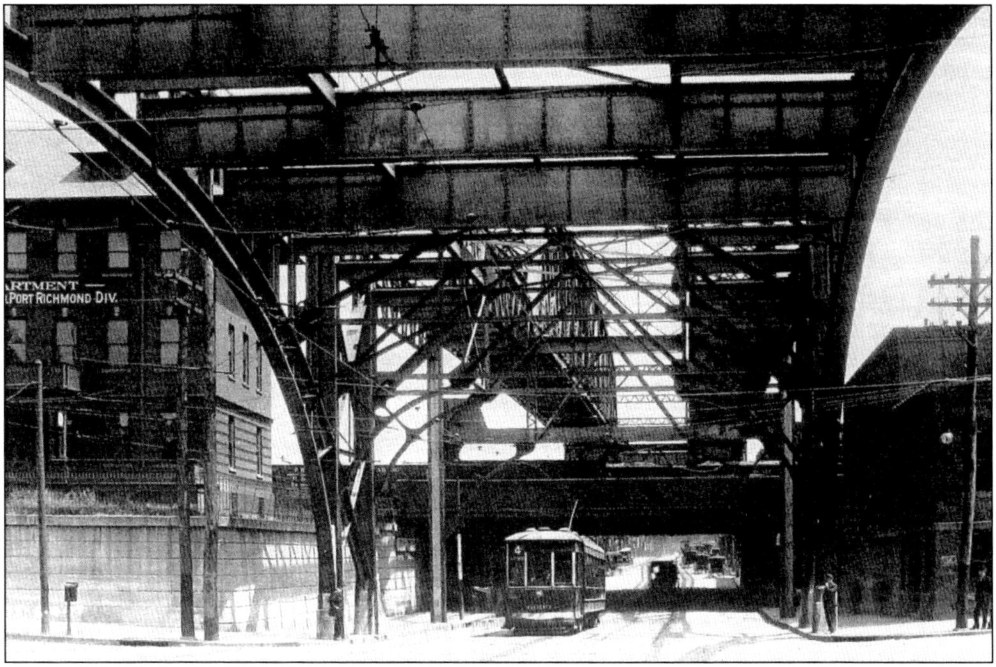

The No. 4 trolley car traveled under the El along Kensington Avenue. As it turned onto Front Street, it became the No. 3 trolley and traveled the same route as the El. These route numbers, though serviced by buses, remain the same today.

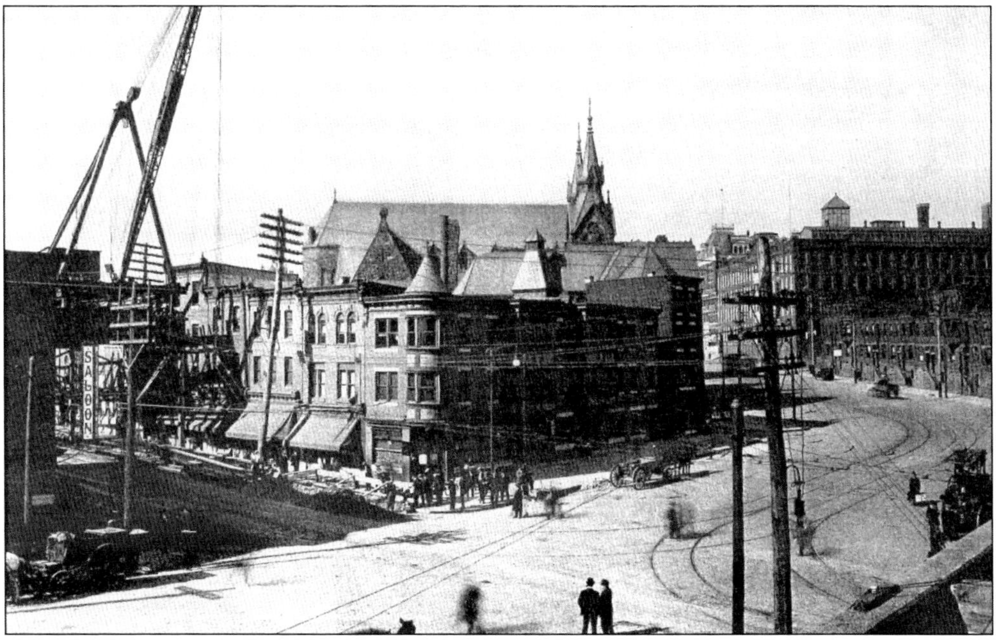

Possibly the only known aerial photograph of the El under construction. This view is from the northeast looking toward the southwest from the rooftop of what was the Strathman Coal Company. Clearly visible is the Tinney Saloon, a neighborhood fixture for over 80 years. Notice the excavation of the intersection and the bend of Lehigh Avenue as it heads west toward North Philadelphia.

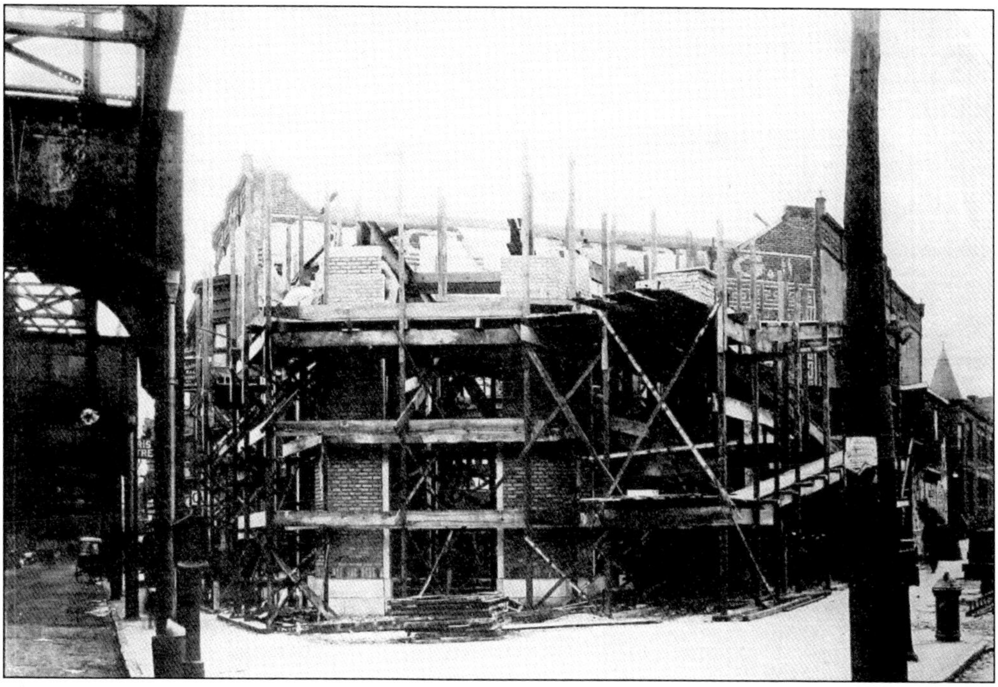

These two photographs are of the construction of the original El stops at the K&A (Kensington and Allegheny Avenues) intersection. The top photograph is of the southwest corner—the southbound stop. The bottom photograph is of the northeast corner—the northbound stop. These longtime landmarks were replaced by new, modern structures in 2000.

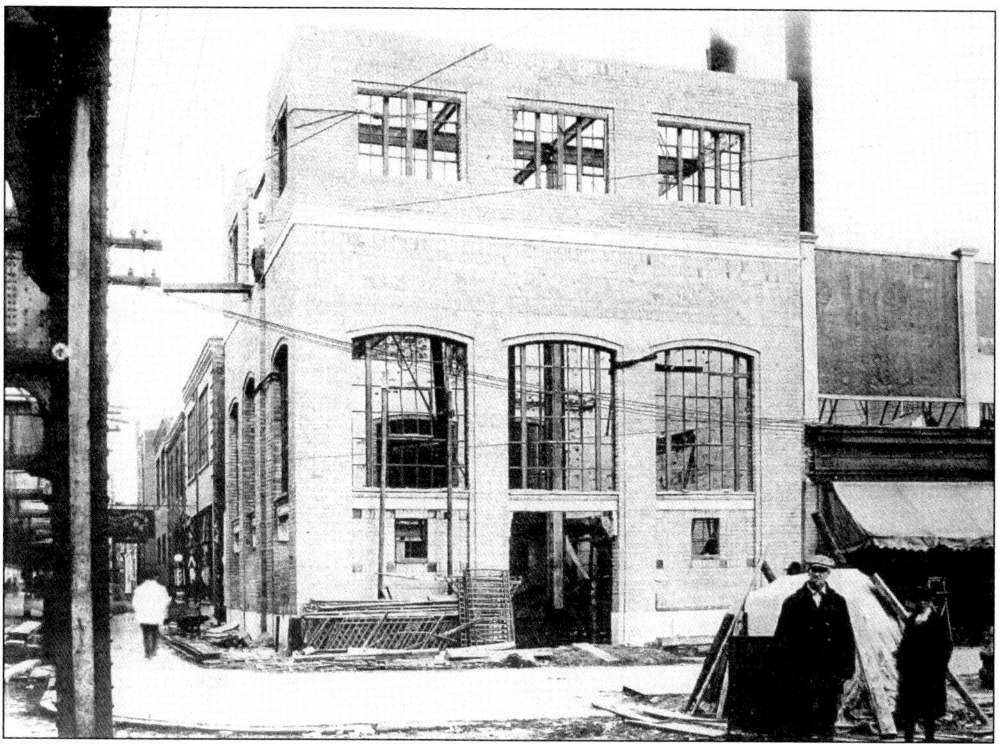

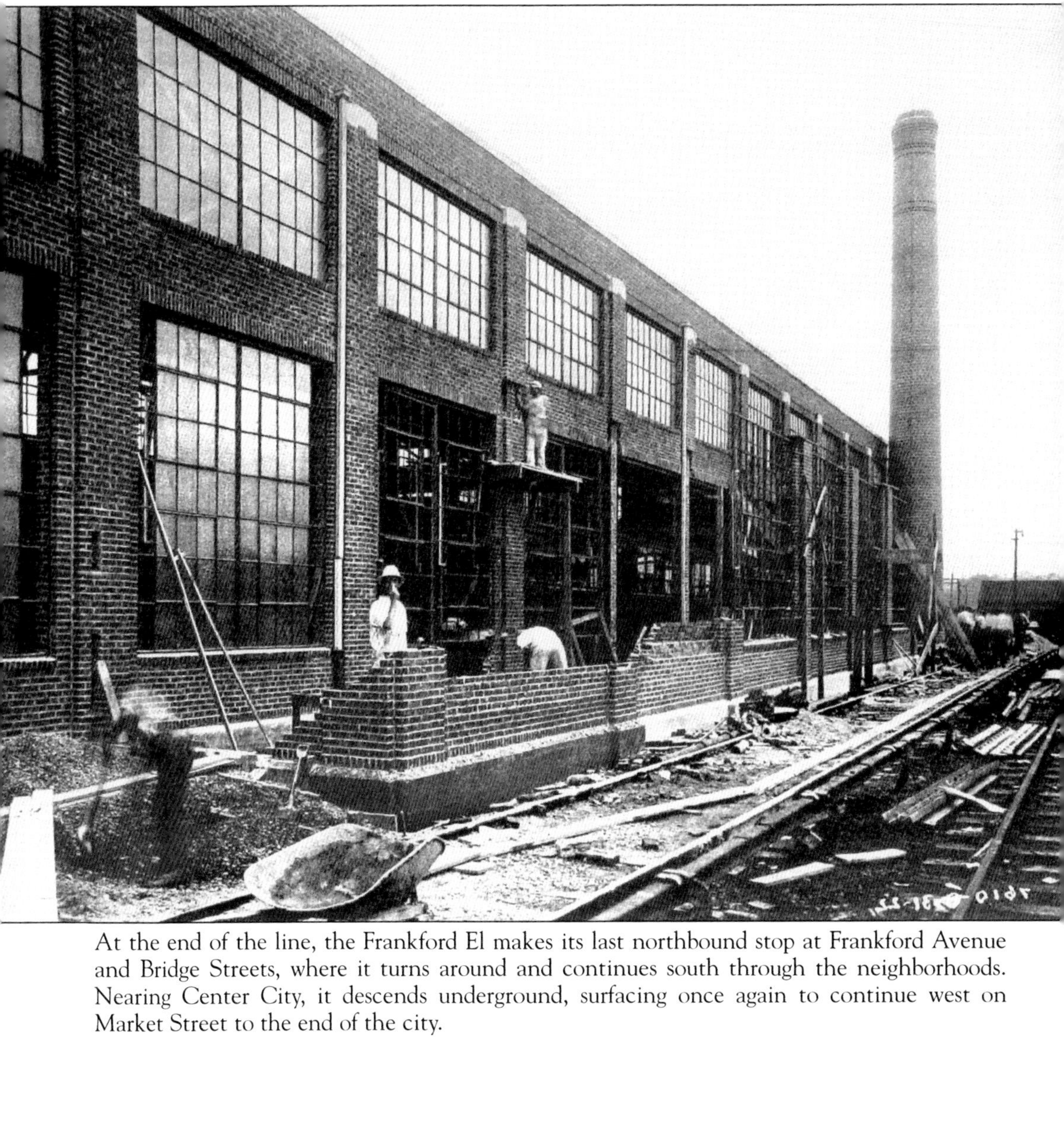

At the end of the line, the Frankford El makes its last northbound stop at Frankford Avenue and Bridge Streets, where it turns around and continues south through the neighborhoods. Nearing Center City, it descends underground, surfacing once again to continue west on Market Street to the end of the city.

Four

THE NEIGHBORHOODS AND THEIR PEOPLE

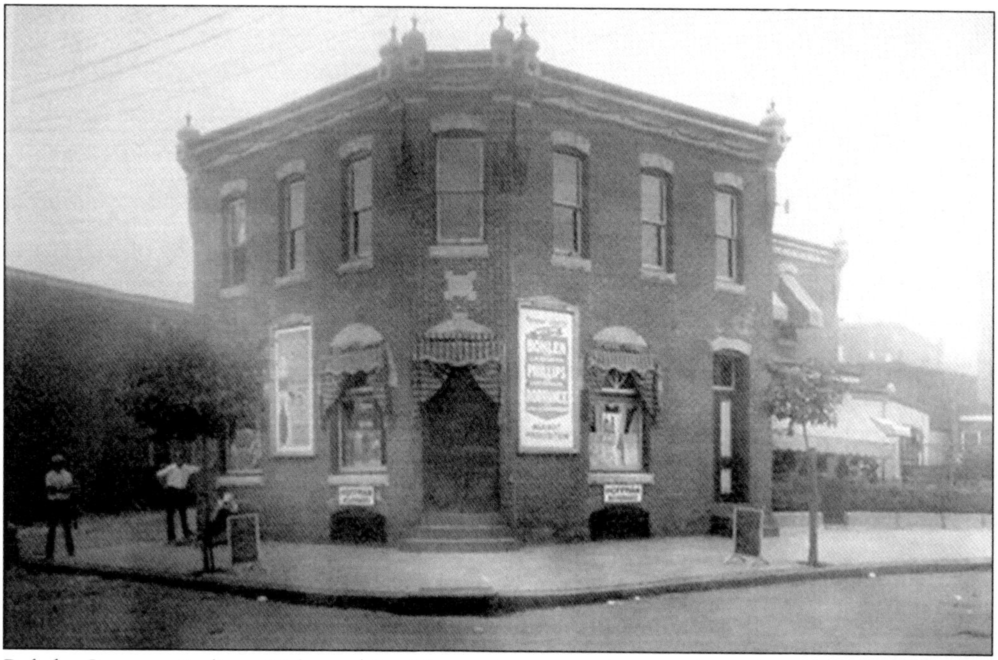

Polish, German, Italian, Irish, and Jewish immigrants each carved out their own small section of the River Wards. Within the neighborhoods, each ethnic group lived closely together, sharing the cultural traditions of their homelands. Most continued to speak in their native tongue, while struggling to learn the language of their new home. In Port Richmond, a tiny neighborhood within a neighborhood sprang up in the area around Cambria and Martha Streets. A Jewish scrap-metal dealer named Yehzekiel Bernstein settled a small cluster of Jews in the area and named it Jerusalem Richmond, which later became known as Jewtown.

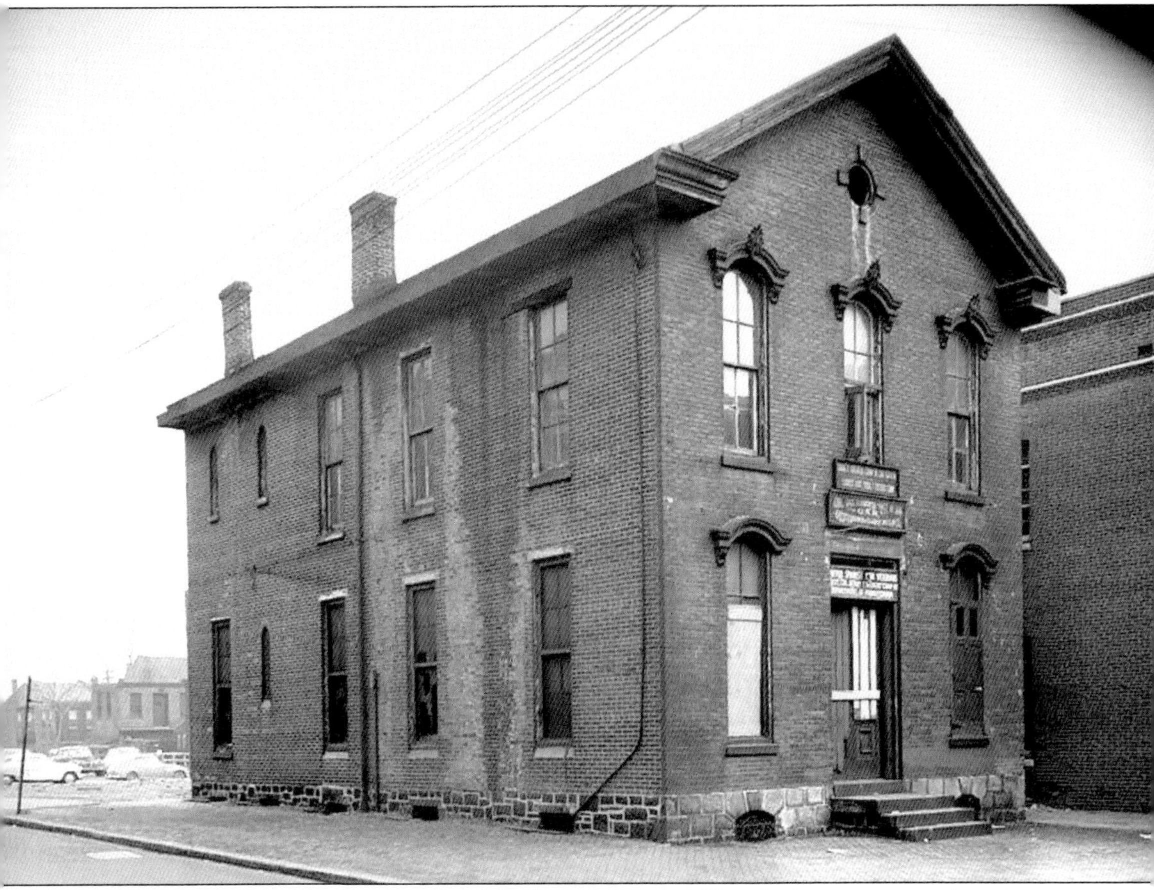

At one time, this building on Frankford Avenue near Church Street was used as the town hall. Every unincorporated township had a town hall or municipal building that managed the day-to-day business of the township.

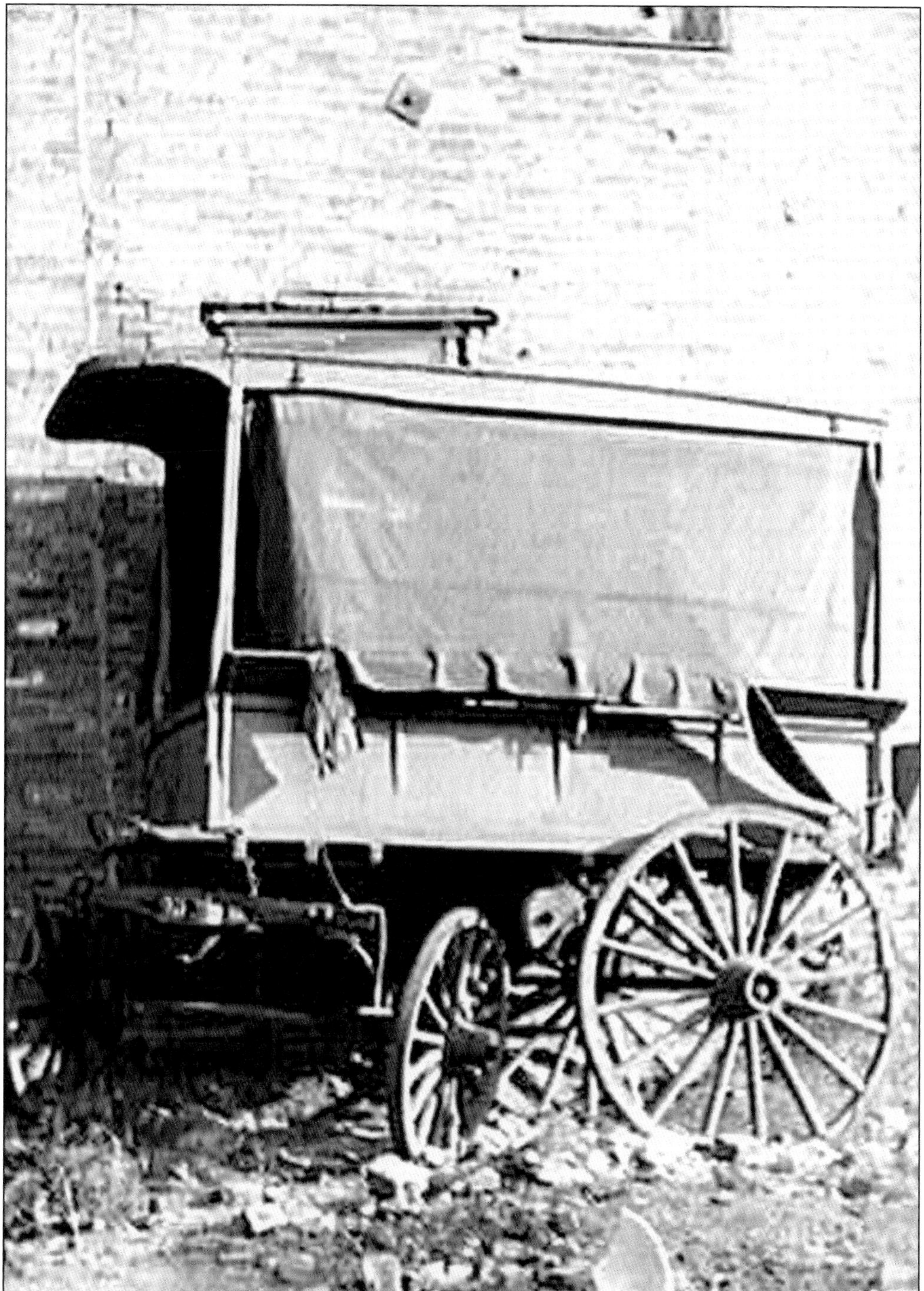

Horse-drawn wagons were a common sight in the early days of the River Wards, and they continued to be used in a lesser capacity by produce sellers until the 1970s. Foster's (or Feorst's) Stables, located on Janney Street between Clearfield and Ann Streets in Port Richmond, housed horses and wagons used in the delivery of fruits and vegetables.

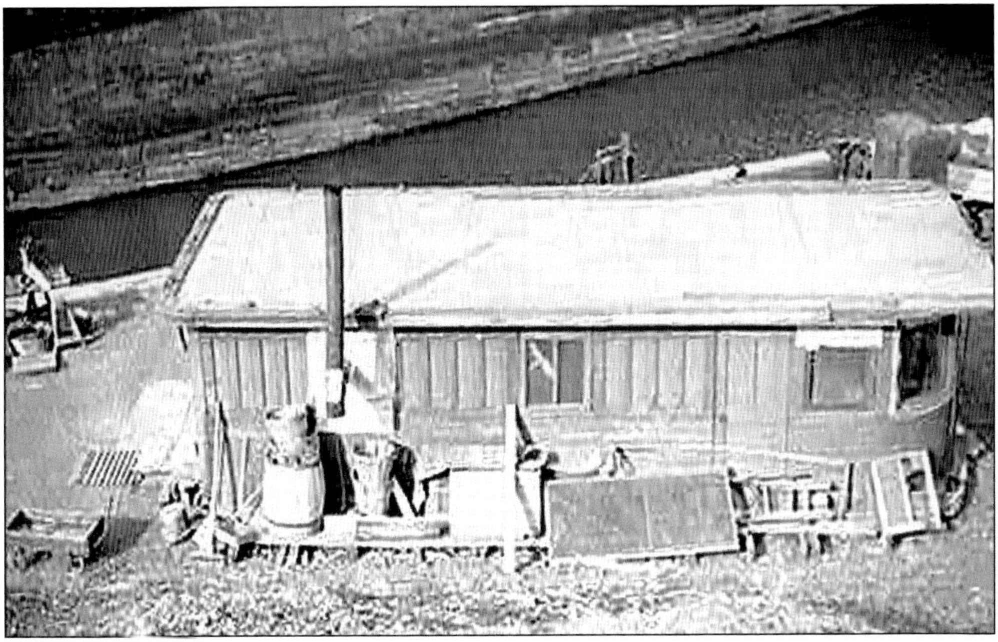

Situated along the Delaware River at the foot of Cambria Street is one of several shacks that dotted the banks of the river in the early and mid-1900s. These shacks were the living quarters of coal company employees who worked on the coal barges.

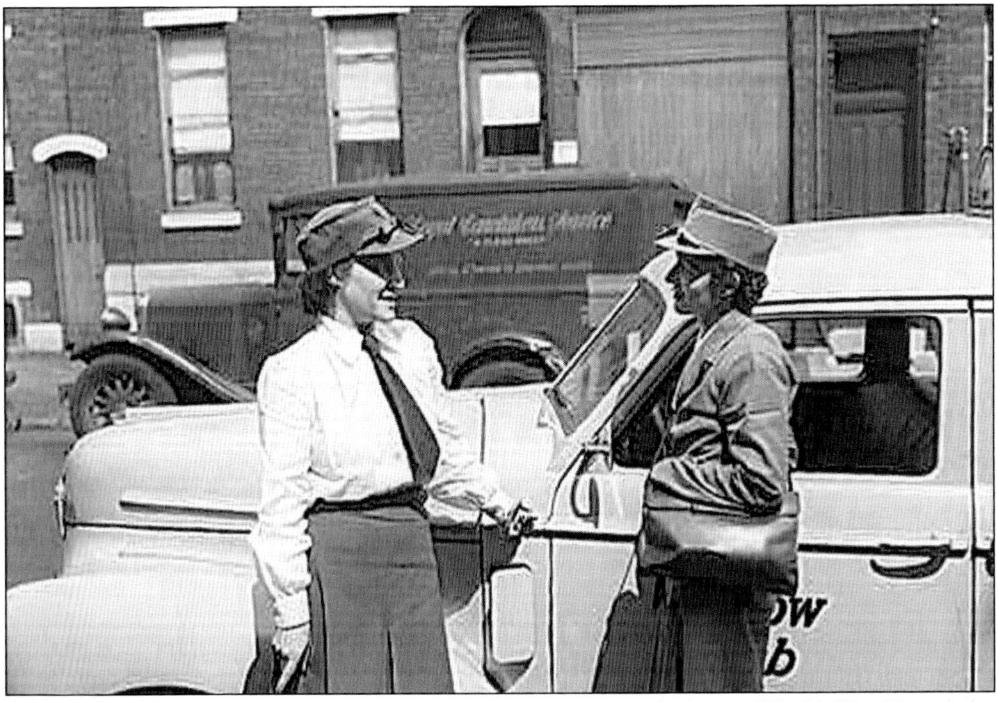

Rosie the Riveter was not the only woman who went to work during World War II and the Korean War. Many women signed on as cabbies to help make ends meet. The Yellow Cab Company was located at Cambria Street and Kensington Avenue and had a very unique entrance ramp that went directly to the second story.

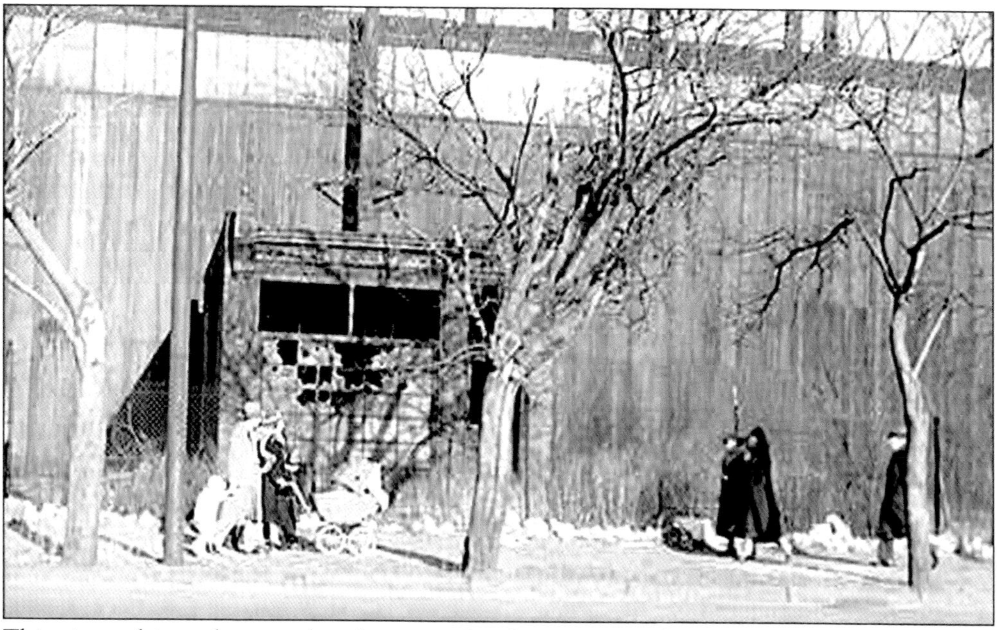

This city archives photograph, taken on a Sunday morning, shows Port Richmond residents, perhaps on their way to church, passing the lumberyard on Aramingo Avenue between Westmoreland and Ontario Streets. The lumberyard was destroyed by a fire in the early 1970s and was replaced by an Acme and a Kmart.

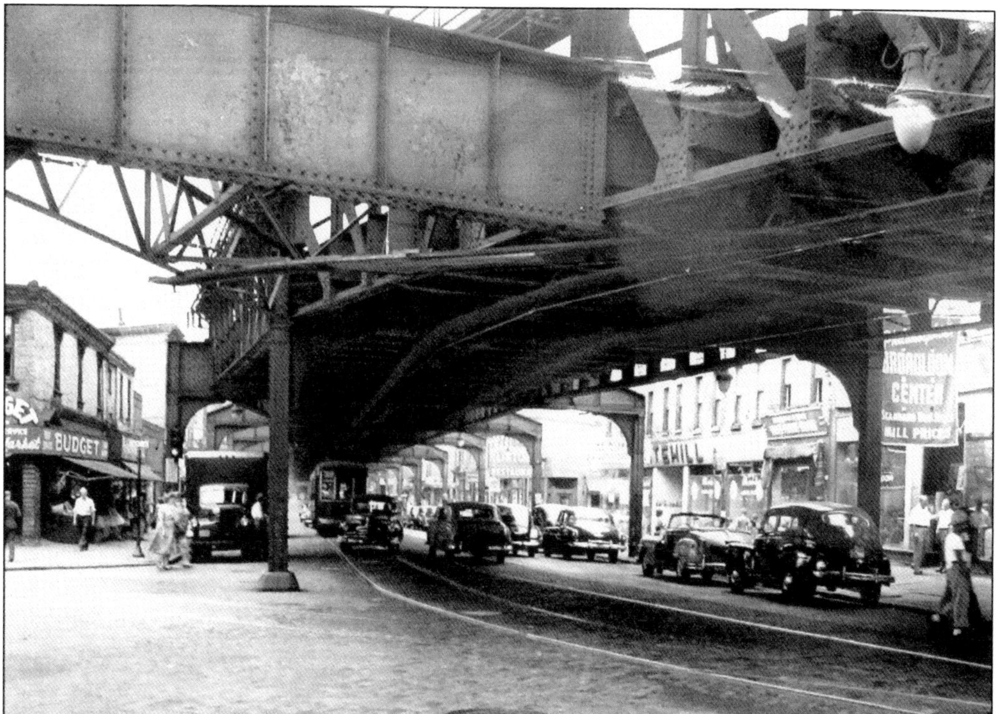

North and southbound El riders are familiar with the ear-piercing screech of metal meeting metal that signals the bend where Kensington Avenue meets Front Street.

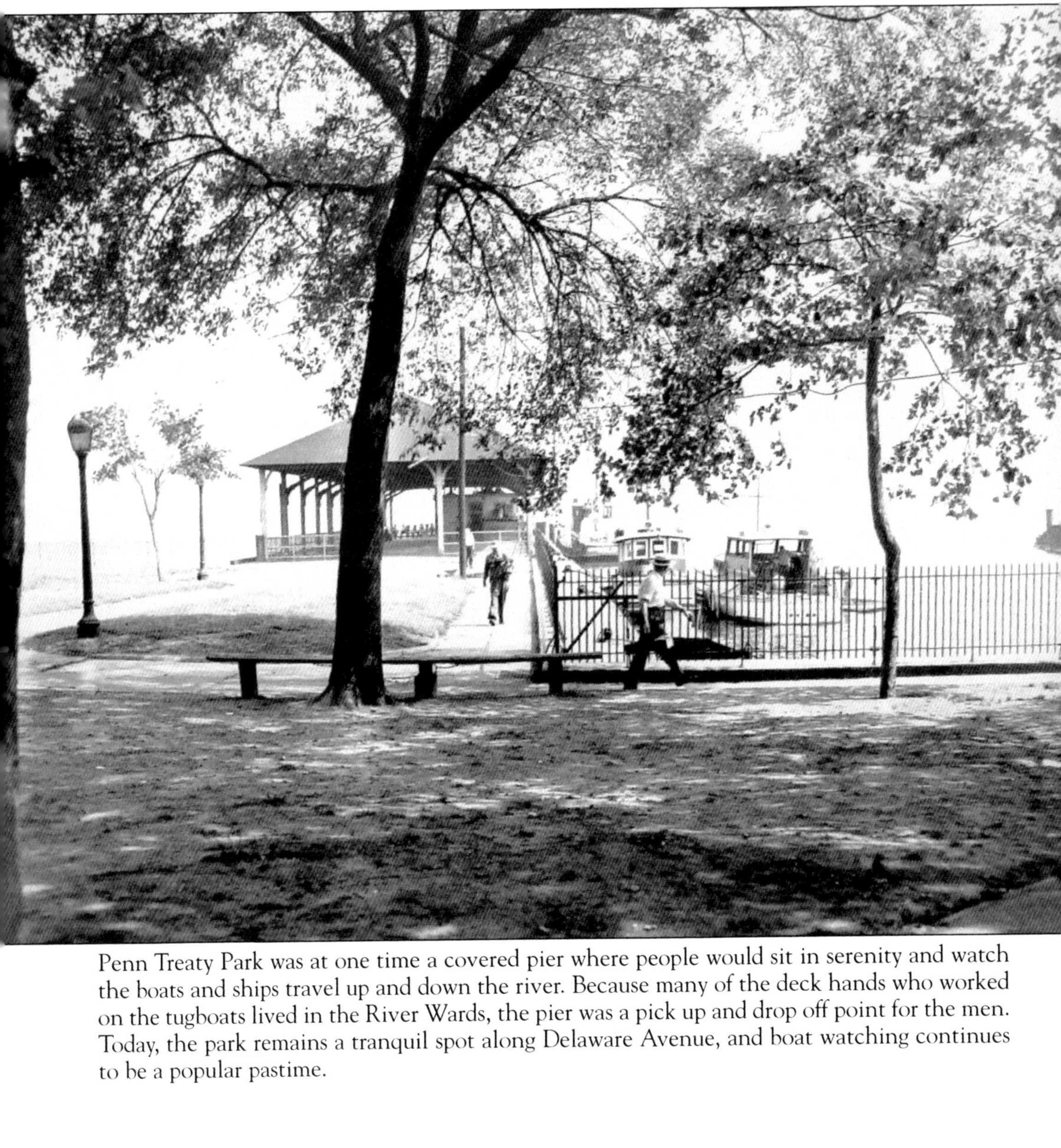

Penn Treaty Park was at one time a covered pier where people would sit in serenity and watch the boats and ships travel up and down the river. Because many of the deck hands who worked on the tugboats lived in the River Wards, the pier was a pick up and drop off point for the men. Today, the park remains a tranquil spot along Delaware Avenue, and boat watching continues to be a popular pastime.

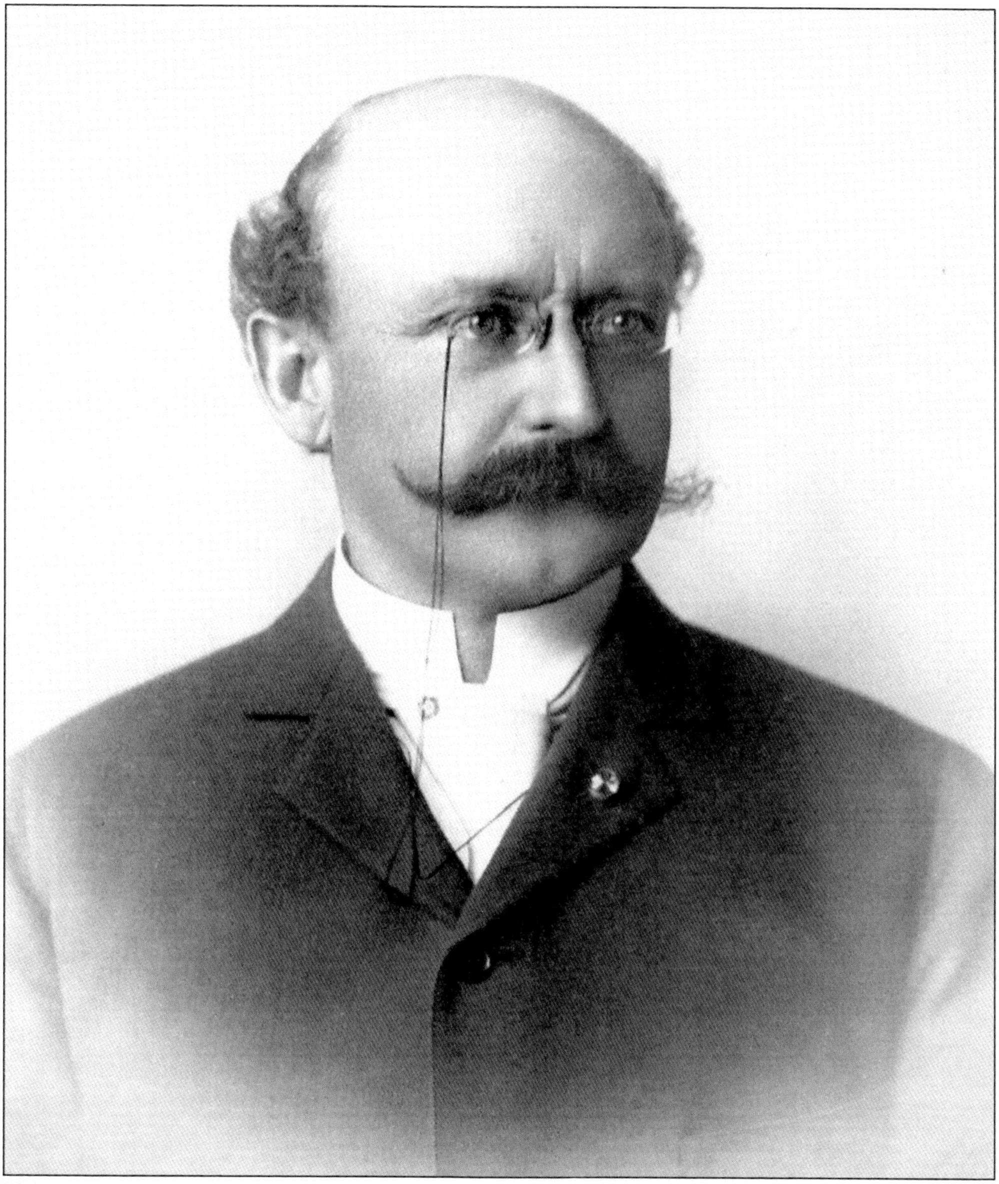

U.S. Congressman Henry H. Bingham, a Frankford resident, was a Civil War Union general who was awarded the Medal of Honor. In a scene depicted in a Gettysburg monument, fatally wounded Confederate General Armistead gives his Masonic bible to Bingham to give to his friend, Union General Hancock. Bingham is buried in the cemetery located at Frankford Avenue and Bridge Street.

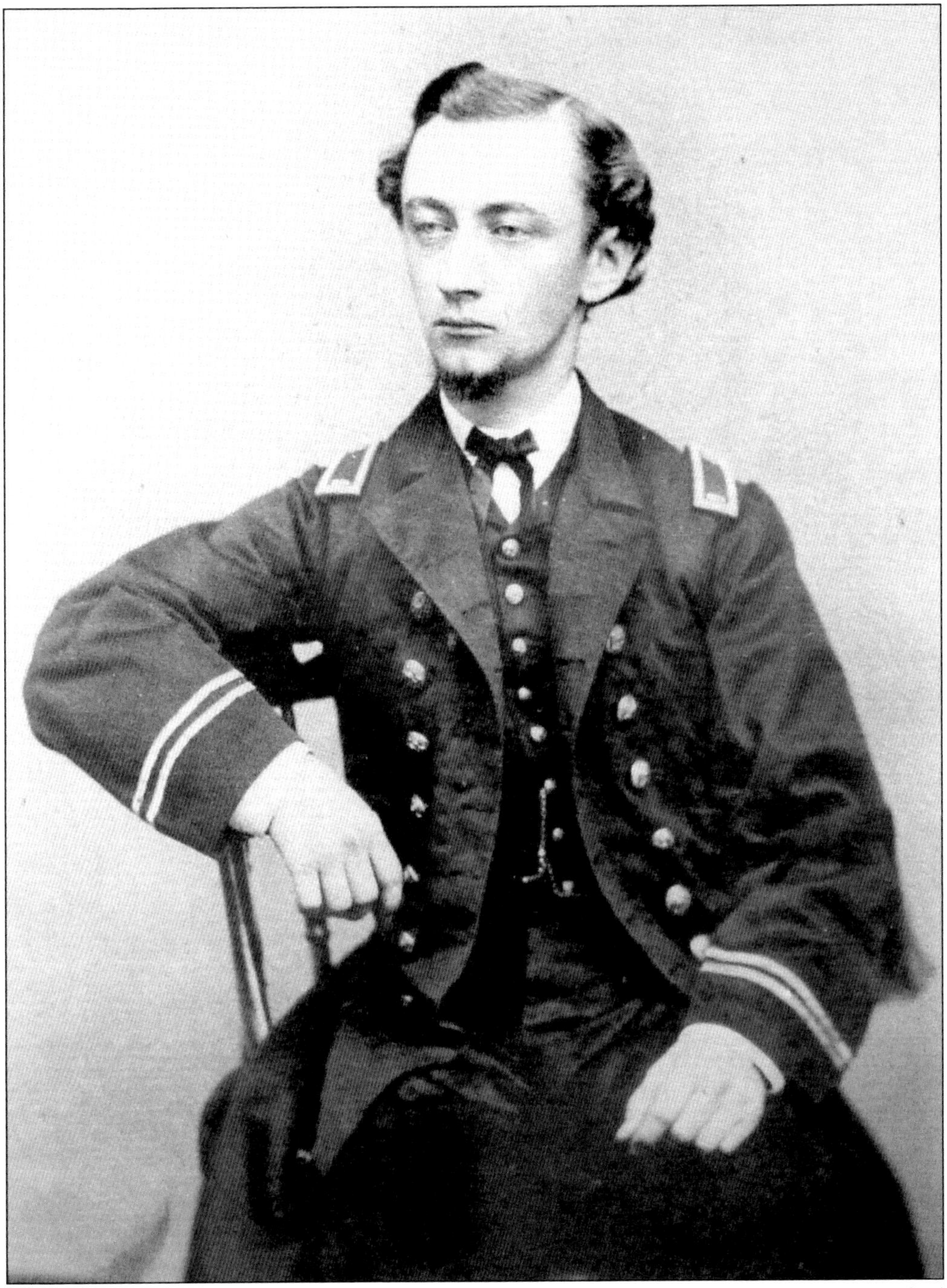

The subject of this photograph is identified as Union officer Rice of Frankford Road, who died in the battle of Antietam. Unearthed at a neighborhood flea market, the photograph was taken by a photographer whose studio was located at 200 Arch Street in Center City.

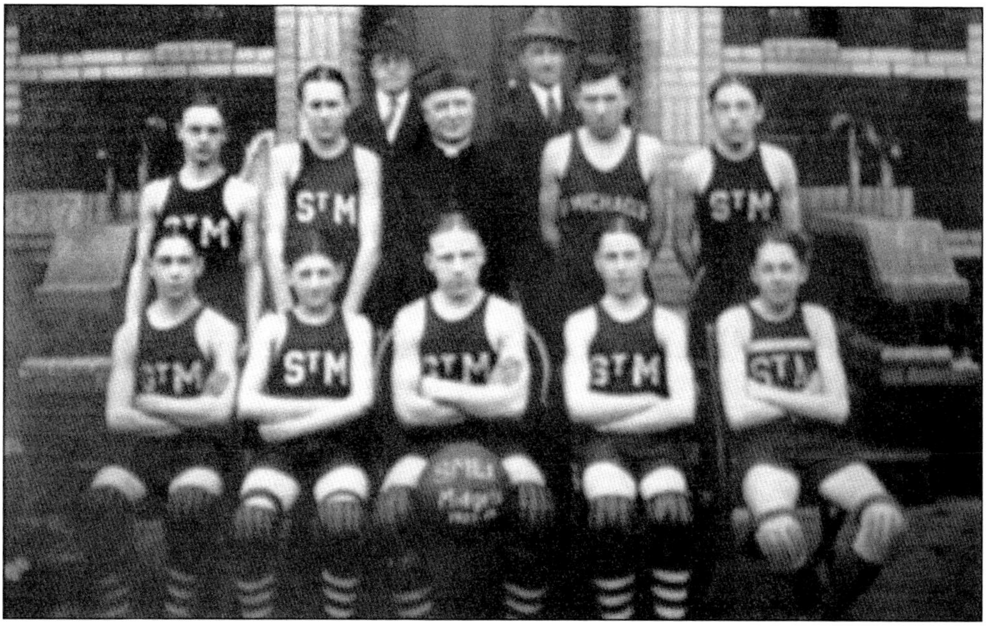

St. Michael's basketball teams pose for championship photographs in 1912 and 1925. This Irish Catholic parish is rich in history. In the early 1800s, St. Mike's, as it is fondly called, was the scene of ethnic strife. The English residents burned the original church building to the ground in the 1840s. For weeks following this event, the entire area was taken over by cavalry and army patrols, sheriffs, and corrupt politicians. The Irish parishioners trusted no one for some time after the torching, but eventually they rebuilt their church. The burning and destruction of St. Michael's is the reason the Cathedral Basilica of SS. Peter and Paul in downtown Philadelphia was built without large stained glass windows.

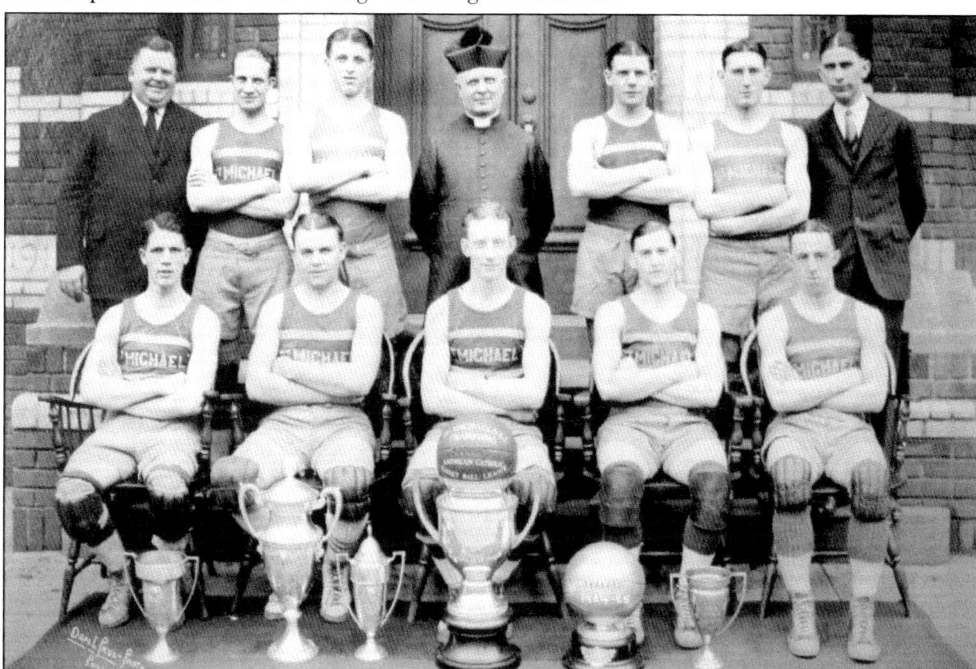

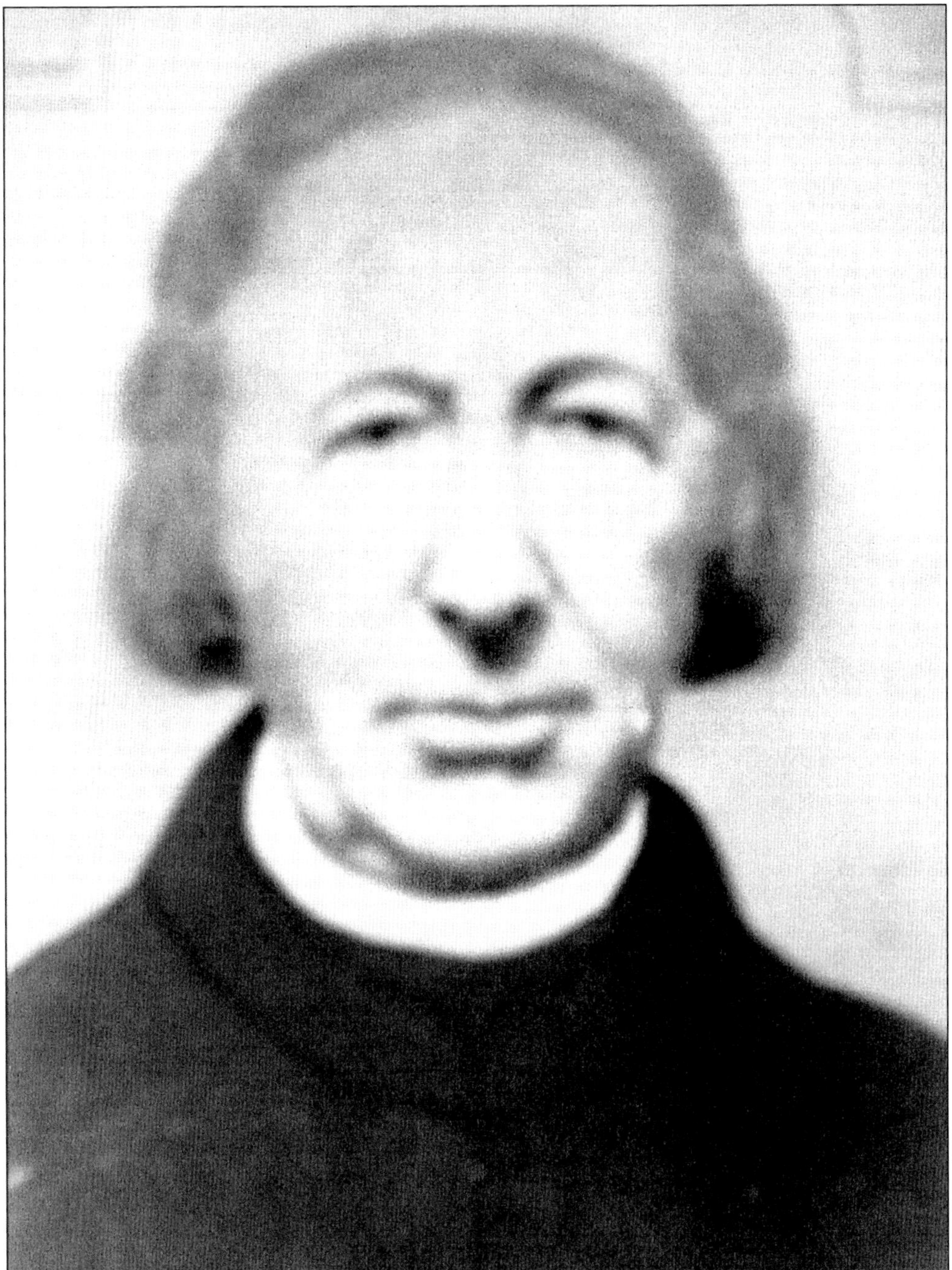

Father Donoghoe, the first pastor of St. Michael's, organized the church and the school, working with a group of women he brought with him from Ireland. Father Donoghoe undertook the task of Catholic education in a time when prejudice against the Irish was prevalent. The parish was built at Second and Jefferson Streets in Kensington. The shops surrounding the church and school area posted signs that read: "Catholic Irish need not apply."

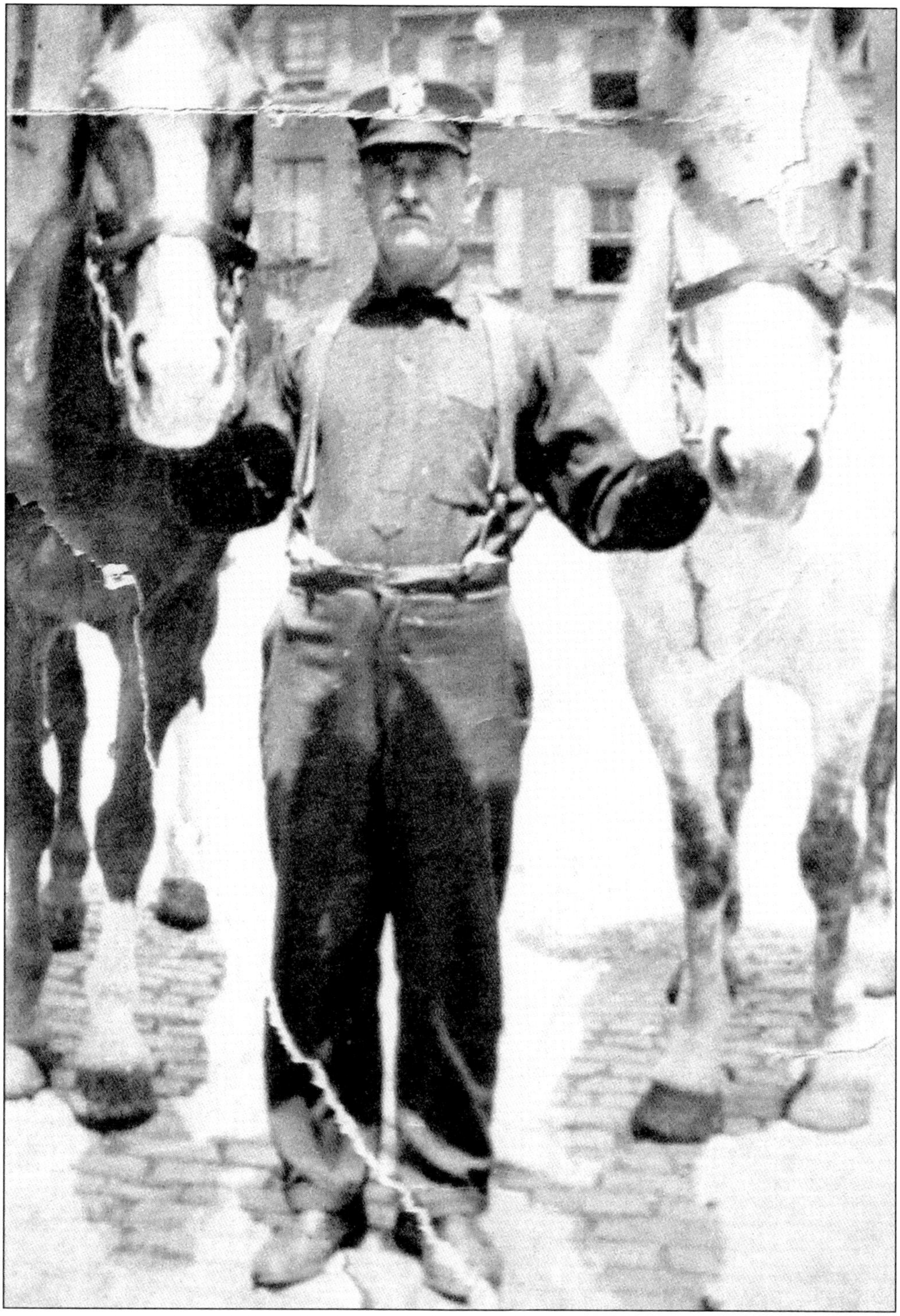

A fireman, from what is believed to be the firehouse at 300 Richmond Street in Old Kensington, is pictured with the firehouse horses whose job it was to pull the hose wagons. In the original, timeworn photograph the horses' names are printed but are now unclear.

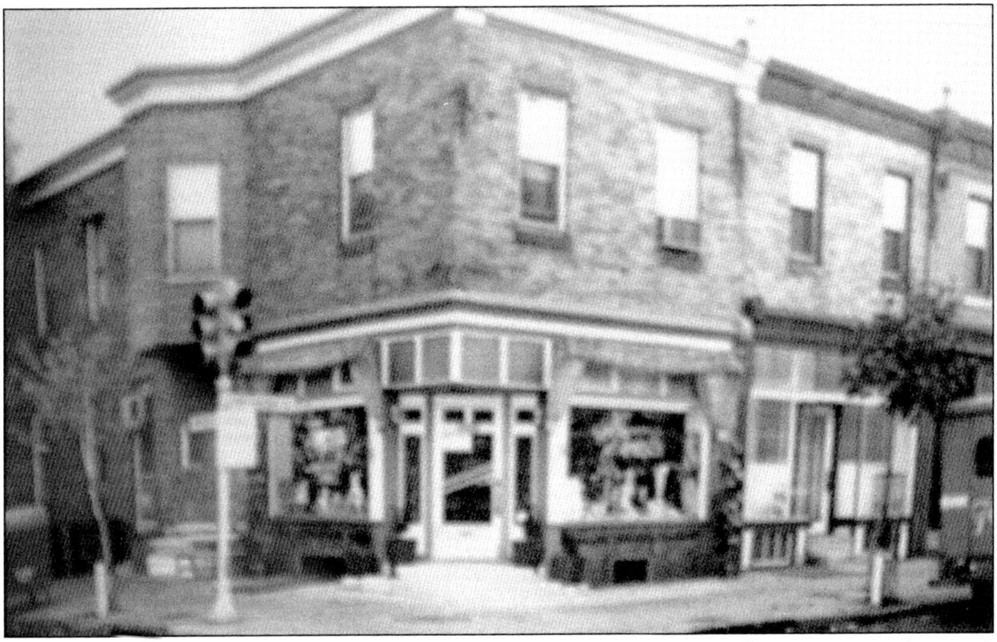

In the 1950s, Bridesburg was predominantly a Polish community. This area near the 2400 block of Orthodox Street was dotted with delicatessens, meat markets, and bakeries. Today, Bridesburg remains a tight-knit community—although more ethnically mixed. Corner stores still feature Polish delicacies.

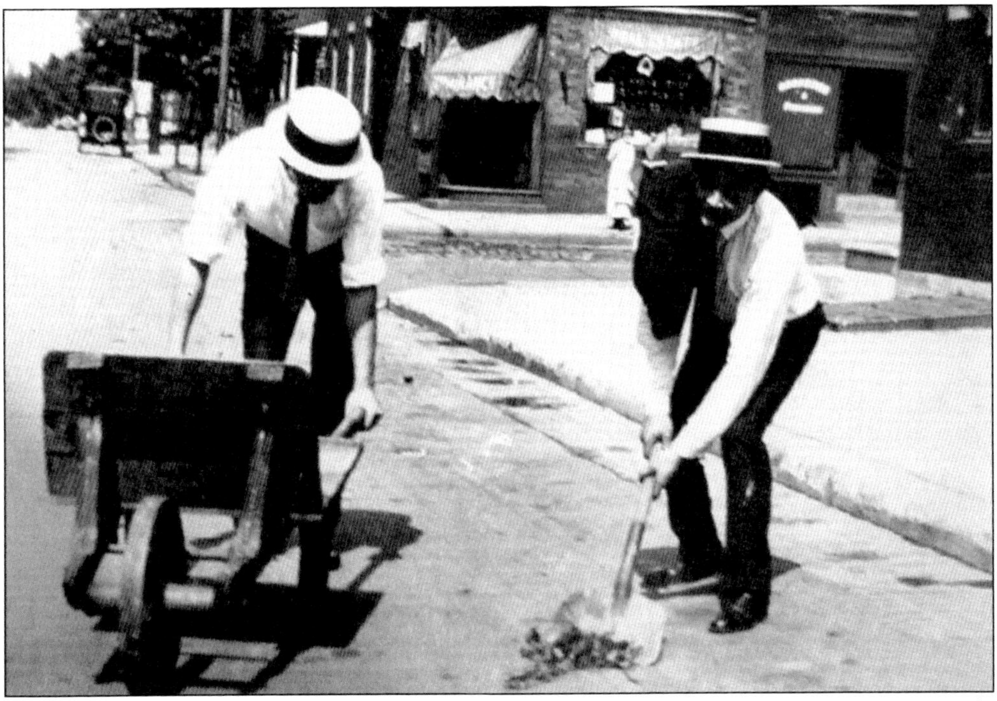

By the look of the cars in the distance, this photograph was taken around the late 1920s or early 1930s. These two dapper fellows are believed to be shoveling horse manure after a parade in Bridesburg. Today, Bridesburg still boasts the largest Memorial Day parade in the area.

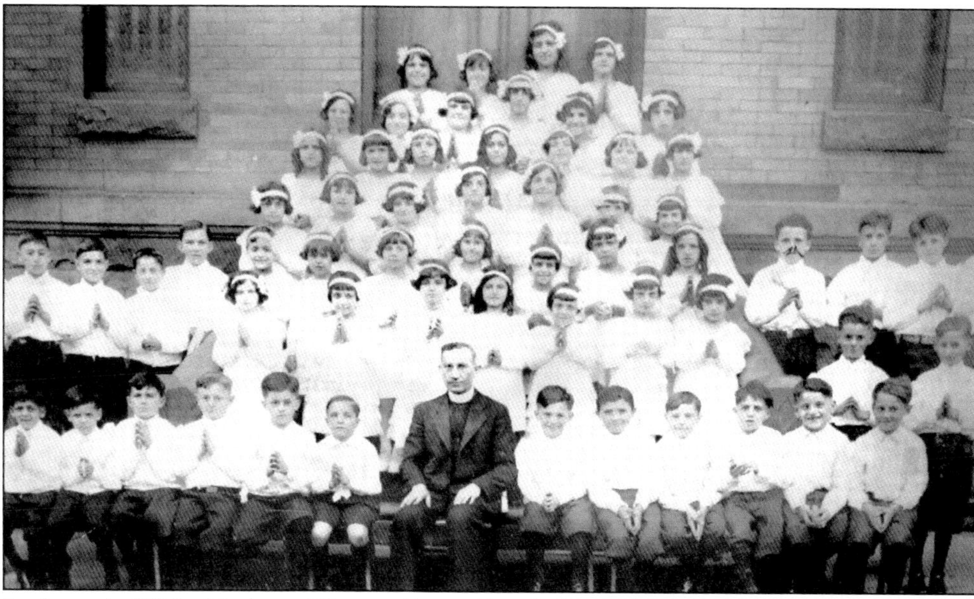

In the early 1900s, Mother of Divine Grace Church, located in Port Richmond at Thompson and Cambria Streets celebrated First Communion services such as this one. Following in the early Philadelphia tradition of ethnic national parishes, Mother of Divine Grace Church began as an Italian parish. The area in Port Richmond where the church and school were located was even called "Little It'ly." Mother of Divine Grace Church remains an active parish today.

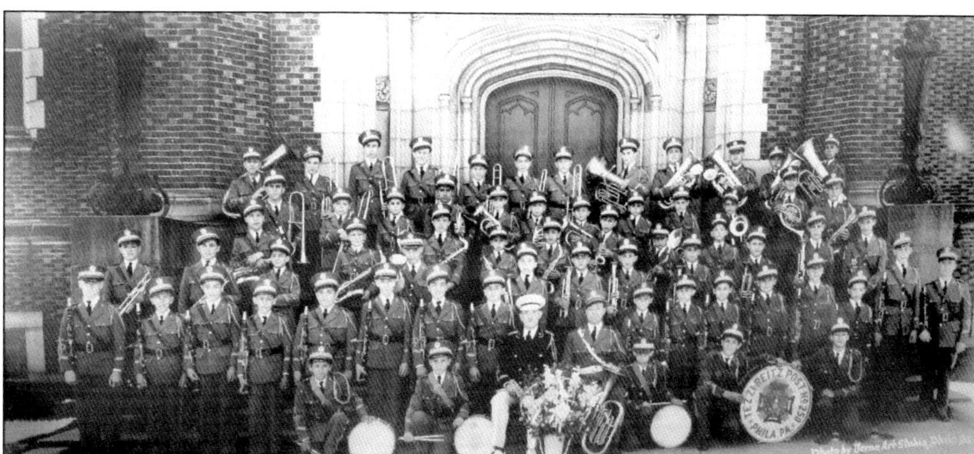

Another Port Richmond landmark is the Richmond Library, the Port Richmond Branch of the Free Library of Philadelphia, located at Almond and Indiana Streets. In this photograph, the Tezzi Reitz American Legion Post No. 250 poses outside the library. The post's marching band participated in many neighborhood and city parades in the early 20th century.

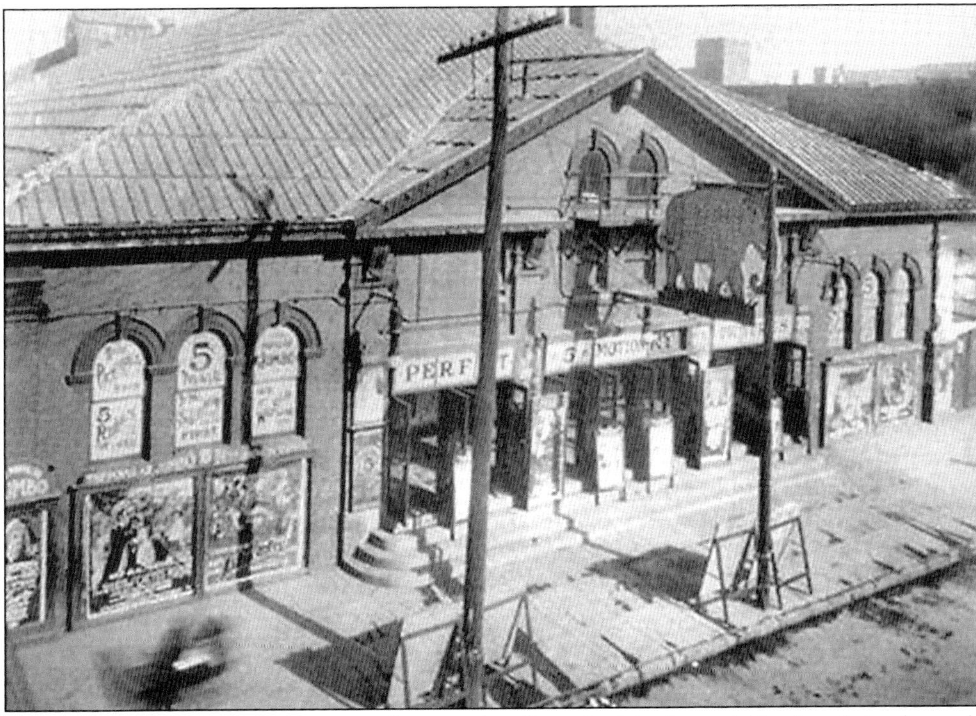

The Jumbo was one of many movie theaters that flourished in the neighborhoods in the early 20th century. Located at Front Street and Girard Avenue, the Jumbo is pictured from the catwalk of the southbound El. With its trademark woodcut elephant, the theater was named for the famous P.T. Barnum pachyderm. Belying its name, however, the theater was small in comparison to others in the area.

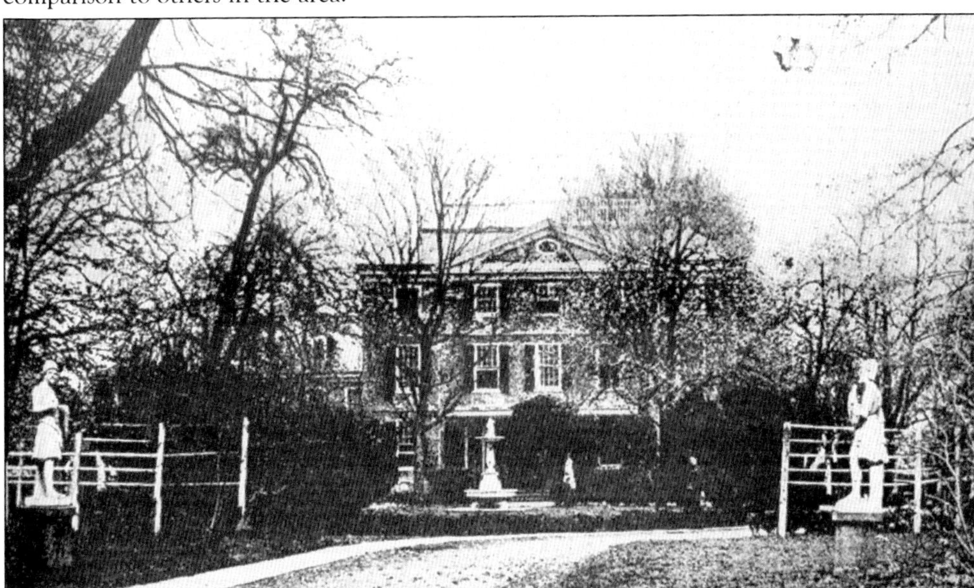

Chalkley Hall mansion stood on the corner of Sepviva Street and Wheatsheaf Lane, Frankford. Thomas Chalkley, a wealthy railroad tycoon, owned it in the early 1900s. One city record places the mansion in Aramingo, below Frankford.

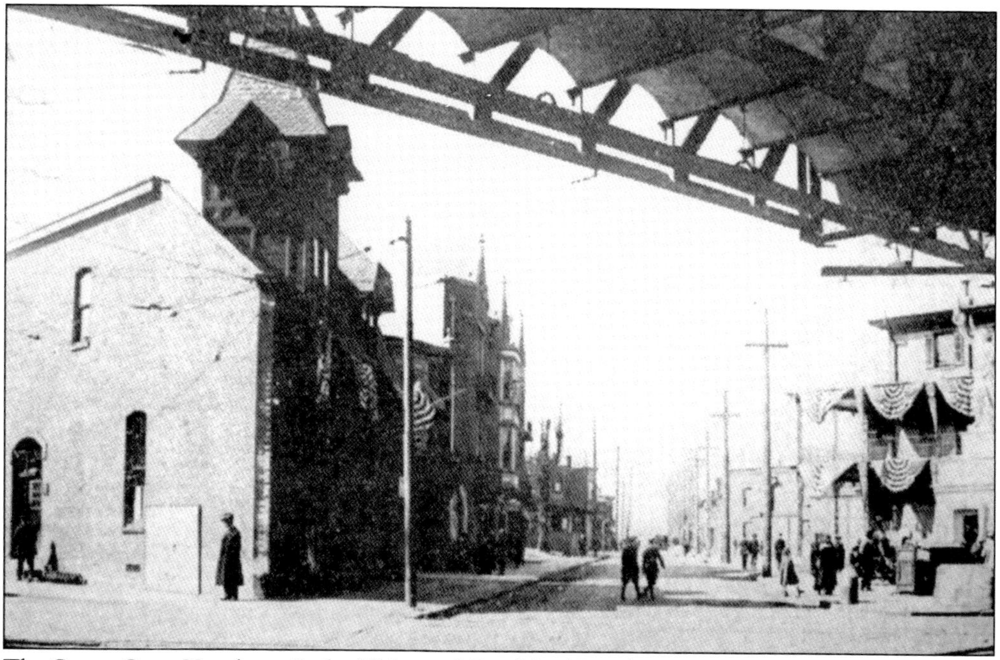

The Seven Stars Hotel, on Oxford Pike and Frankford Road, is thought to have been 100 years old when this photograph was taken in 1919. In the shadow of the Frankford El, the carriage depot to the right of the hotel seems to be draped with half-circle, American flag regalia.

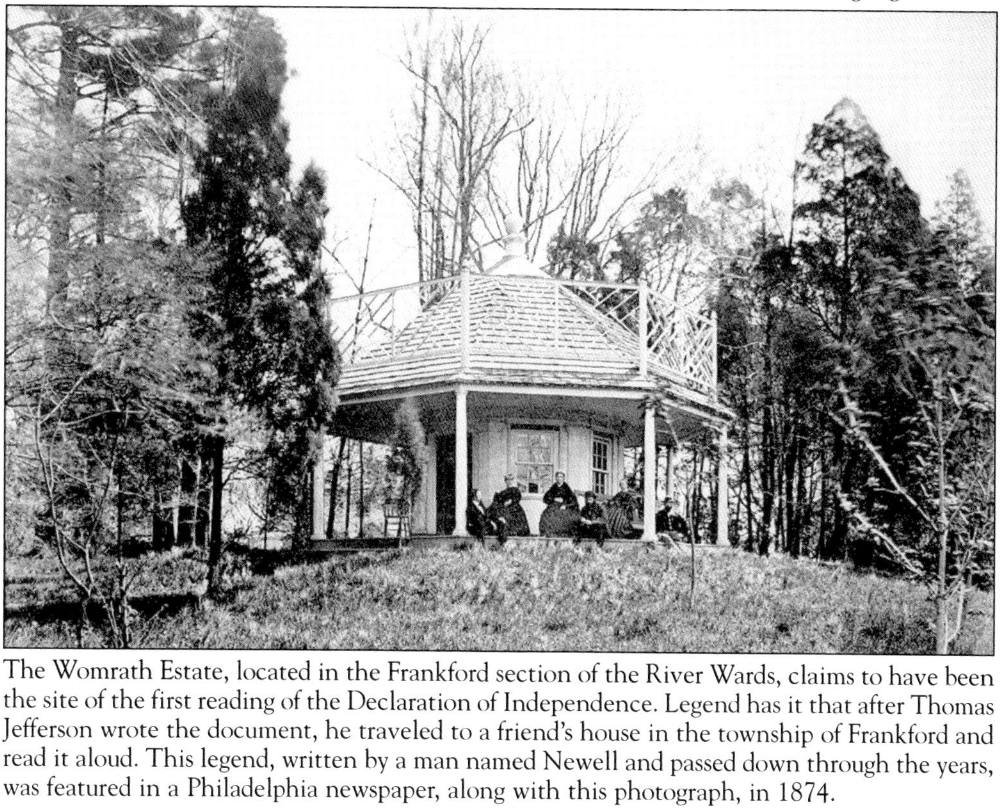

The Womrath Estate, located in the Frankford section of the River Wards, claims to have been the site of the first reading of the Declaration of Independence. Legend has it that after Thomas Jefferson wrote the document, he traveled to a friend's house in the township of Frankford and read it aloud. This legend, written by a man named Newell and passed down through the years, was featured in a Philadelphia newspaper, along with this photograph, in 1874.

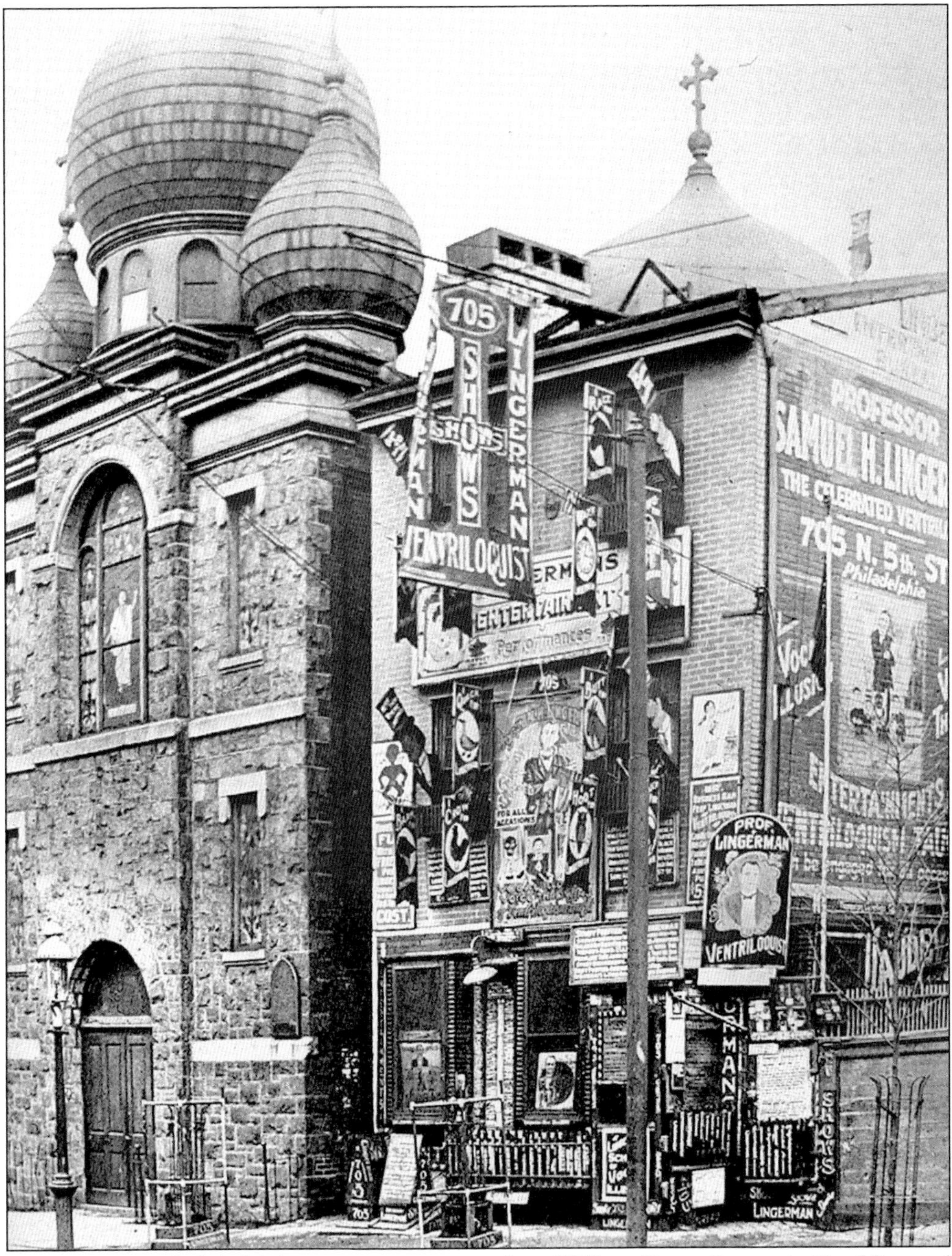

The early days of Philadelphia saw great men, such as William Penn, Benjamin Franklin, and George Washington, walk the streets of Northern Liberties. The turn of the 20th century brought a new kind of celebrity to the neighborhood, however. In this property on Fifth Street, north of Springarden Street, the somewhat infamous ventriloquist, Antonio Blitz, mesmerized audiences by making decapitated chickens speak to the crowds. Blitz later teamed up with magician Samuel Lingerman, and together they entertained audiences for years. Eventually, they were shut down by pressure from the Russian Orthodox Church next door under claims the performers practiced black arts and voodoo.

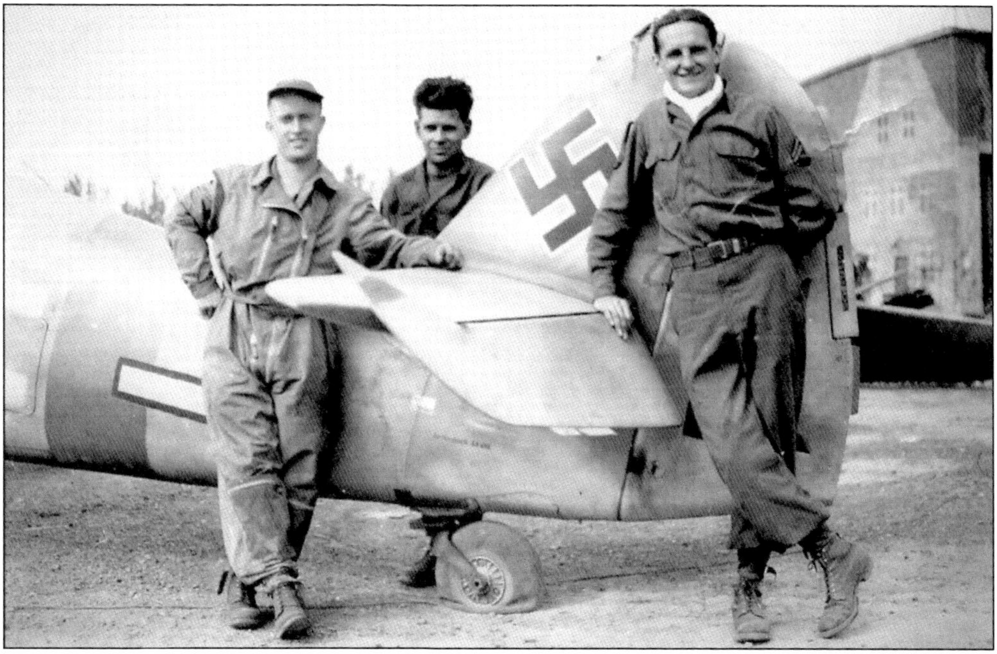

Cpl. Stanley Szklarski (at right) stands by a captured Nazi plane, along with two of his army comrades in Schwerin, Germany, near the end of World War II. A life-long Port Richmond resident, Szklarski left his home and his new bride in 1941 to serve in the United States Army. He fought in Normandy, Northern Africa, and then in Germany during the final days of the war. Like many other young men from the River Wards, Szklarski considered it an honor to serve his country and remained a proud veteran for the rest of his life.

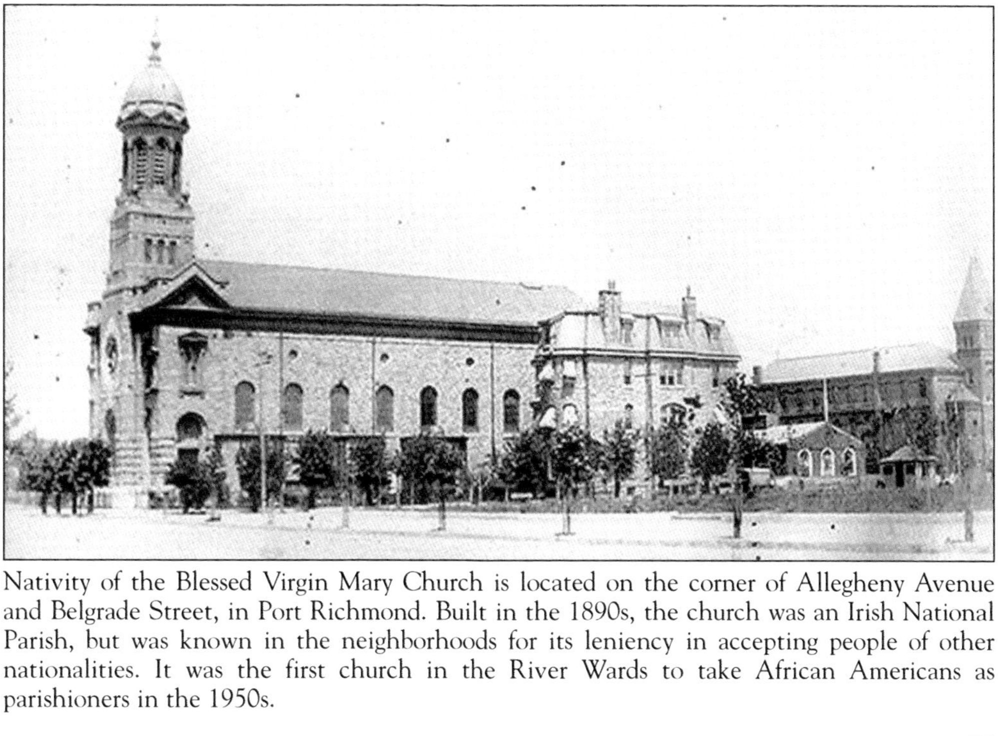

Nativity of the Blessed Virgin Mary Church is located on the corner of Allegheny Avenue and Belgrade Street, in Port Richmond. Built in the 1890s, the church was an Irish National Parish, but was known in the neighborhoods for its leniency in accepting people of other nationalities. It was the first church in the River Wards to take African Americans as parishioners in the 1950s.

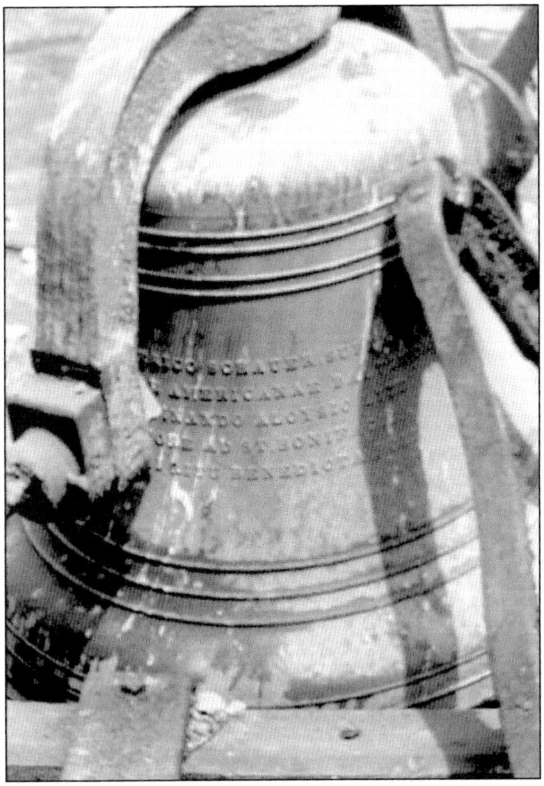

The tower room of the Nativity Church's original school building was a place of mystery to latter-day students, but this old bell was its only treasure. The old school was located at Belgrade and Madison Streets, across the street from the much bigger structure that replaced it. The old school was torn down in the late 1990s to make room for a parking lot.

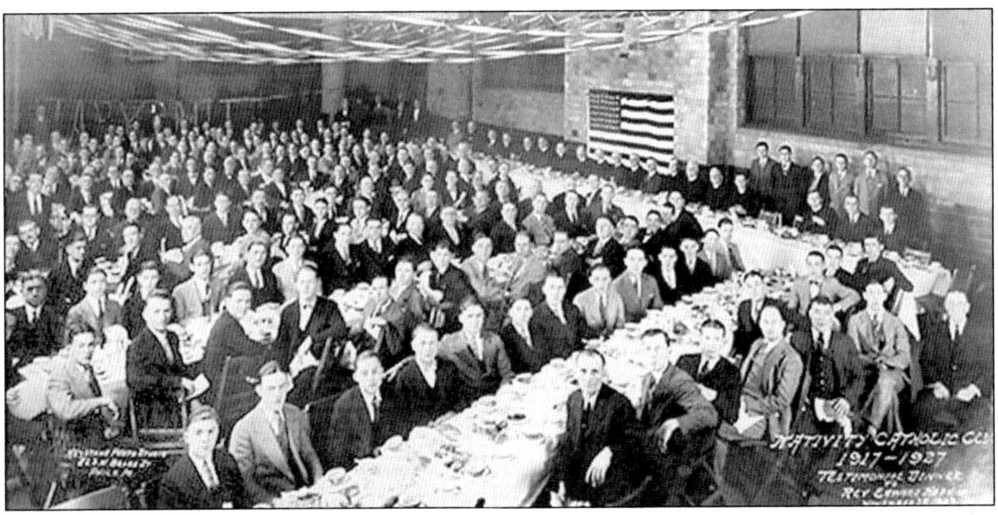

The tenth anniversary of the Nativity Catholic Club was a standing-room-only event. The club originated in 1917, just a few months after the school was built at Madison and Belgrade Streets. The basement was large enough to handle the crowd shown here.

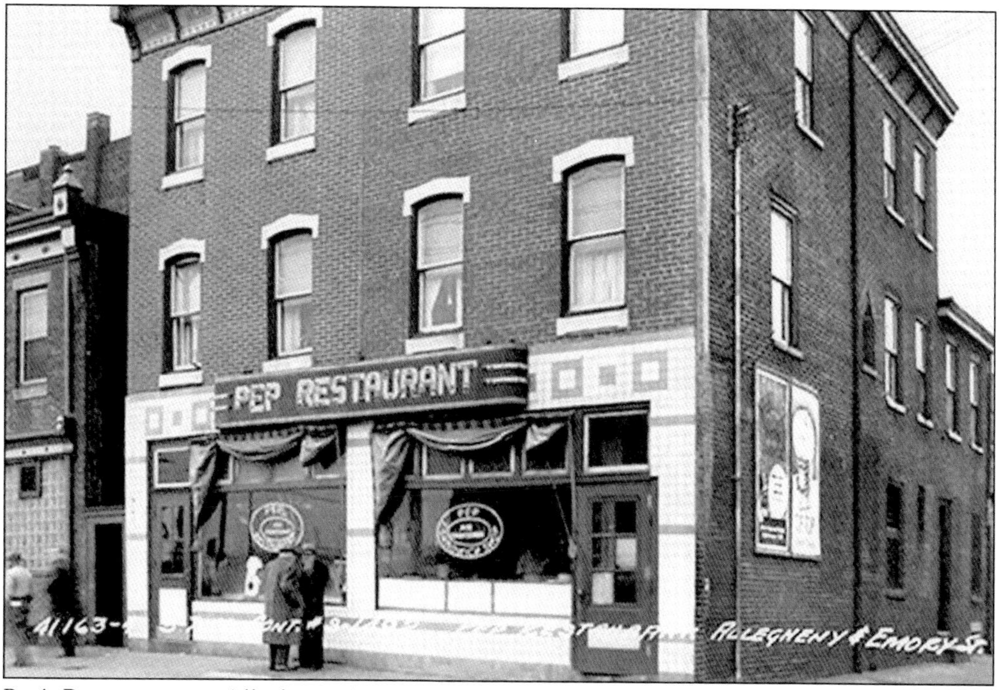

Pep's Restaurant on Allegheny Avenue and Emery Street in Port Richmond was not just an eatery but also a neighborhood institution. Sunday morning churchgoers had only a short walk to go for a hearty breakfast. Interestingly, some of the infamous K&A Irish burglary teams planned their heists over meals at Pep's.

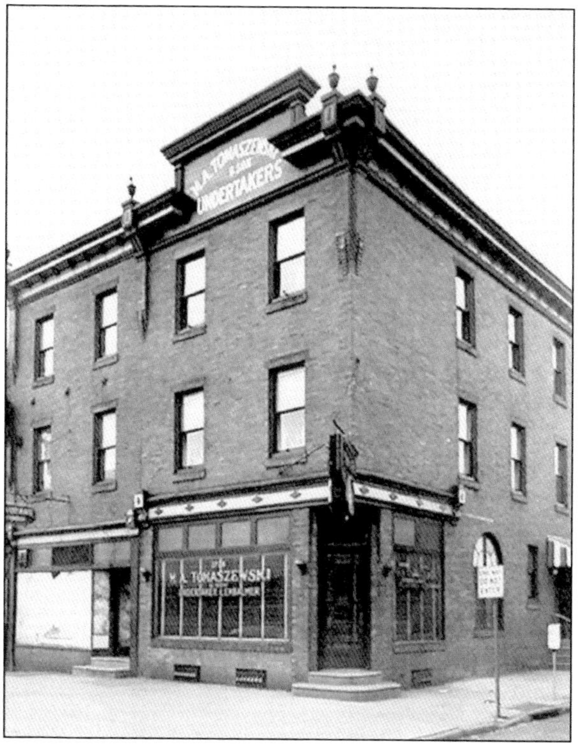

Just as the Catholic parishes were ethnically segregated, the neighborhood funeral homes operated in much the same fashion. Allegheny Avenue in Port Richmond had several funeral homes that serviced the ethnic parishes. Tomaszewski Funeral Home, located on the corner of Salmon Street and Allegheny Avenue, has been a family run business for three generations. Marie Tomaszewski, grandmother of the present owner, was one of the first female licensed morticians in the state of Pennsylvania. The home was one of several that provided service for the predominantly Polish parishioners of nearby St. Adalbert's Church throughout much of the 20th century. Today, Tomaszewski's continues its tradition of dignified, caring service to a more ethnically diverse neighborhood.

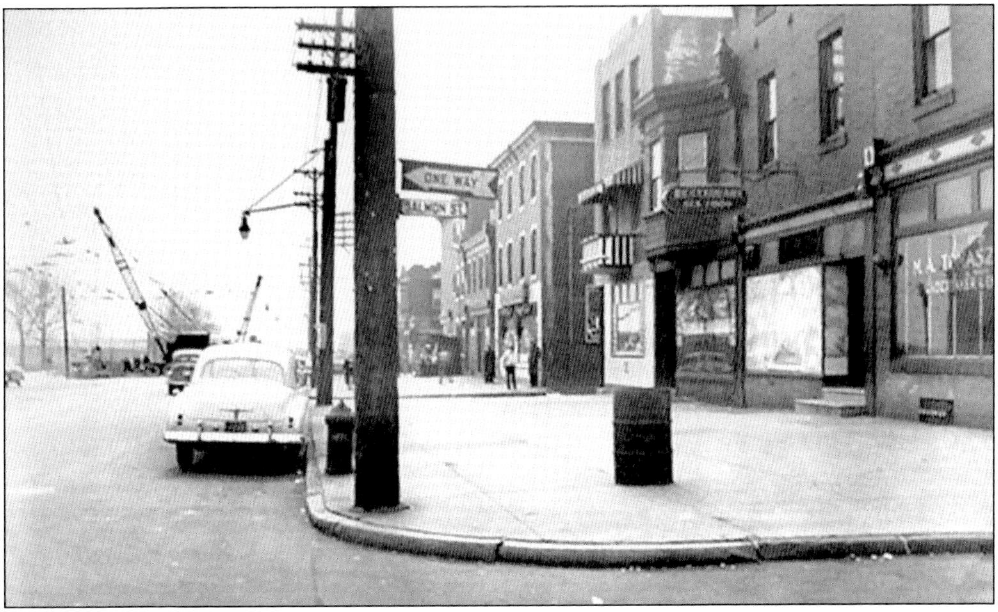

Looking east to Richmond Street shows major construction of large water mains along Allegheny Avenue. The installation of the 48-inch distribution lines, used to pump water to other neighborhoods, took place in March 1951. The area behind the trees where the crane is rising in the sky is where Interstate 95 crossed Allegheny Avenue almost 20 years later.

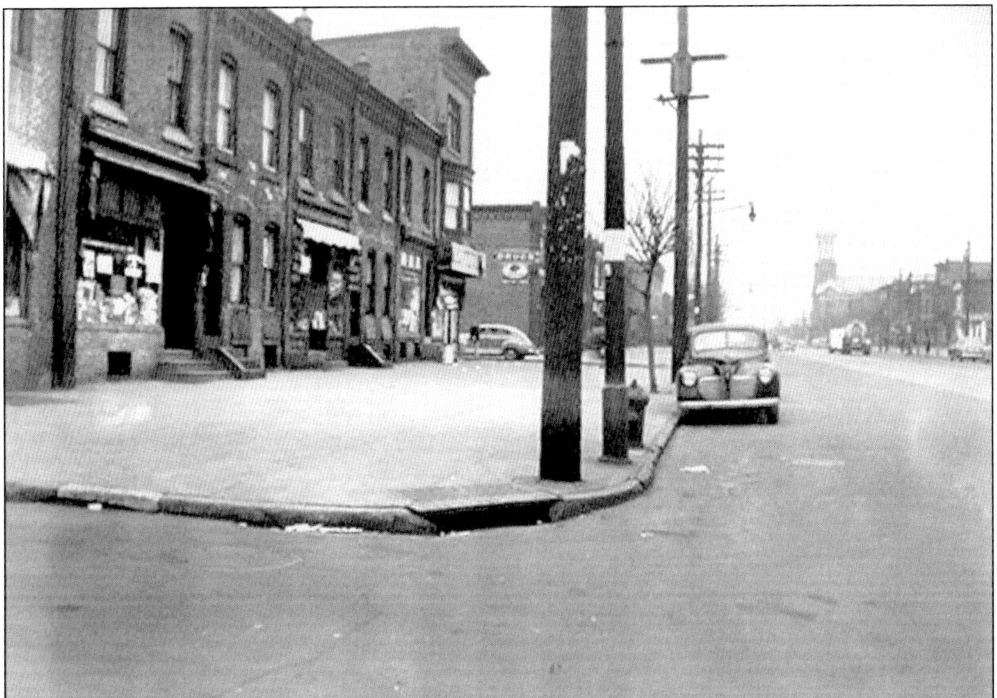

This view is looking west up Allegheny Avenue from Richmond toward Kensington Avenue. The steeple of the Nativity of the Blessed Virgin Mary Church can be seen in the distance.

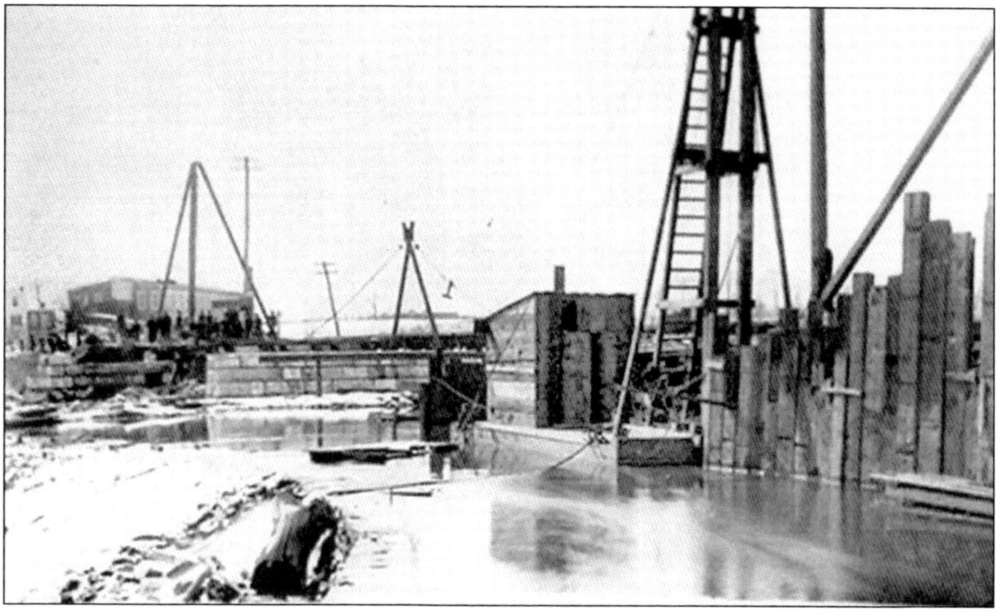

The stretch of Kensington Avenue that travels through the Frankford section has seen many changes over the years. This rebuilding of the bridge over the Frankford Creek took over two years to complete. It has since been rebuilt three more times. Note the large amount of water, enough to float small, wooden work barges. Today, the creek is fewer than 3 feet across and fewer than 12 inches deep.

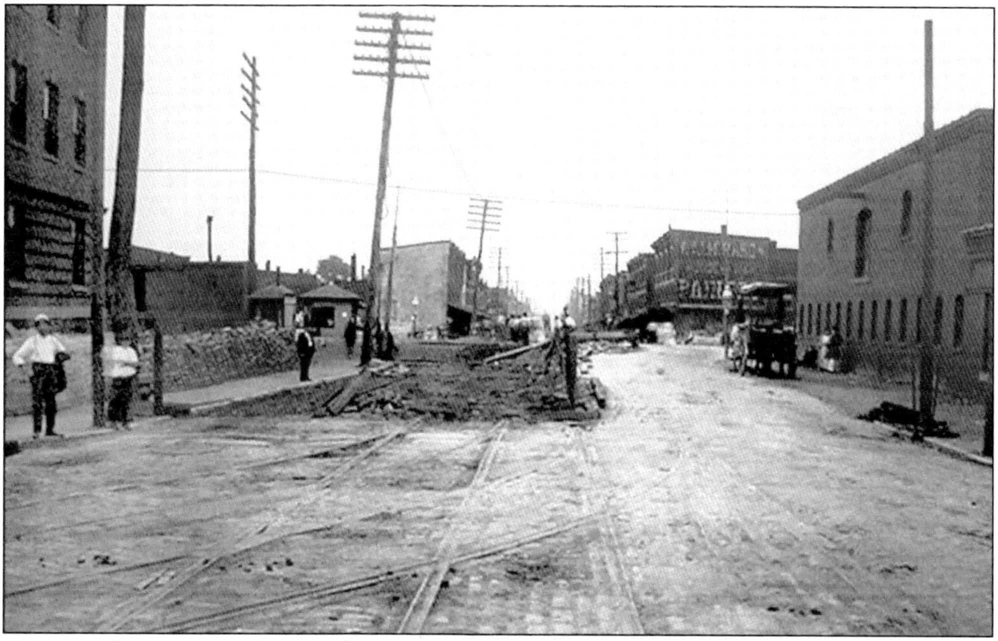

Taken in the summer of 1912, this photograph shows street work going on where there is no street today. City records label this as Trenton Avenue traveling through Aramingo Valley. The location is between Orthodox and Margaret Streets along the Pennsylvania Railroad line. Today, boundary lines in this area are unclear and are often hotly debated by the residents. Some say it is part of Bridesburg, others call it Frankford Valley.

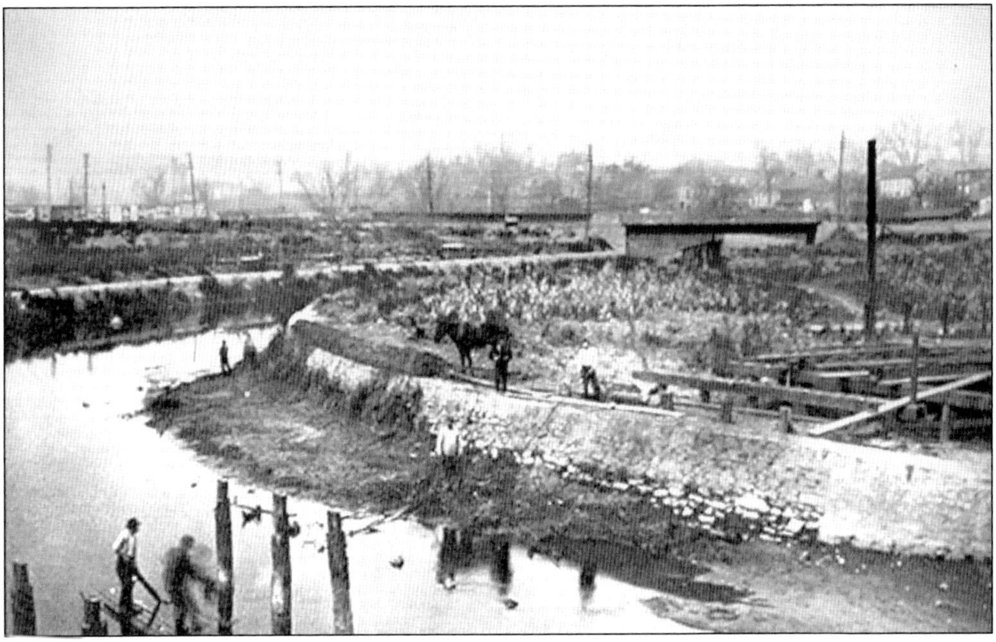

November of 1902 was a time of major bridge abatement construction throughout the neighborhoods. City planners, looking to the future settlement of the area, saw the bridges as a way of connecting Kensington, Fishtown, and Richmond to the Harrowgate and Frankford areas of the city.

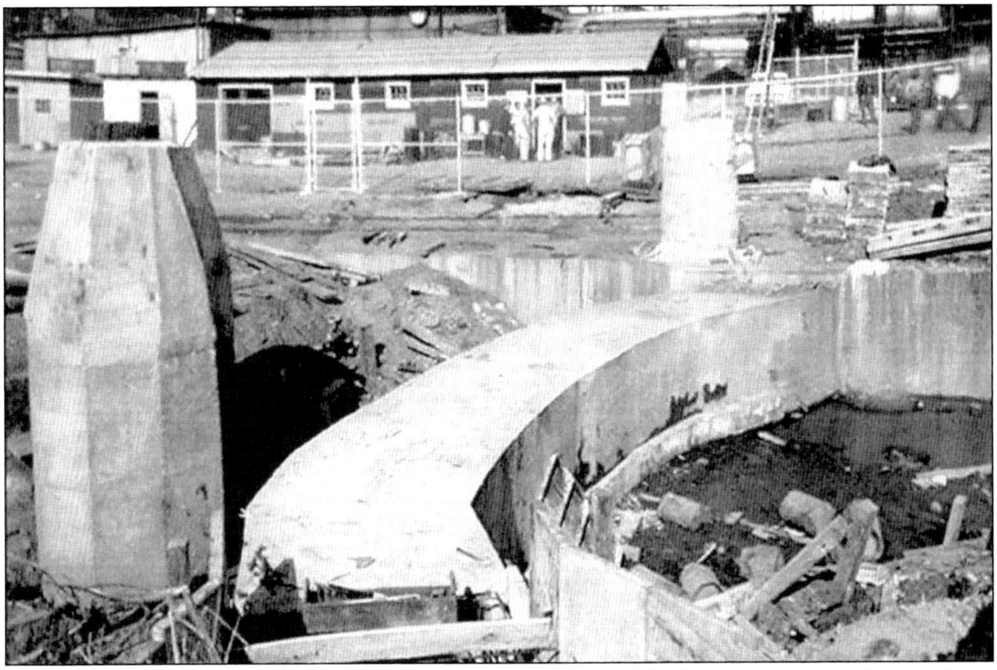

In the mid-1950s, as roads and bridges connected the neighborhoods, water and sewer lines needed to be updated. Due to the massive growth of the River Wards area, the city found it necessary to install new sewer lines through the Frankford Creek at Ash Street in Frankford. As the neighborhoods grew, so did the needs of the people. The city strove to meet these needs.

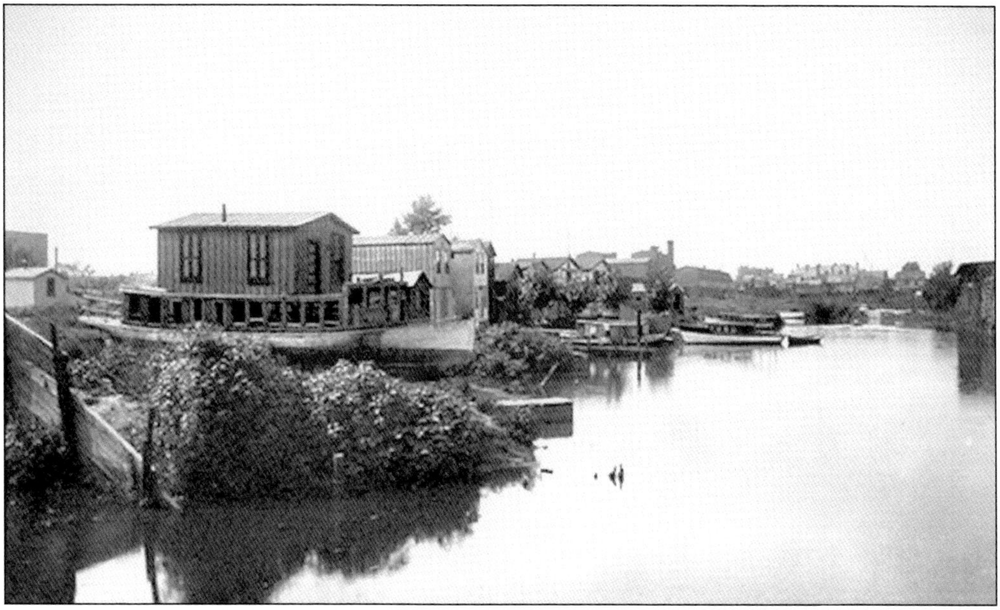

In the early 1900s houses were built along many creeks throughout the city. This 1914 photograph shows waterfront property on Frankford Creek. Small boats were docked in the rear of the houses, giving the residents access to the Delaware River. As industry along the riverfront grew, these residences disappeared, but the homeowners profited handsomely from their sales.

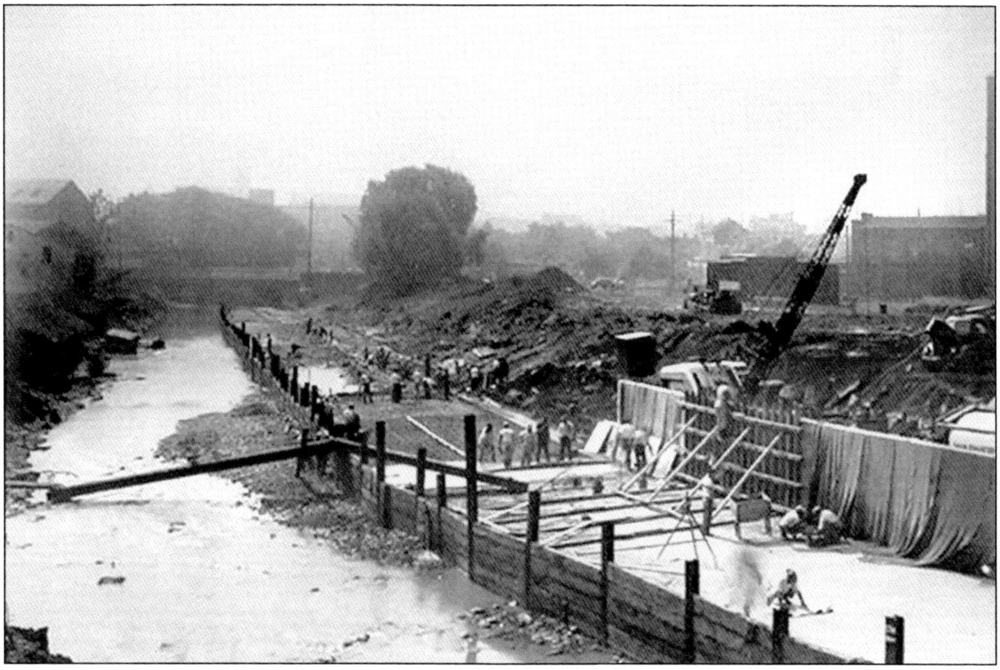

Prior to 1940, flooding was a serious problem along the Frankford Creek. As the population density of the River Wards increased, the city of Philadelphia had to deal with this headache. In 1949, the city commenced one of the country's largest flood-control projects, with huge success.

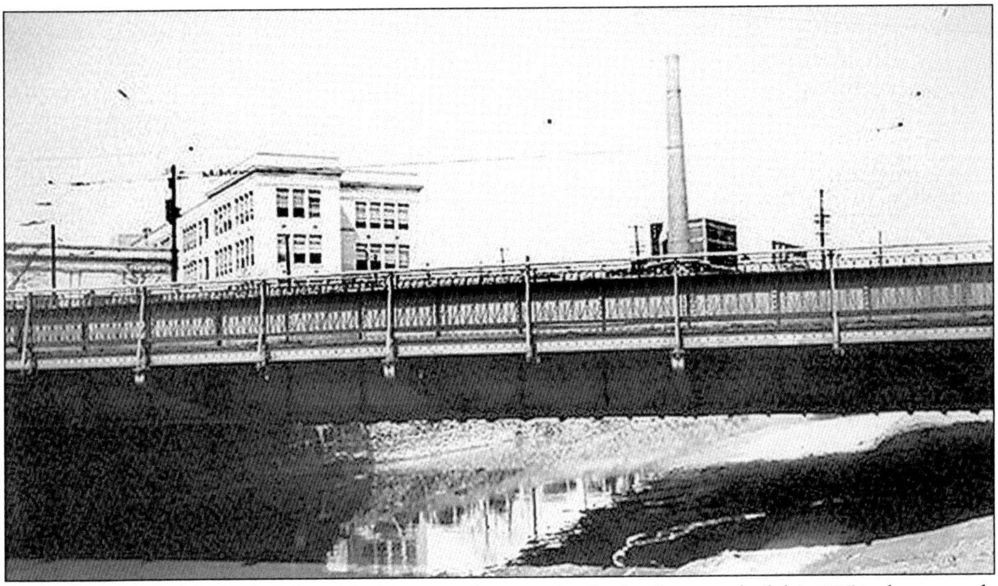

Northeast Catholic High School for Boys can be seen in the background of this 1951 photograph looking south along Frankford Creek. Established in 1926, North was the high school to which the River Wards' Catholic grade schools sent their male graduates. Today, as one of the few all-male Catholic high schools in the city, North enjoys a fine reputation as an institution devoted to quality education. The school also has a tradition of cultivating friendships that last a lifetime. "Once a North boy, always a North boy."

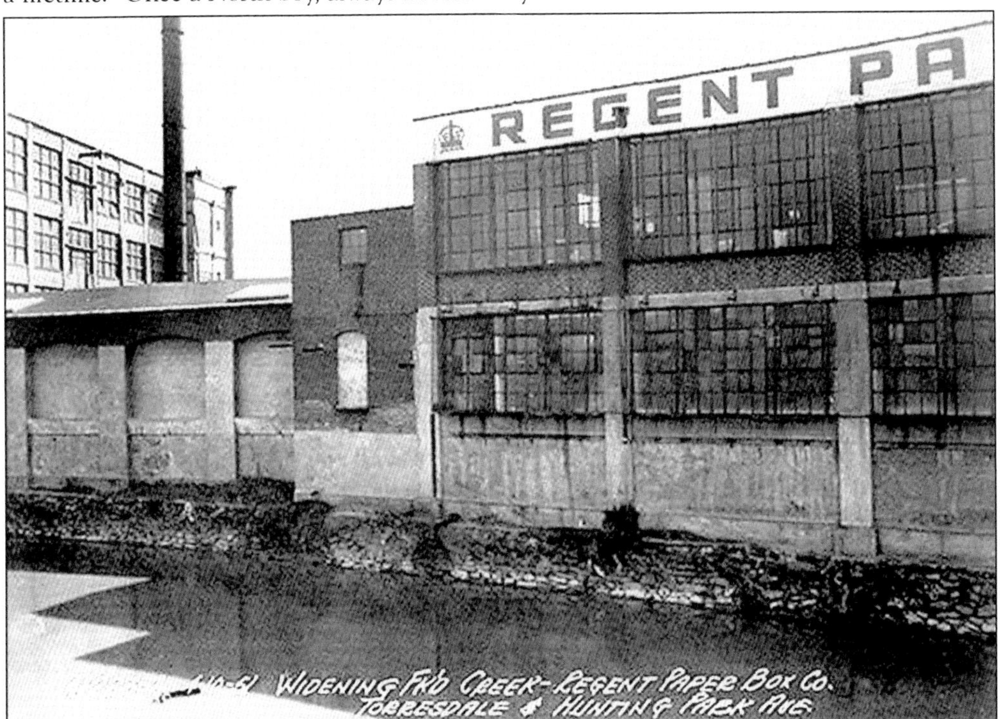

Some companies along the Frankford Creek changed the natural contours of the creek in an attempt to curb flooding and expand their property.

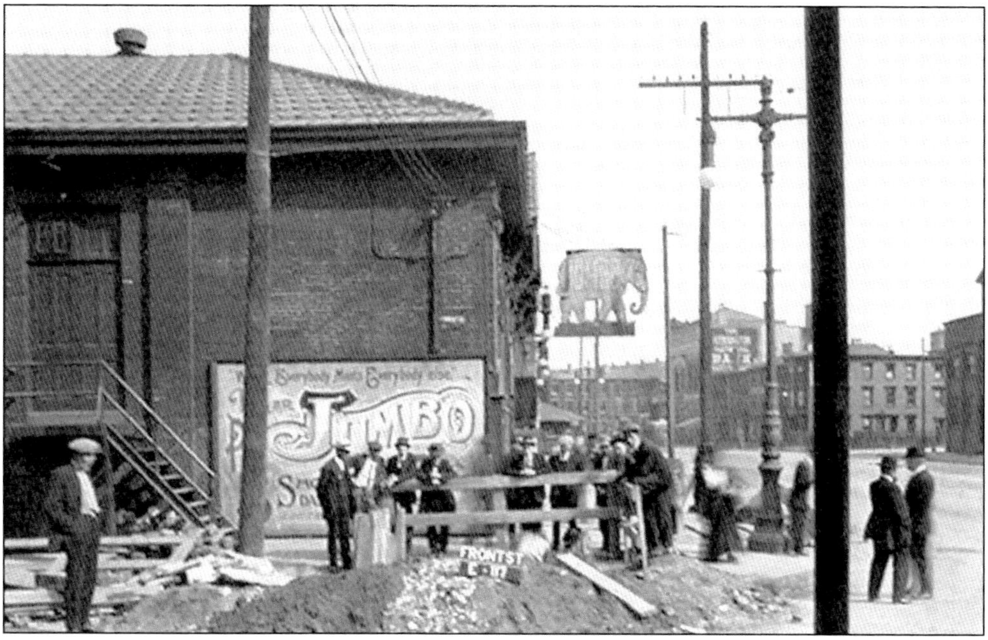

This photograph, taken prior to the construction of the Frankford El, shows the Jumbo Theater's slogan: "where everybody meets everybody else." Looking west up Girard Avenue, this 1915 photograph shows Cadwalder Street in the distance, the point were Girard Avenue turns west from Front Street.

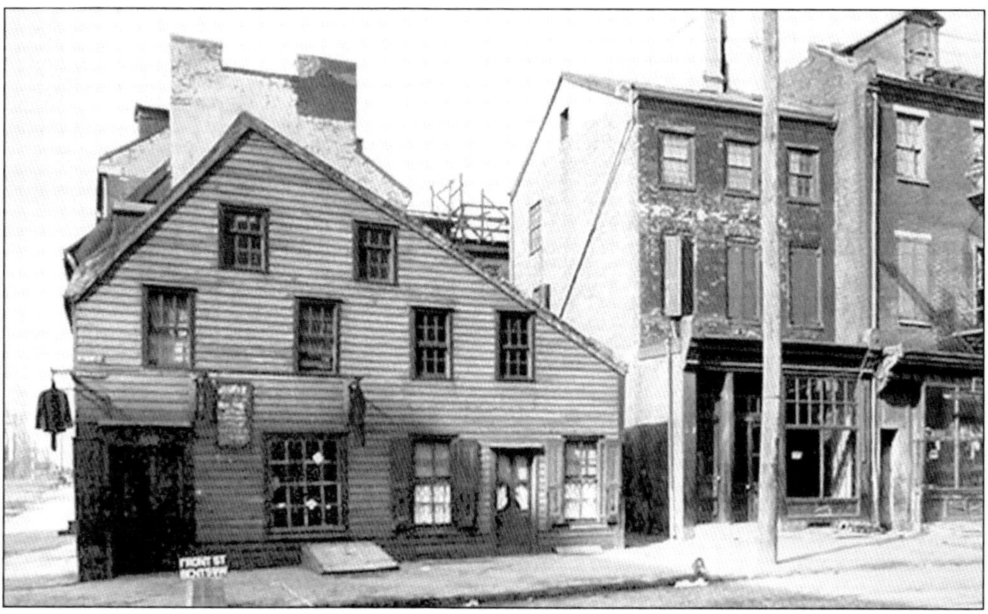

Northern Liberties, the River Wards neighborhood closest to the city proper, was the first to see the beginning of modernization. This Civil War–era house on the corner looks quite unusual due to the large number of windows as compared to its size. This is indicative of the fact that homes at the time were made up of many small rooms, each room having its own heat source. Rooms that were not in use could be closed off, saving on heating and lighting costs. The windows, of course, offered natural light to each room.

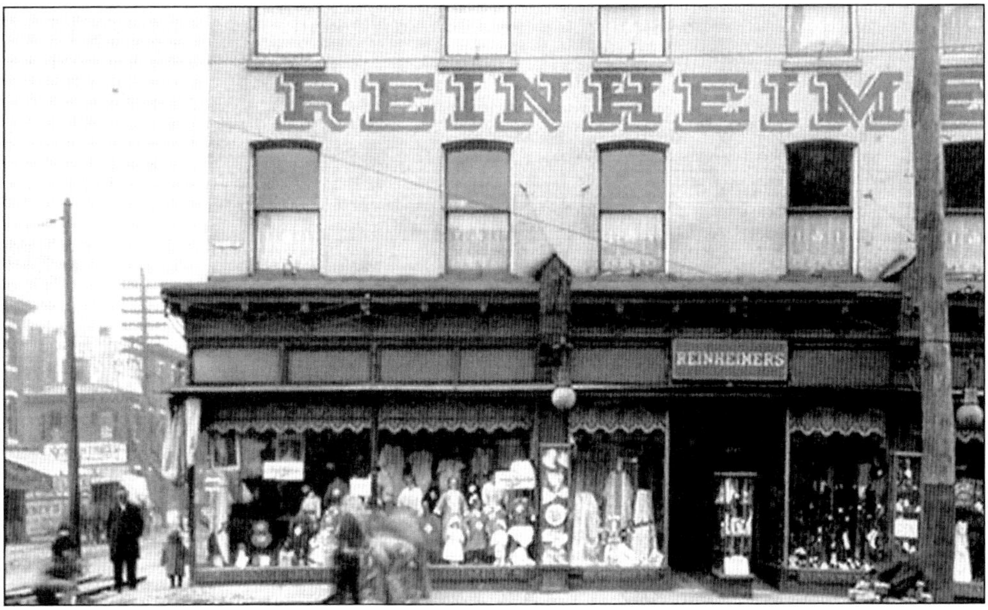

Reinheimers Men and Women's Clothing Store, located on Front Street near Berks Street, is a perfect example of the shops that lined Front Street, Frankford Avenue, Kensington Avenue, and Richmond Street in their heyday as shopping meccas. Residents seldom needed to venture outside of their own neighborhoods to shop because everything they needed could be purchased close to home.

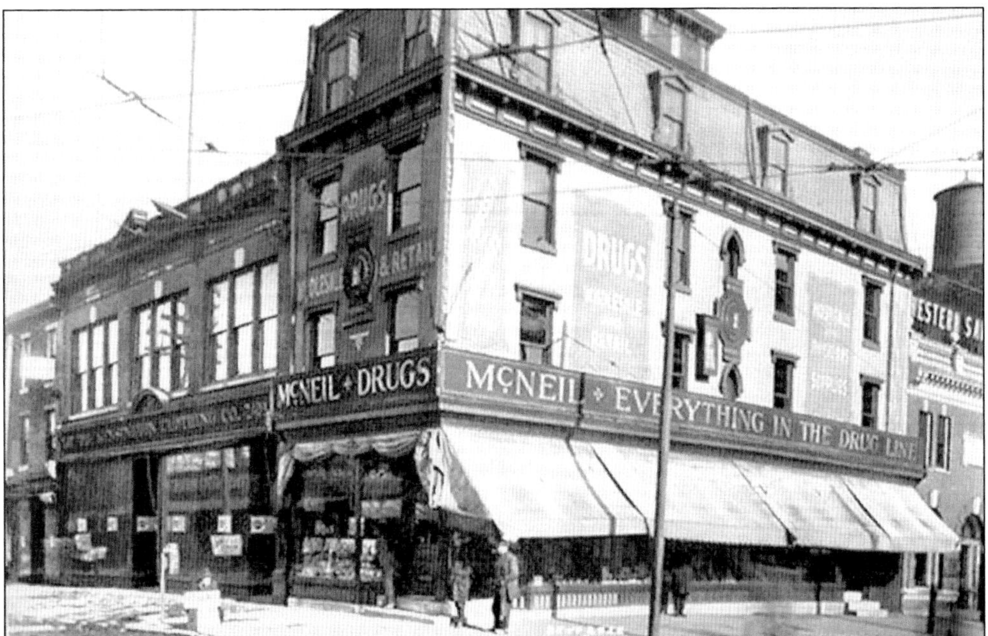

McNeil Drugs, a retail and wholesale drugstore located on Front Street in the Northern Liberties area, was also a showpiece of 17th-century architecture. In this photograph, taken before the construction of the Frankford El, you can see the trolley car wires above the street. Trolleys sometime traveled in four different directions at major intersections.

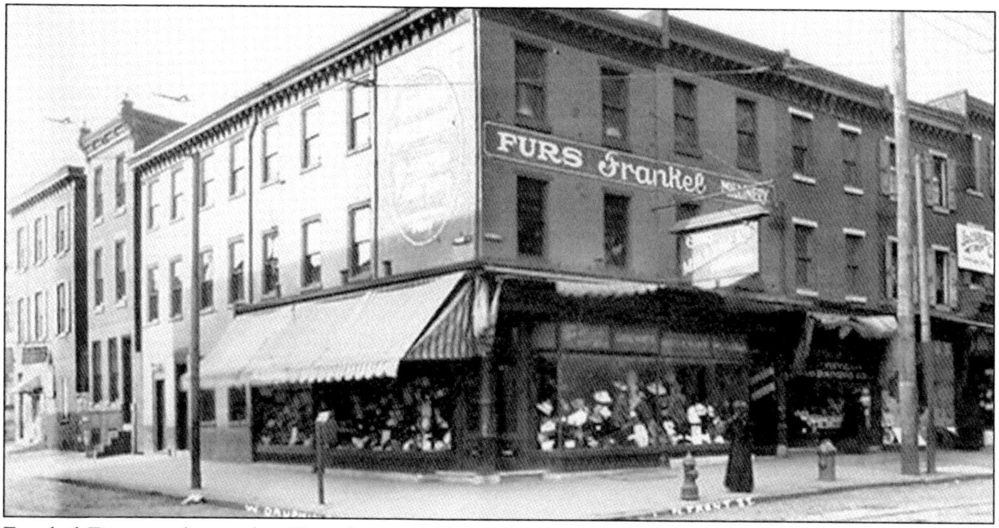

Frankel Furs was located at Dauphin and Front Streets in what some maps label as Kensington, others as Fishtown. Of interest are the two different types of fire hydrants on each side of the woman on the corner. The hydrant to the left is a filtered freshwater hydrant that is used for drinking. The hydrant on the right is a high-pressure hydrant that takes its water directly from the river and is used for fighting fires. As any youth raised in the River Wards will tell you, the high-pressure hydrants were the best ones to play under on a hot summer day. High-pressure hydrants were built in the River Wards due to their heavy concentrations of industry.

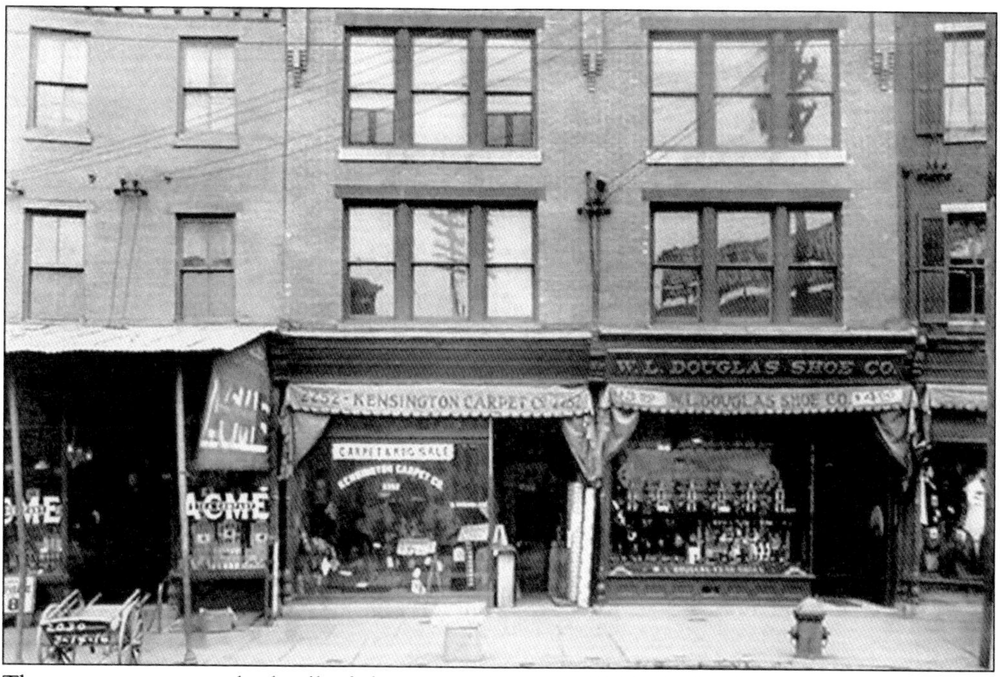

The same contractor built all of the stores along the 2200 block of Kensington Avenue, as is evidenced in this photograph, taken before the El construction. Note the cart in front of the Acme Food Store. This photograph was probably taken at either opening or closing time, otherwise the cart would have been loaded with fresh fruit and vegetables, ready for sale.

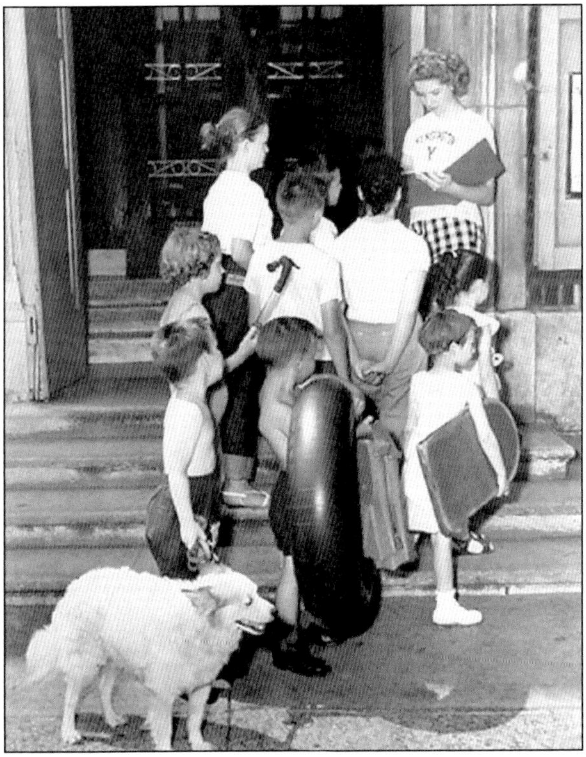

In the 1950s, YMCAs and YWCAs were located in every neighborhood, and each one had an indoor pool. This one on Berks Street was no exception. Although they were popular swimming holes (apparently even for the family dog), only the "Frankford Y" remains open today.

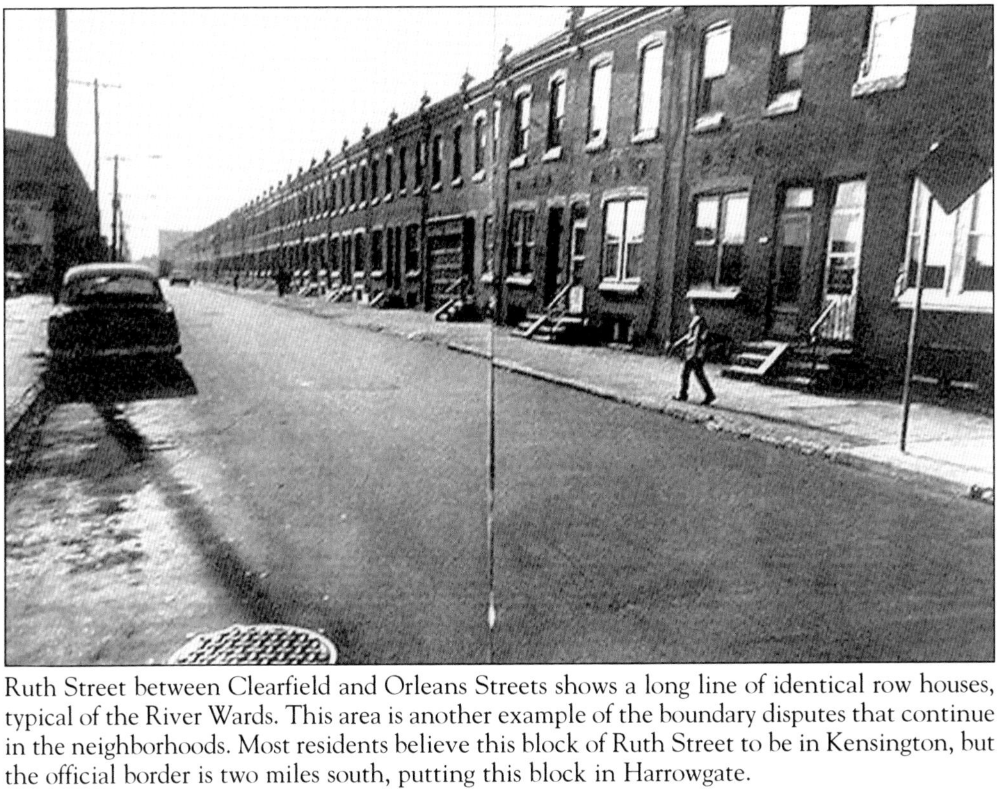

Ruth Street between Clearfield and Orleans Streets shows a long line of identical row houses, typical of the River Wards. This area is another example of the boundary disputes that continue in the neighborhoods. Most residents believe this block of Ruth Street to be in Kensington, but the official border is two miles south, putting this block in Harrowgate.

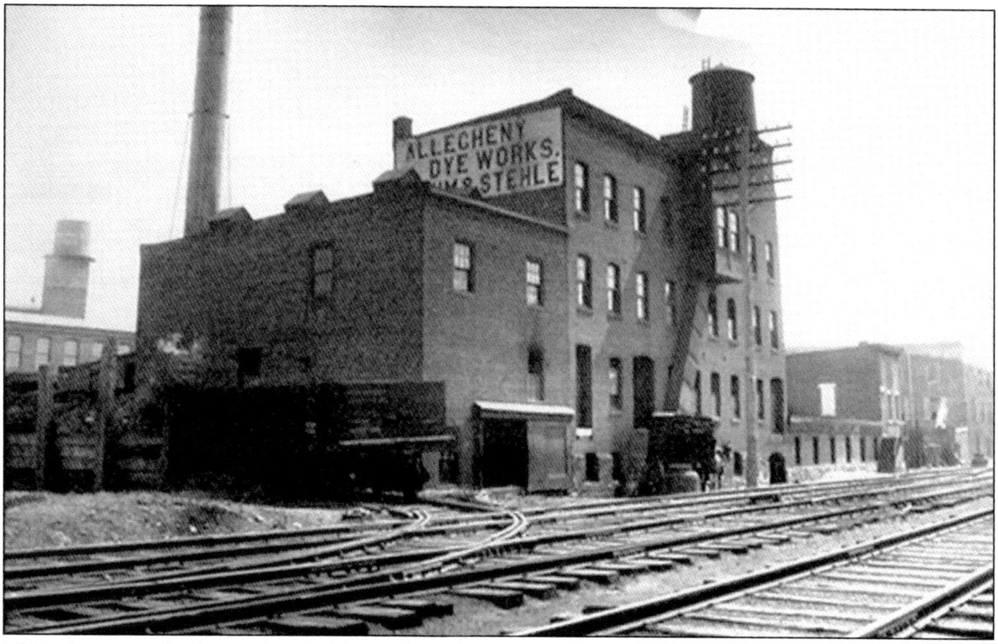

This photograph along Martha Street (also known as Trenton Avenue) near Lehigh Avenue in Port Richmond shows the railroad at ground level. In the early 1900s, the railroad was rebuilt about two stories higher, with dirt and cinder. Today, almost 100 years later, the railroad is no longer used.

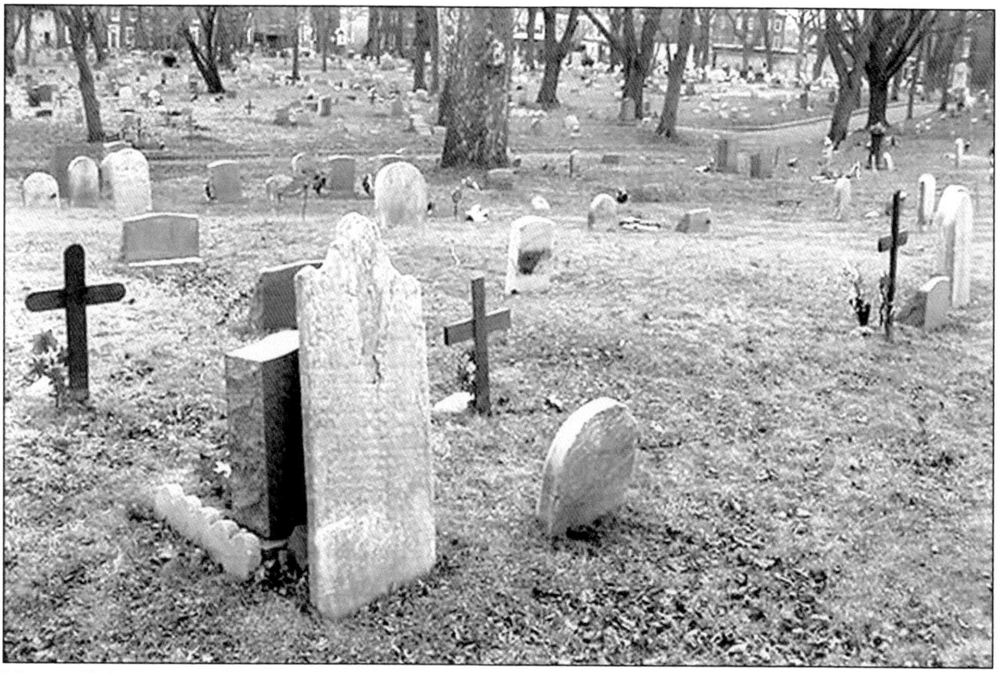

Native Fishtown residents are entitled to be buried in Palmer Cemetery. Located in the original Kensington, this burial ground is the final resting place for many American patriots from the Revolutionary War. Surrounded by residential and industrial areas, Palmer Cemetery is a city square block of peace and tranquility.

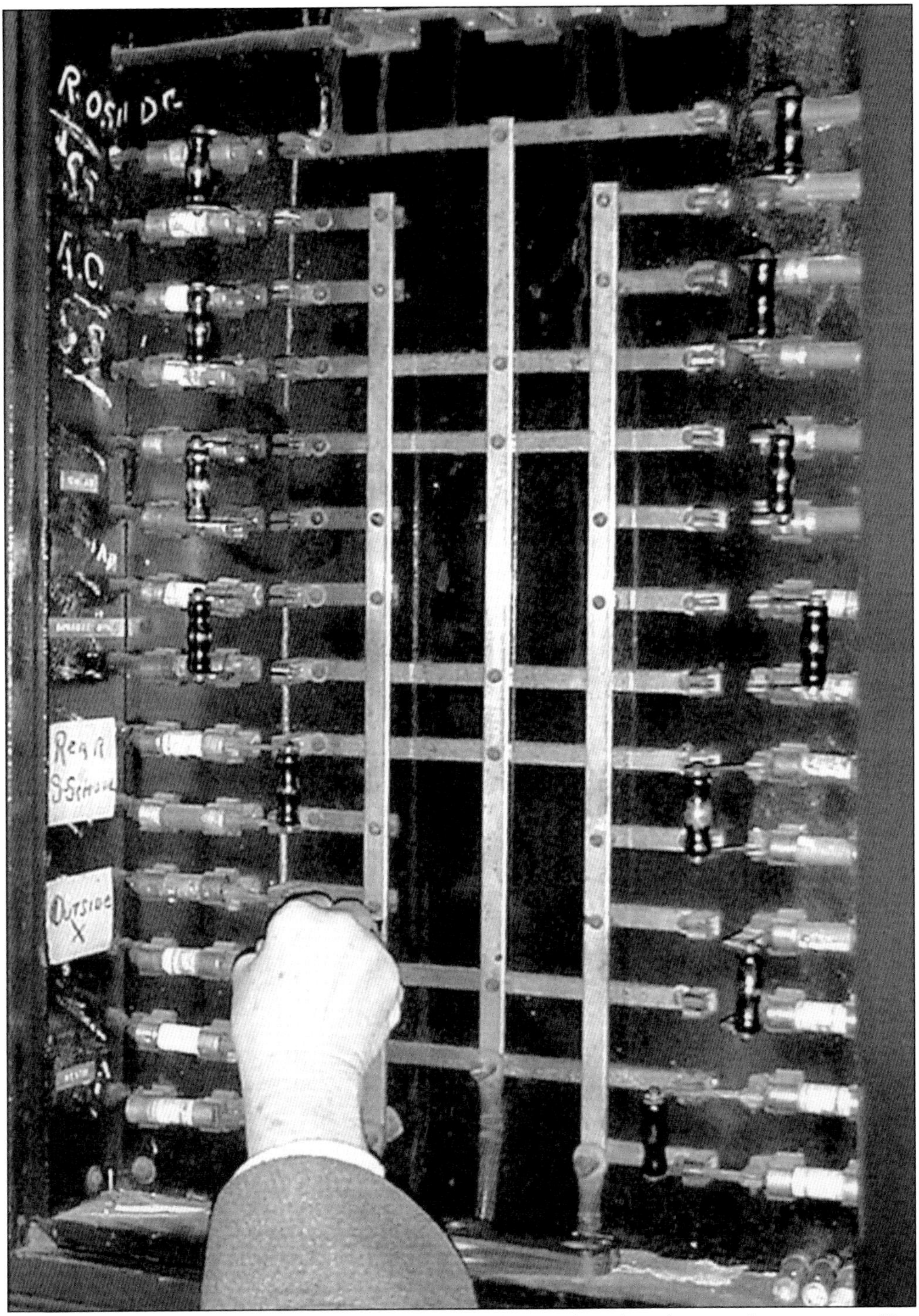

Compared to circuit breakers, most people would consider glass fuses to be antiques. But many churches and historic buildings throughout the River Wards still use the brass switch connectors, although they are against city building codes. Updating these electrical systems would be devastating financially to many of these institutions.

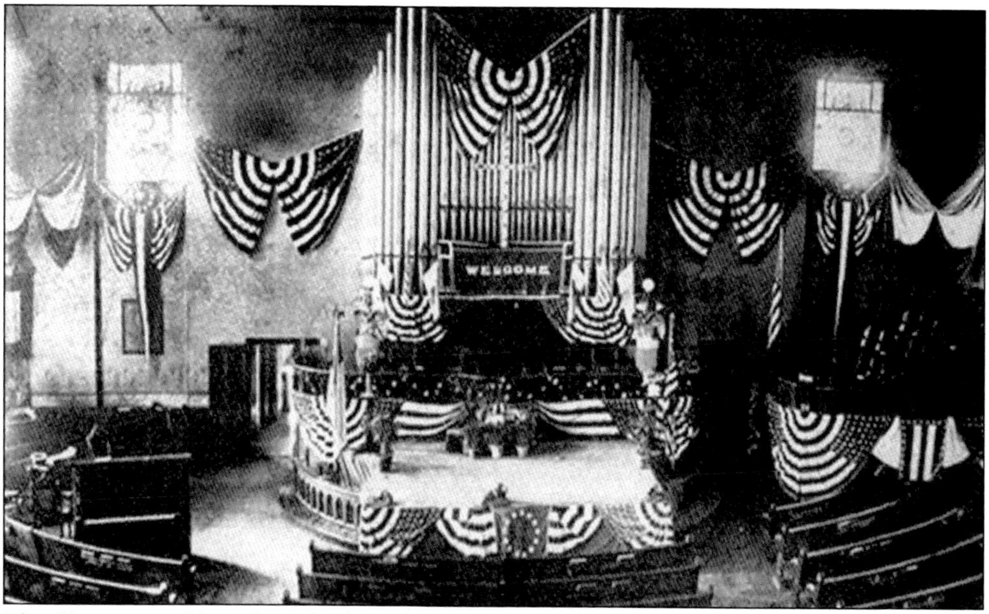

The Kensington United Methodist Church, founded in 1804 and located just yards west of the Delaware River, was the church where Revolutionary War hero John Hewson worshiped. He also started a school here with the profits from his Calico Printing Company. Today, the organ house inside the church is of great historic interest. In the year 2000, the Historic Organ Association awarded it a citation.

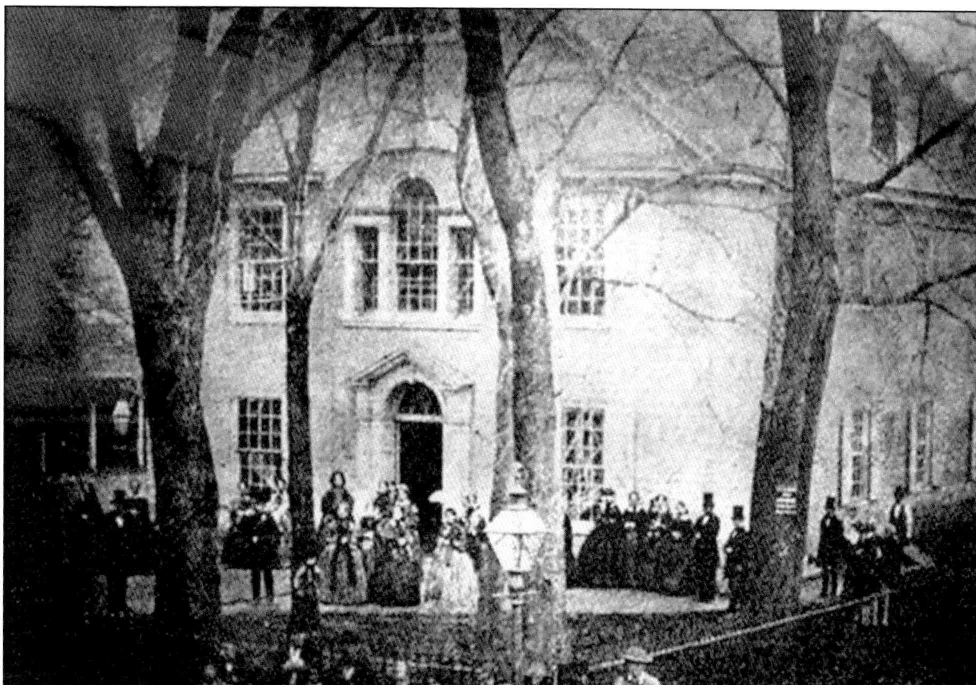

This Protestant church, located on Frankford Avenue and Unity Street in Harrowgate was one of many churches that bade final farewells to Civil War Union soldiers who lost their lives in battle. Although not confirmed, this photograph is said to have captured a funeral for a fallen soldier.

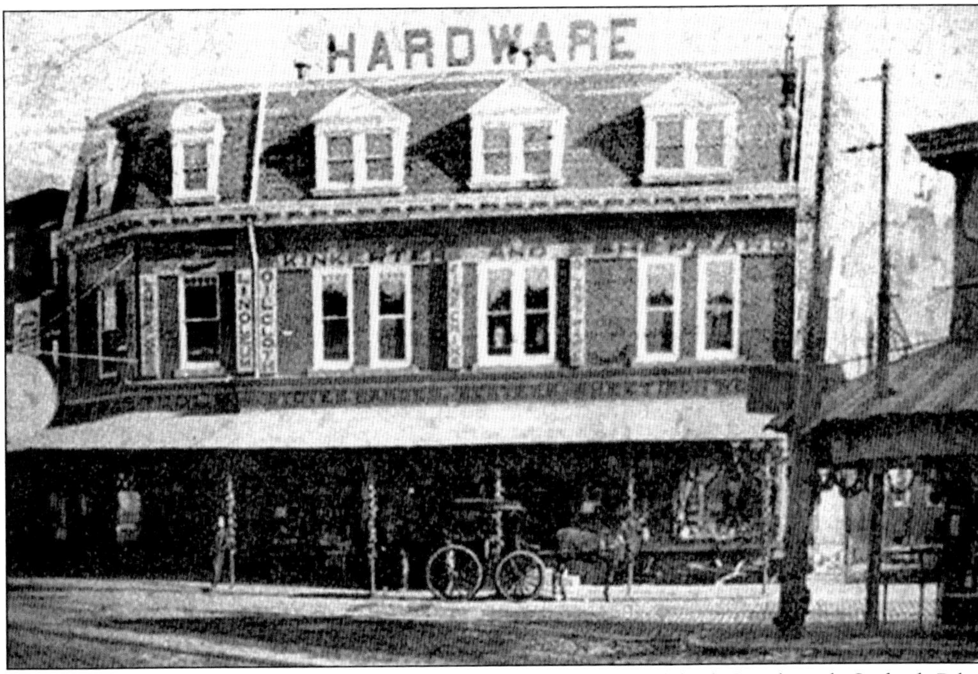

Kinkerter and Sheppard's Hardware Store, located on Frankford Road and Oxford Pike, supplied the residents of Frankford and Harrowgate with their building needs. The building in the lower right was a stagecoach depot and later became an El stop.

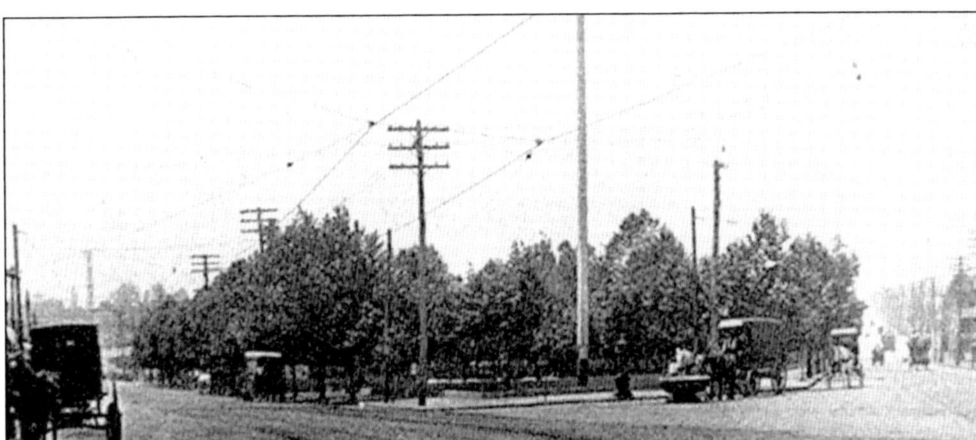

Womrath Park is located where Frankford Road and Kensington Avenue meet. Notice the horse trough at the point where the roads converge. The road to the left looking south is Frankford Road that traveled to Harrowgate and Port Richmond. To the right is Kensington Avenue that led to the mill sections of the city.

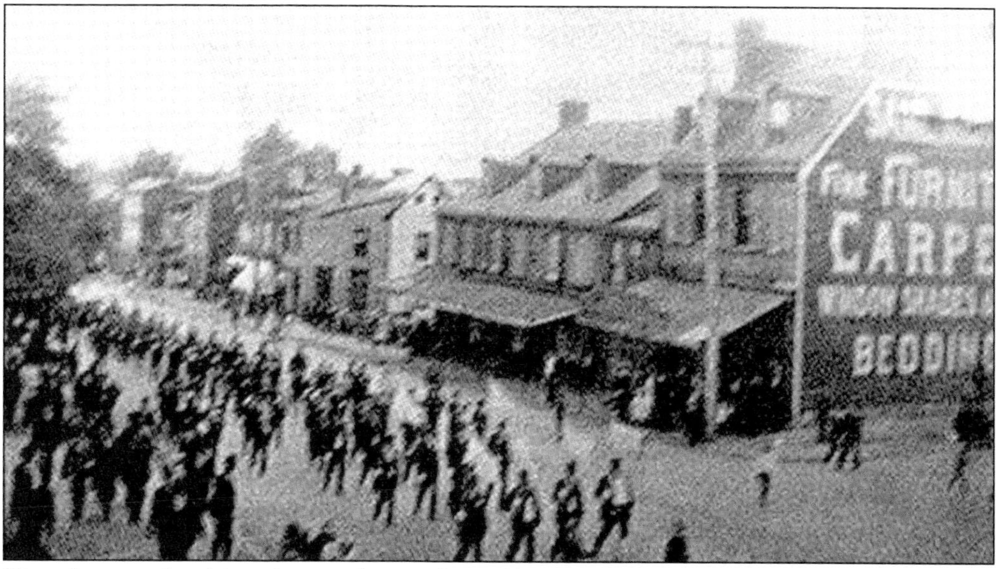

This photograph, although very distorted, is of historic interest. Some local historians claim the photograph was taken in 1865, at the end of the Civil War, from the church steeple at Frankford Road and Sellers Street. The parade was a welcome home celebration for returning Union soldiers.

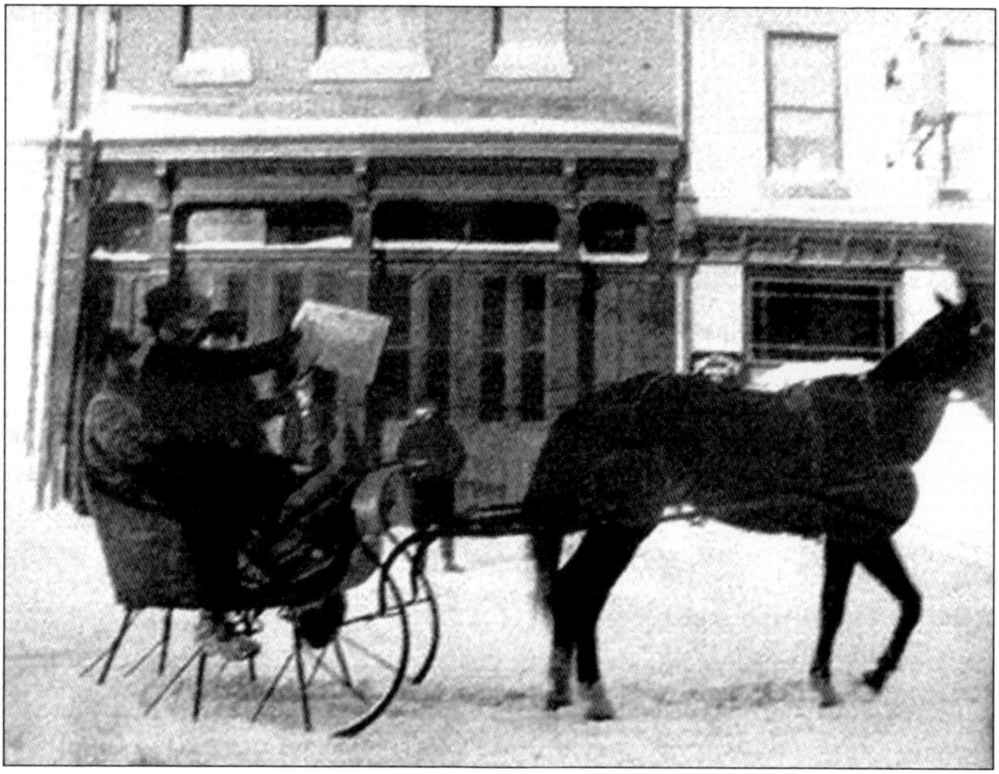
This man is believed to be delivering the *Philadelphia Public Ledger*. The horse and carriage soon gave way to motorcars, but this quaint means of transportation is still popular, especially among tourists, in Old Philadelphia and Northern Liberties.

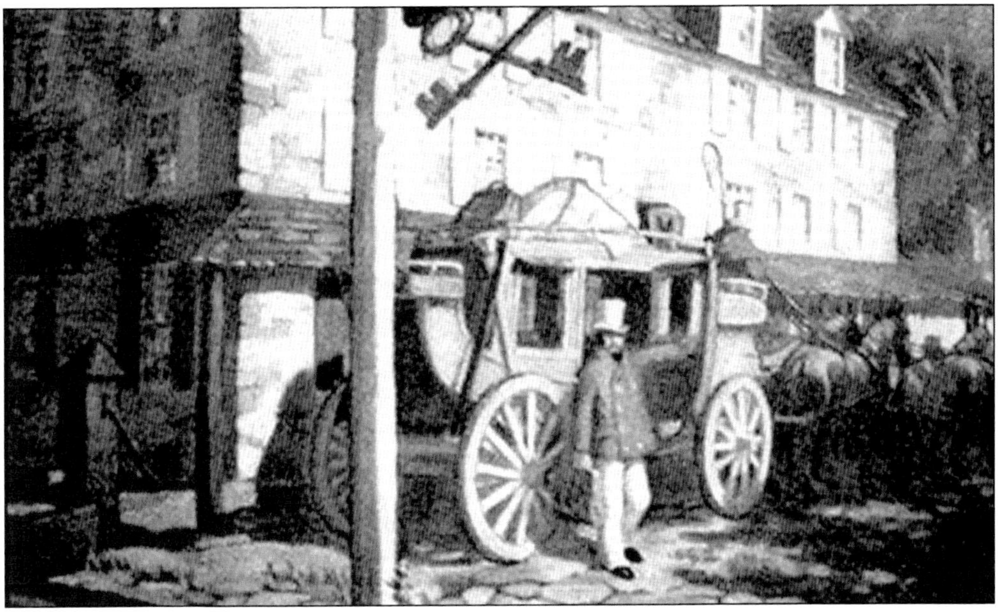

The Inn at the Two Keys was located along Frankford Road at Penn Street. The inn was a popular stop on the road from New York to Philadelphia. It was famous for selling Peggy Mullin beef sandwiches, thinly sliced beef served on a baked roll. This sandwich originated in a restaurant around Northern Liberties, but it soon gained popularity in the northern neighborhoods.

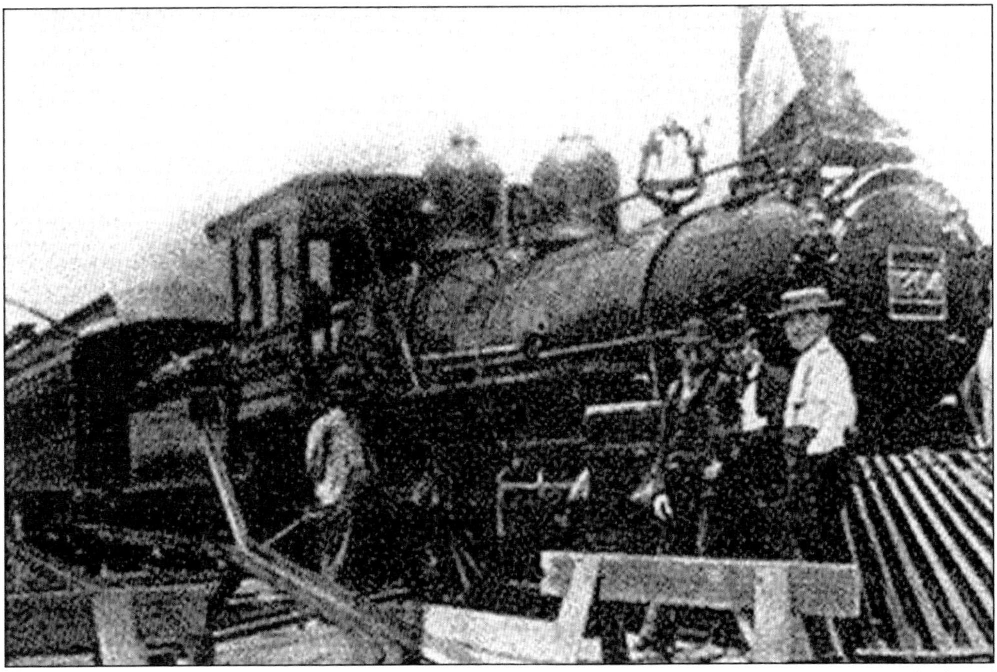

The great train wreck of the early 1900s along Frankford Avenue and Sedgley Street killed and maimed many people. The accident was national news and tied up roads for days afterwards. To the amazement of many, not even a scratch was found on the Baldwin locomotive.

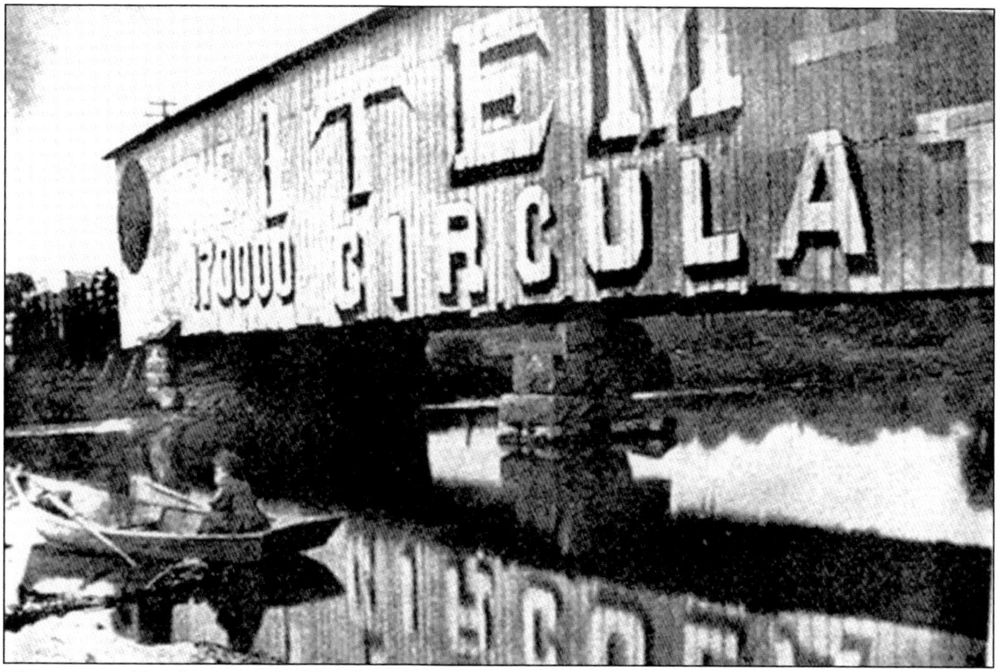

This covered bridge over the Frankford Creek appears to bear an advertisement for a local paper called the *Item*. There is not much information to be found concerning the *Item*, but it claimed a circulation of 170,000, which seems questionable for the time period.

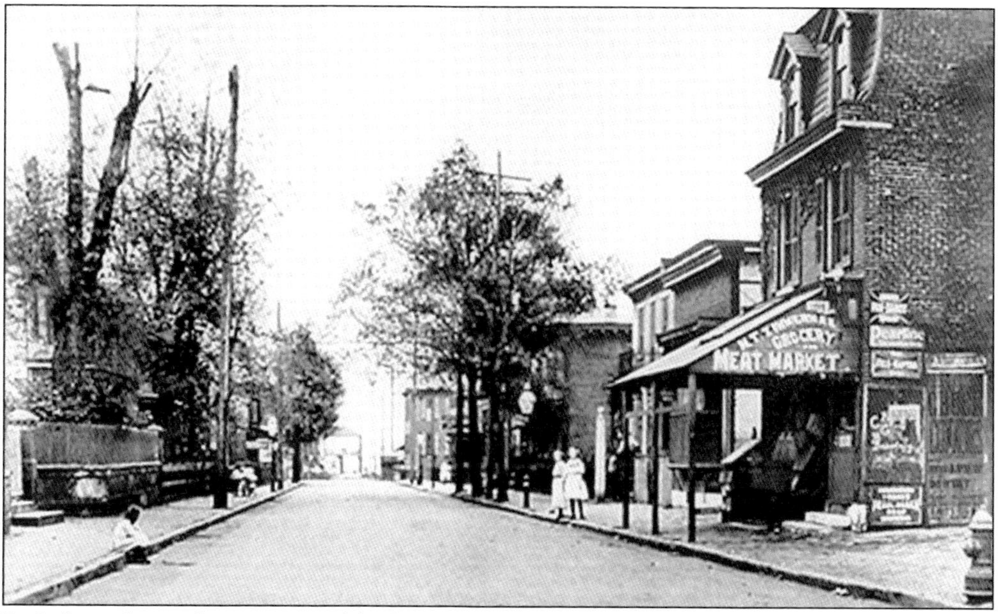

Bridesburg, the northern most neighborhood of the River Wards, was originally named Kirkbridesburg after its founder. This photograph, looking east toward the Delaware River from Richmond Road on what is now Bridge Street, shows a concentration of homes leading to the waterfront. Today, Ellis Coffee Company occupies the left-hand corner of Richmond and Bridge Streets, in front of the Rohm and Haas Chemical Company, a major employer of Bridesburg residents.

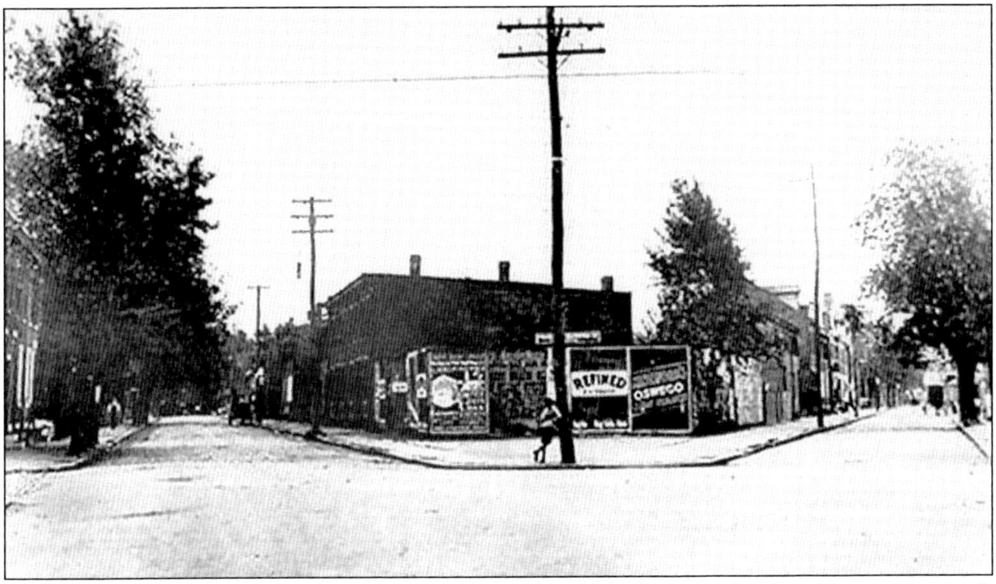

Thomas Holme, Williams Penn's surveyor, painstakingly laid out a plan for the city in which the streets ran true north, south, east, and west. As the River Wards stretched northward along the Delaware River, however, the streets in some of the neighborhoods turned in different directions due to the twists and turns of the river. This location at Thompson and Ash Streets in Bridesburg demonstrates the V point that became prevalent as the street layouts were adapted to the river's bends.

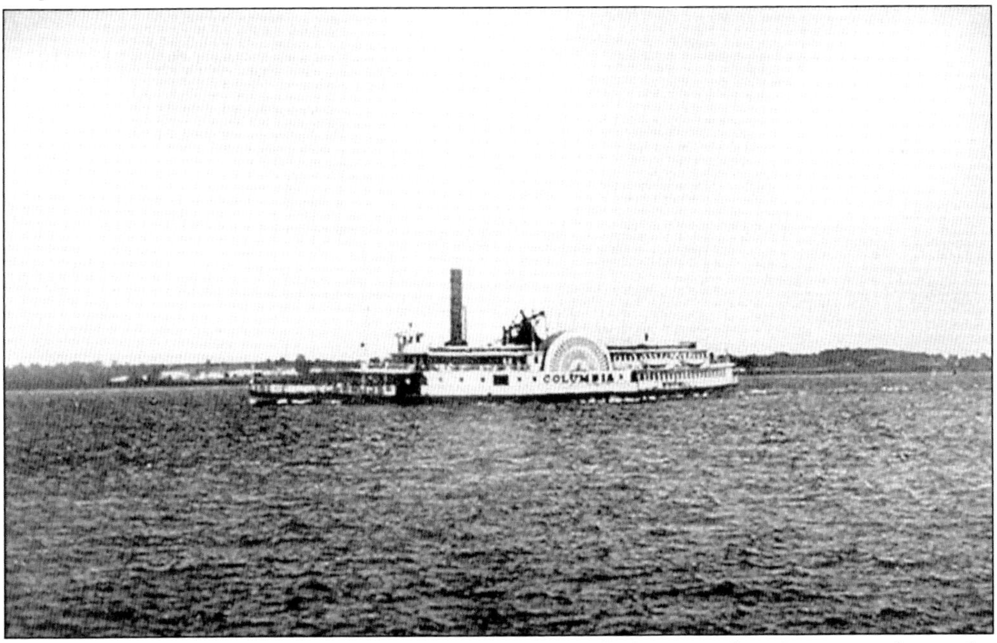

The wheel ferryboat *Columbia* traveled from its main dock at Market Street north up the Delaware River then back and forth across the river from Philadelphia to New Jersey. On Saturdays and Sundays, River Wards families from Northern Liberties to Bridesburg would be picked up from their neighborhood docks to spend an enjoyable day cruising along the Delaware River.

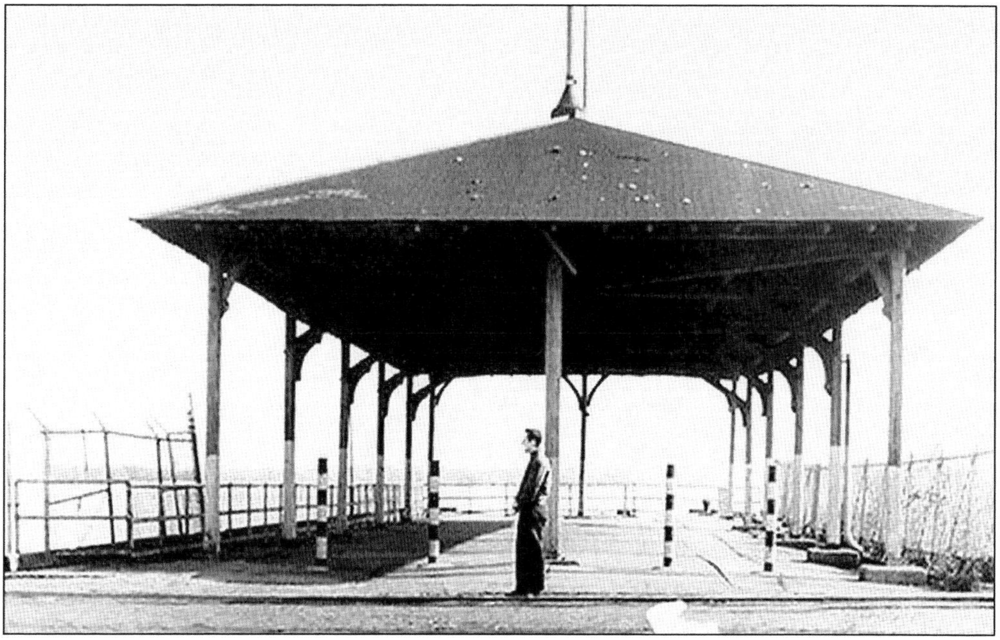

Located at the foot of Bridge Street in Bridesburg, this was one of many public piers the city built along the Delaware River. These piers were popular recreation areas and were used for picnics in the spring and summer. Swimmers would jump from the piers into the cool river for relief from the heat of summer in Philadelphia.

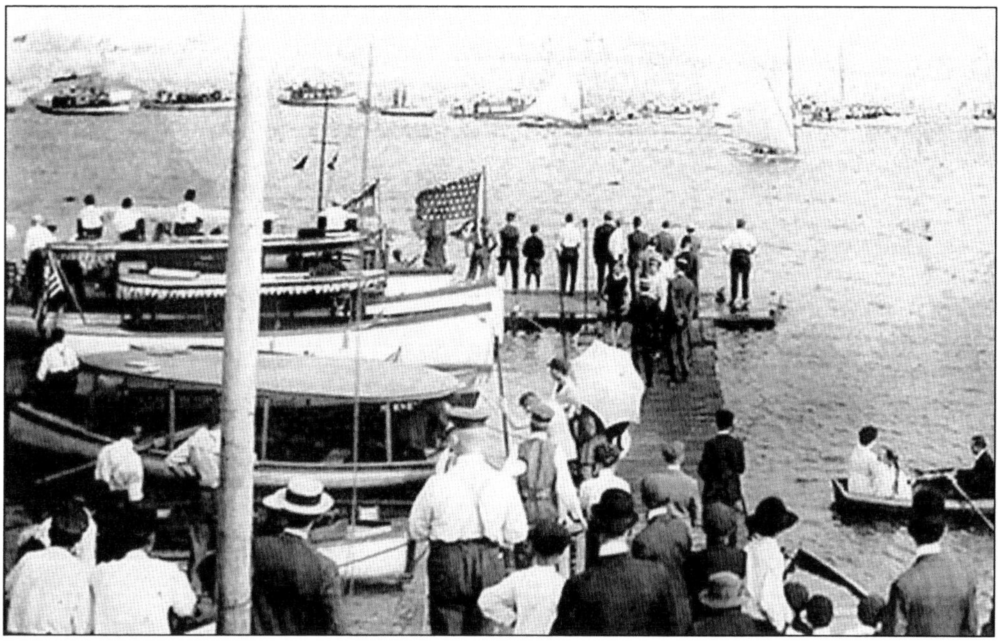

The Bridge Street pier was a gathering spot for watching boat races. Access ramps were available for launching small boats from the pier. In the early 1900s, the city had a lot to offer the River Wards residents in the way of recreation along the waterfront. As commerce grew along the Delaware River, the uses for the riverfront properties changed, and recreation gave way to industry.

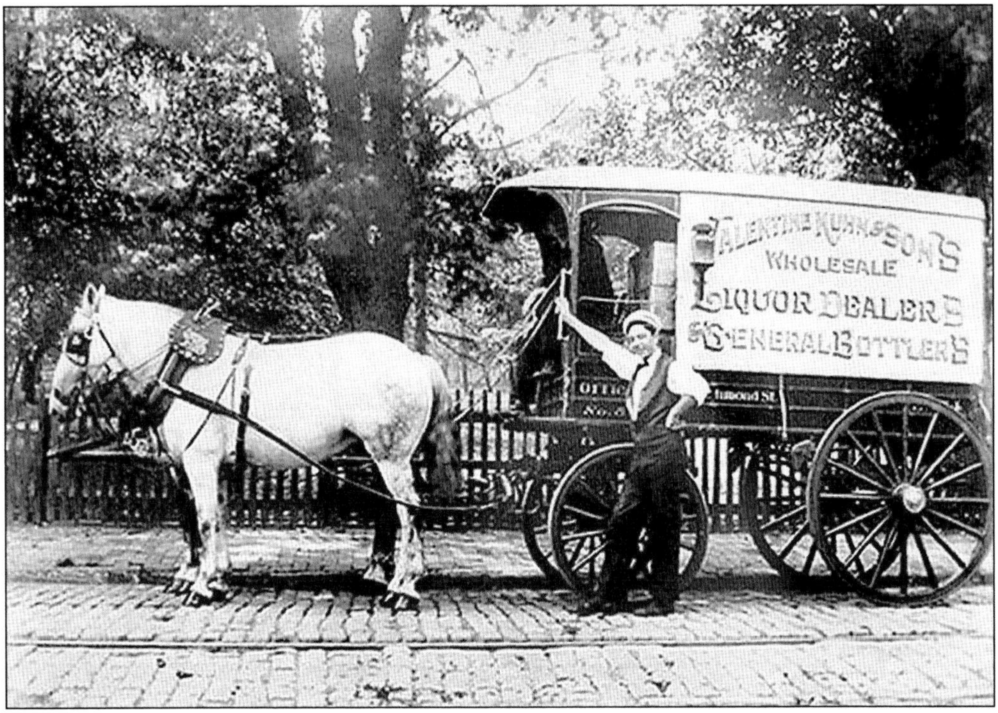

The liquor delivery business was lucrative throughout the River Wards following Prohibition. Liquor distilleries, such as Publicker, Kessler, and Old Grand Dad, popped up all over the city. With no laws governing its sales, deliverymen would buy liquor wholesale and peddle it through the streets. But it was not long before Pennsylvania took control of liquor sales. Today, the state still governs, controls, and taxes the sale of liquor and wine.

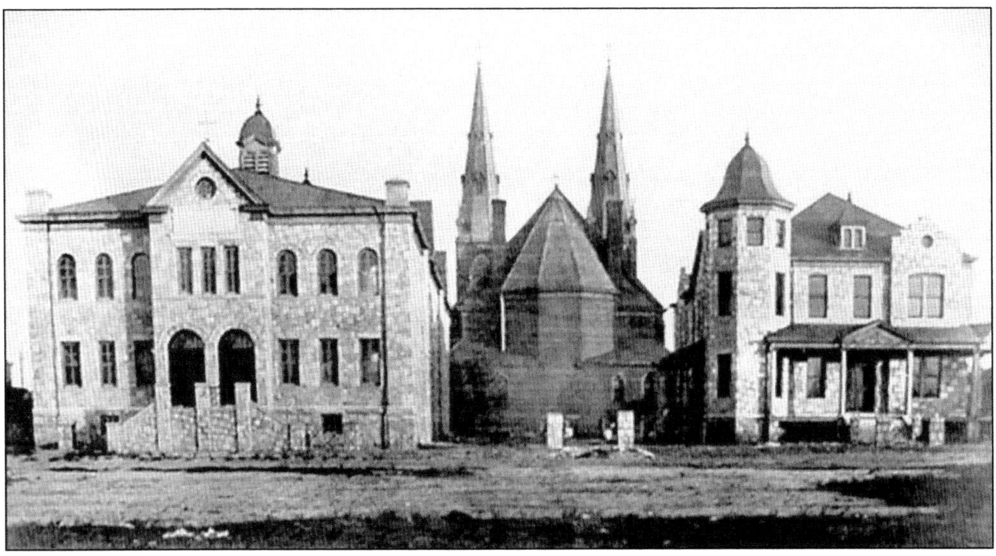

St. John Cantius, Bridesburg's Polish National Church, was built in the early 19th century, a few blocks south of All Saints Church, the only other Catholic parish in the neighborhood. The photograph shows the rear of St. John's fronting Thompson Street and the entrances of the school and rectory on the dirt road that is now Almond Street.

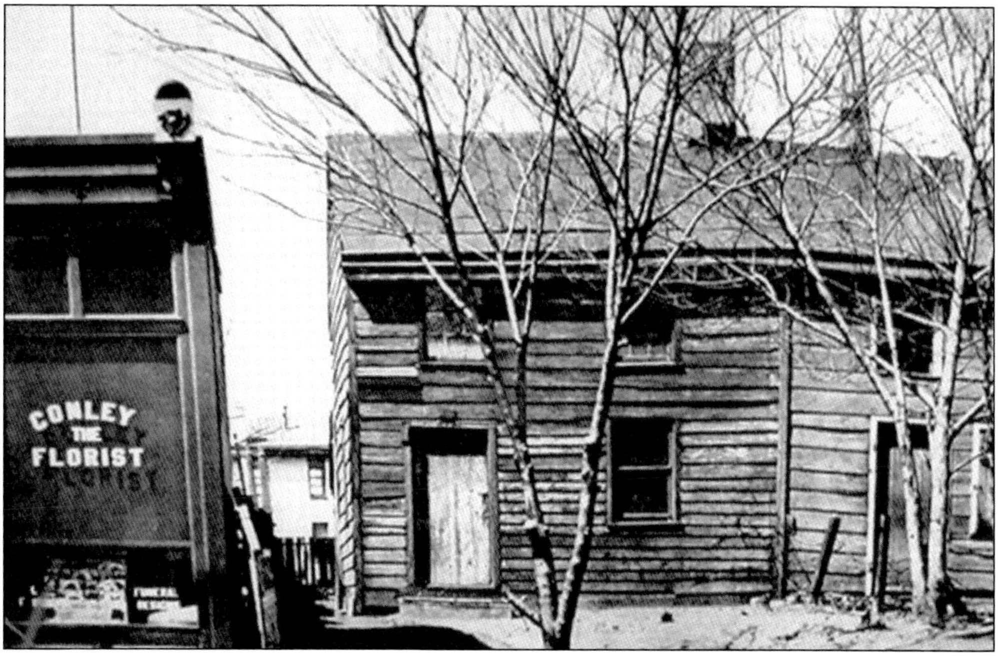

This old wooden house was built on Richmond Road in Bridesburg, near the entrance of what is now the Rohm and Hass Chemical Company. Next to the dilapidated house is Conley Florist, which occupied the site before moving to a new location farther north on Torresdale Avenue.

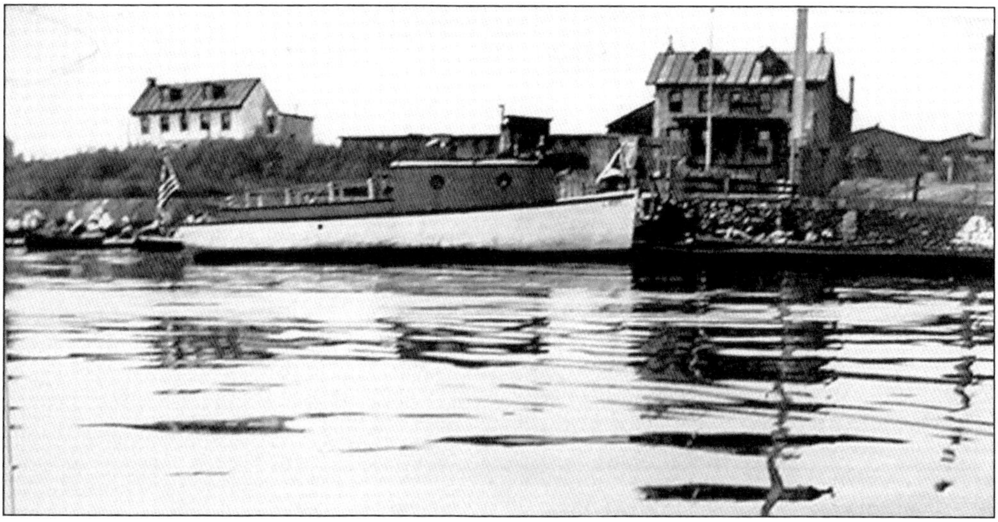
This photograph of Bridesburg, taken from a boat on the Delaware River, shows recreational activity on the river. Early 20th-century Bridesburg residents spent many happy, carefree hours picnicking and socializing on the two neighborhood piers at Lewis Street and Bridge Street.

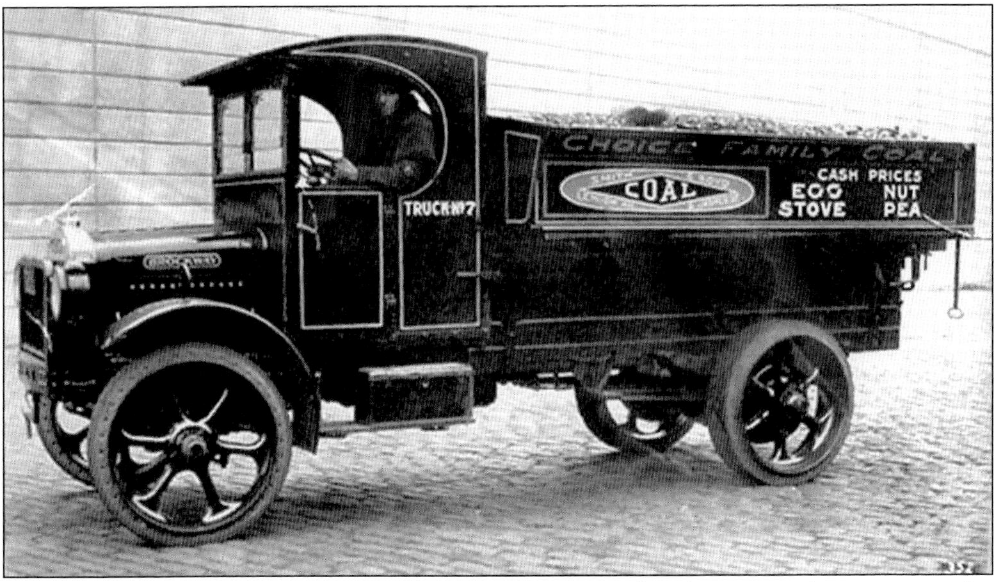

Coal was the main source of home heat in the early to mid-20th century. Some present-day residents of the neighborhoods can still recall the sound of the coal going down the chutes into the basement coal bins. Delivering coal was not an easy job. The driver in this photograph is wearing a heavy leather cape over his shoulders. The cape offered the driver protection when carrying buckets of coal to be used in potbelly stoves in kitchens and when lifting the heavy chutes into position in the small basement windows.

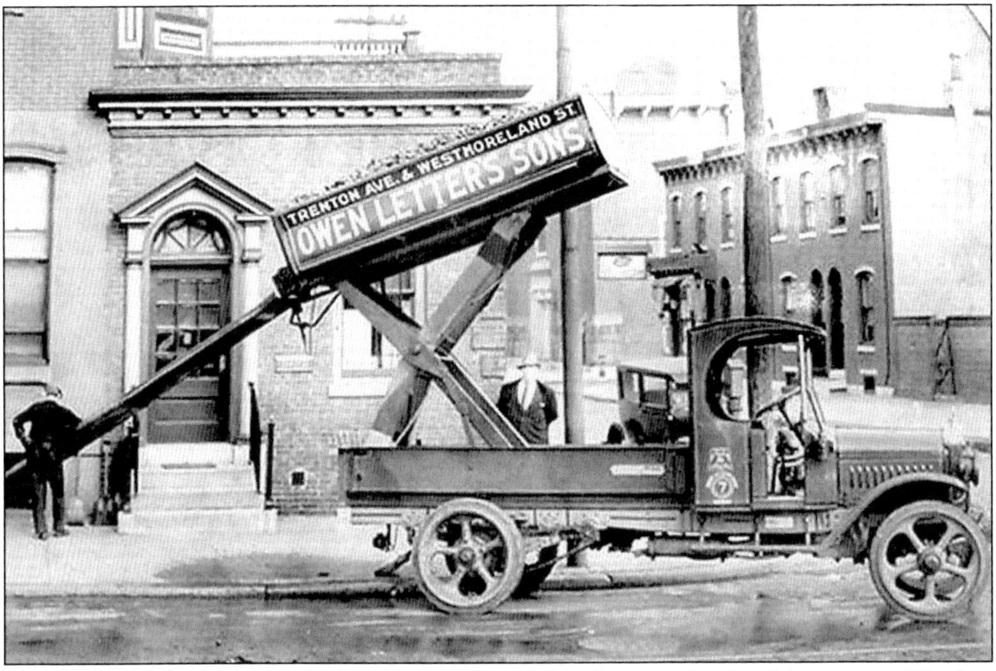

This coal truck had a hydraulic lift, making the job much easier for the deliveryman. The bin of the truck had three dividers that separated the coal for individual deliveries. Coal also had a useful purpose after it was burned. When it snowed, residents would spread the coal ashes over the streets and pavement, giving traction for cars, trucks, and pedestrians.

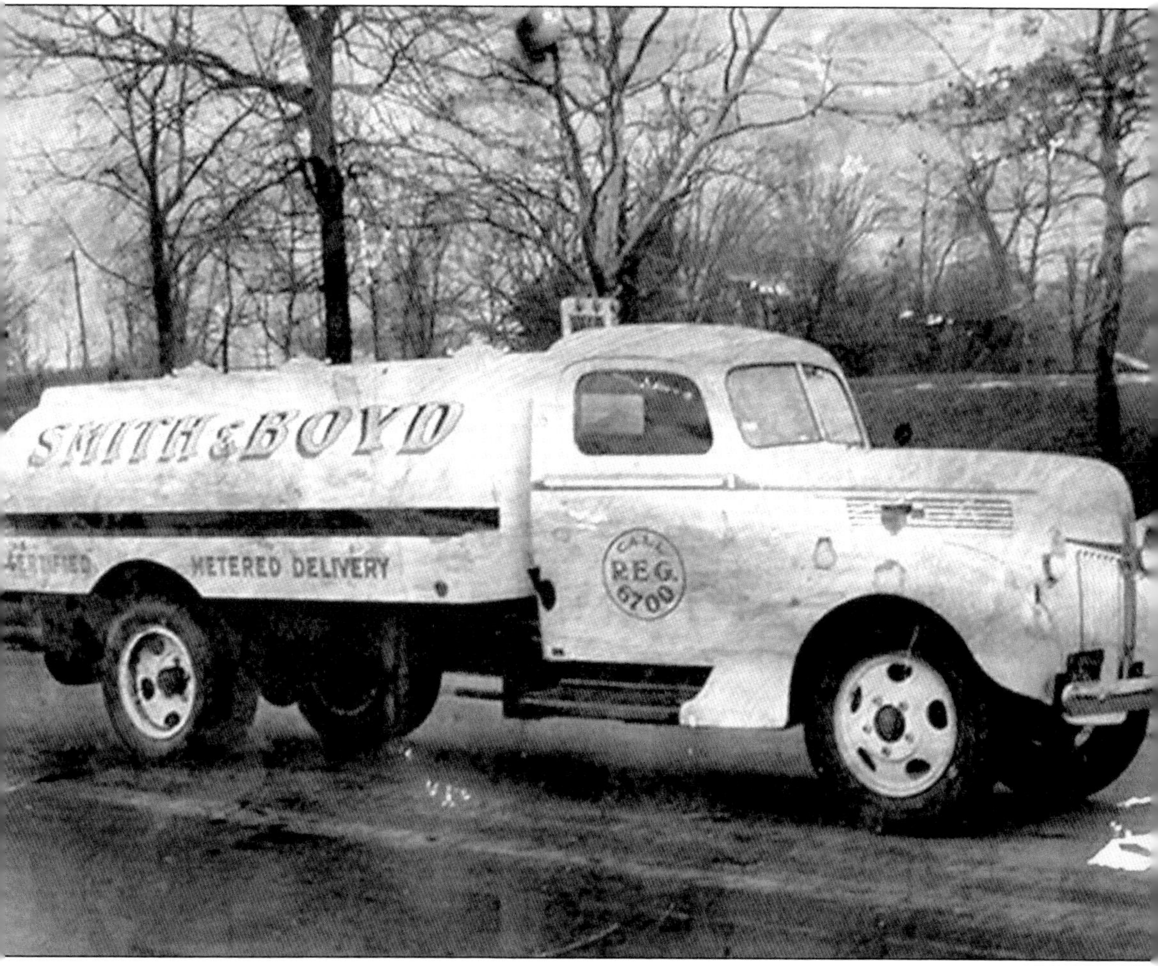

Smith and Boyd, a coal and heating company that advertised heavily in the neighborhoods in the early 20th century, first established its office at K&A, the intersection of Kensington and Allegheny Avenues. After the construction of the El, Smith and Boyd moved its location to Lehigh Avenue in Port Richmond, gaining better access to the trains coming from the Carbon County coal region.

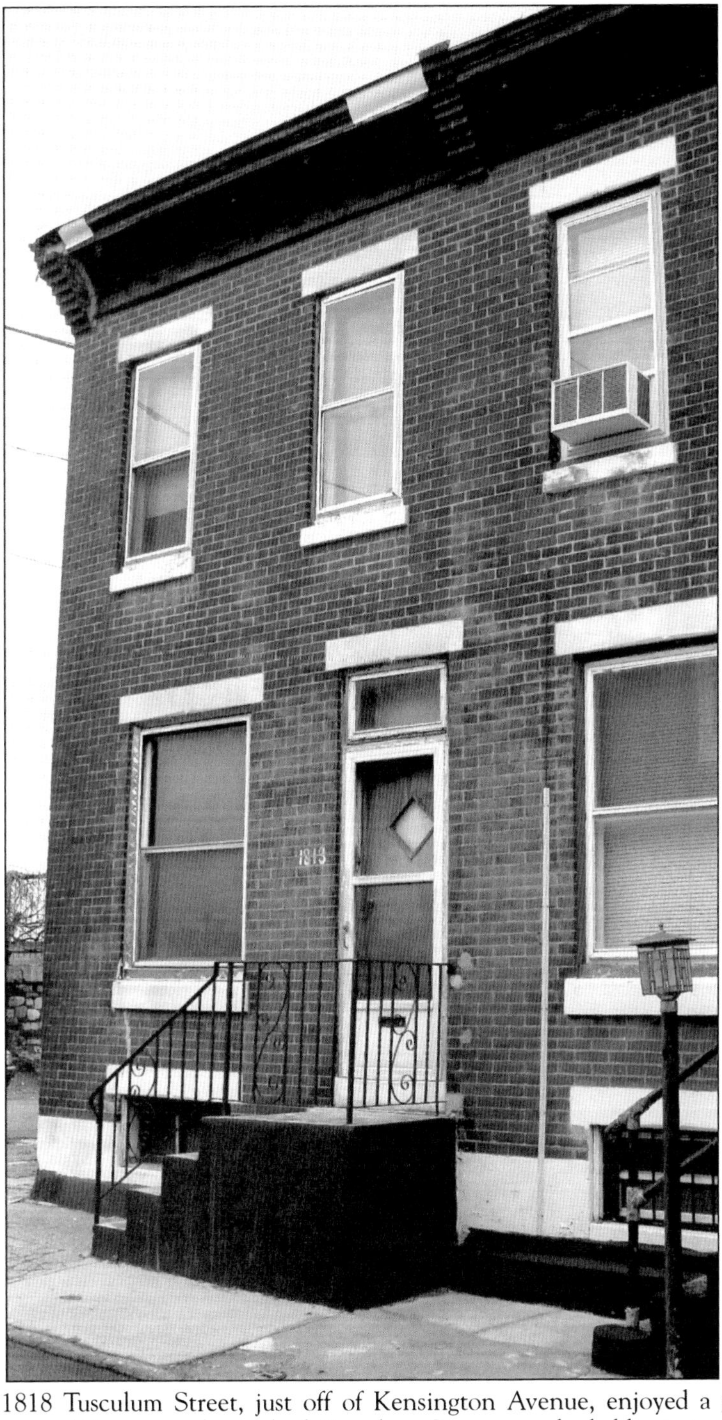

For a time, 1818 Tusculum Street, just off of Kensington Avenue, enjoyed a good deal of celebrity. This small home at the end of Tusculum Street may look like just another River Wards row house, but it became notable as the home of Rocky Balboa in the popular Sylvester Stallone movie *Rocky*. In addition to the house, much of Kensington was featured in the film, including the Frankford El.

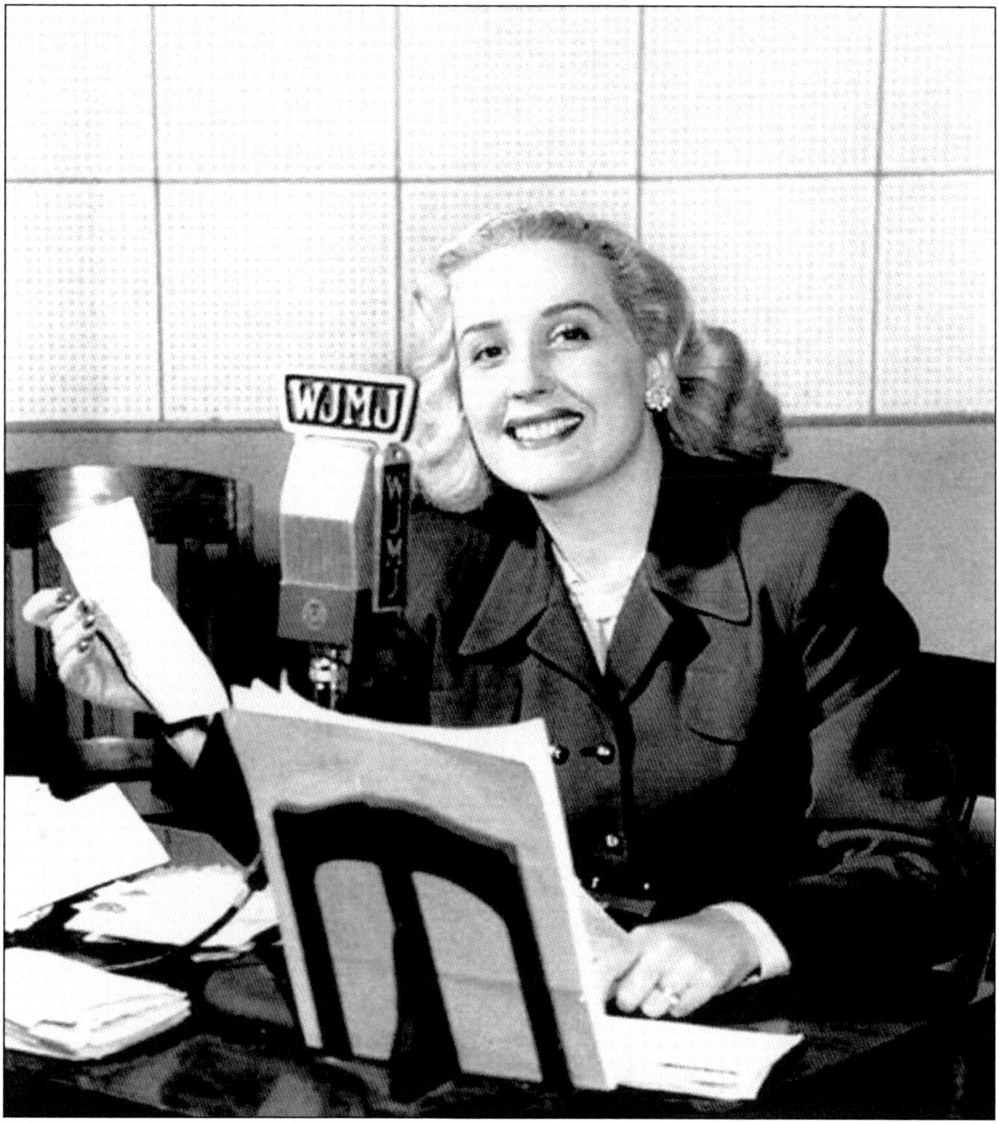

Sally Starr is a Philadelphia institution and local celebrity who hosted an after-school television show for children called *Popeye Theater*. Dressed in her cowgirl outfit with her blonde hair in a long ponytail, "Our Gal Sal" brought hours of enjoyment to the baby-boomer generation. In addition to *Popeye* and other cartoons, Sally featured the Three Stooges shorts on her show. The Philly cowgirl had ties to the River Wards through her friendship with Jack Howard, a record producer who owned Arcadia Recording Studio, located on Kensington Avenue near Tusculum Street. Both Sally Starr and Larry Fine of the Three Stooges were regular visitors to Howard's studio.

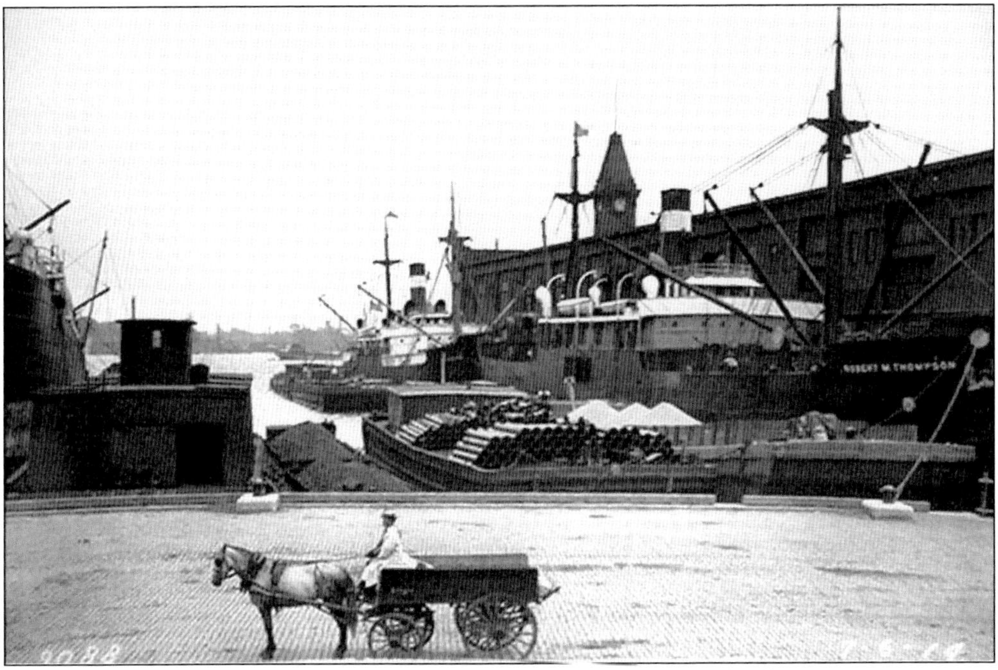

In 1914, this was a commercial area along the Delaware River at the foot of Vine Street in Northern Liberties. Docked along the river are diesel tugboats, as well as steamships with sails. Industry, at the time, was a mixture of small businesses and major companies.

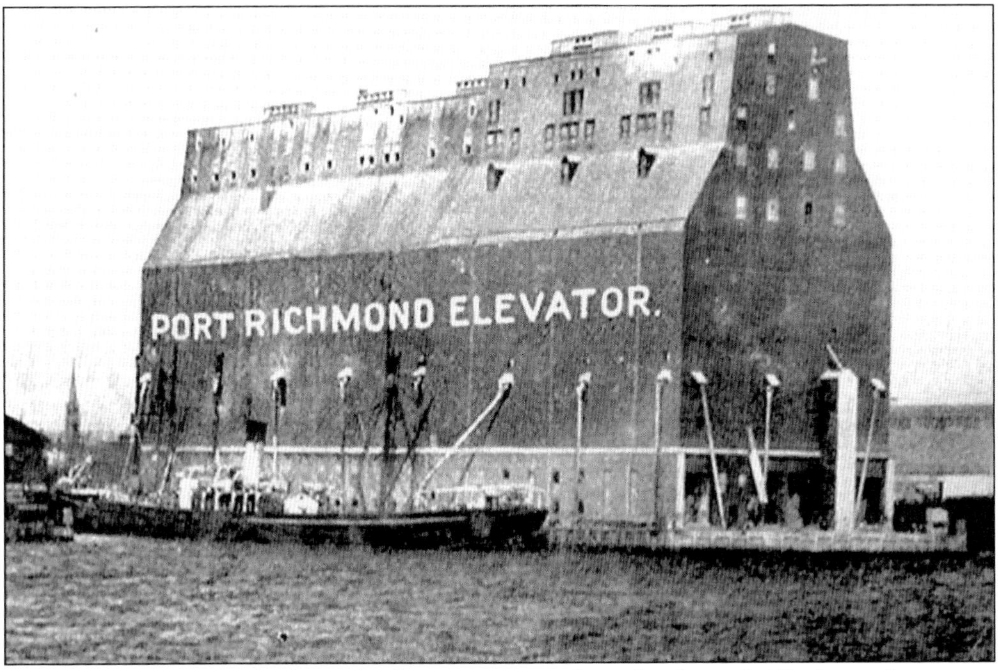

A concrete grain silo, built in the late 1800s, stood at the foot of Allegheny Avenue at the Delaware River. In the distance is the steeple of Our Lady Help of Christians Church, established to serve the German Catholic community in the River Wards. The clock in the church steeple is a neighborhood landmark.

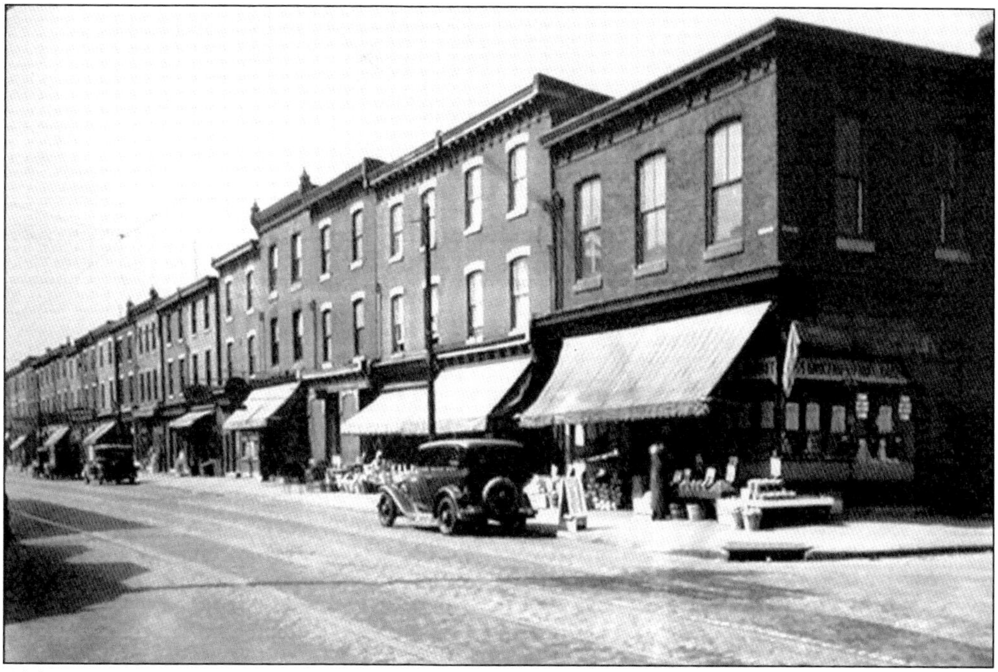

Old-time Richmondites remember when Richmond Street, from Cambria Street to Allegheny Avenue, was a shopping strip equal to the Frankford and Kensington Avenues shopping districts. In this 1935 photograph, shop owners prepare for a busy day.

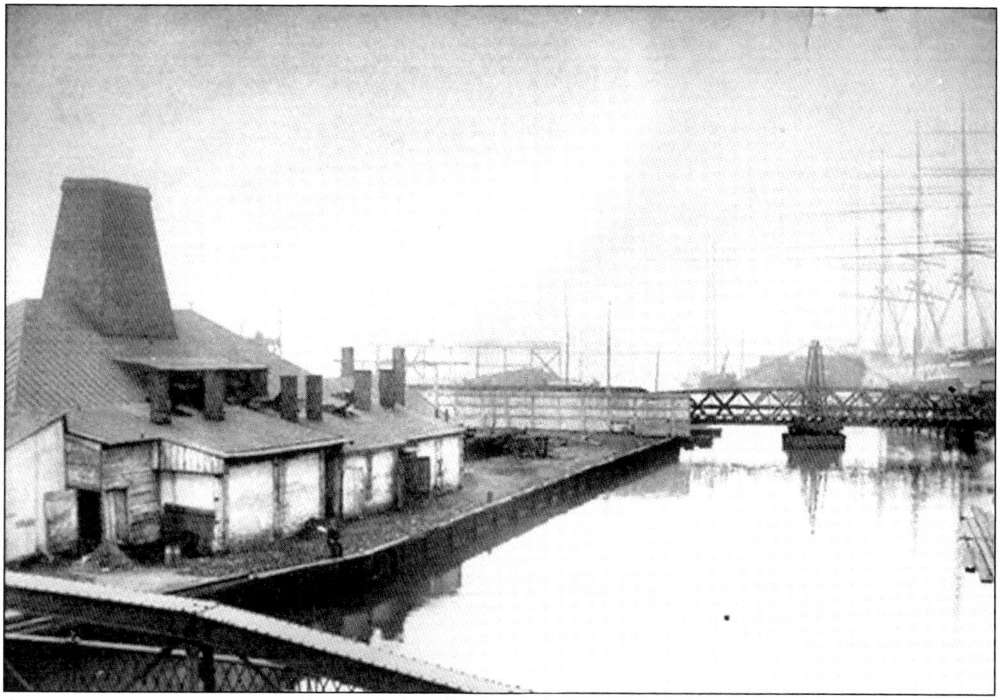

Aramingo Avenue, a major thoroughfare that travels from Girard Avenue in Kensington north to Bridesburg, was built over a creek. Just beyond the turnstile bridge where the creek met the Delaware River, a three-mast sailing ship can be seen.

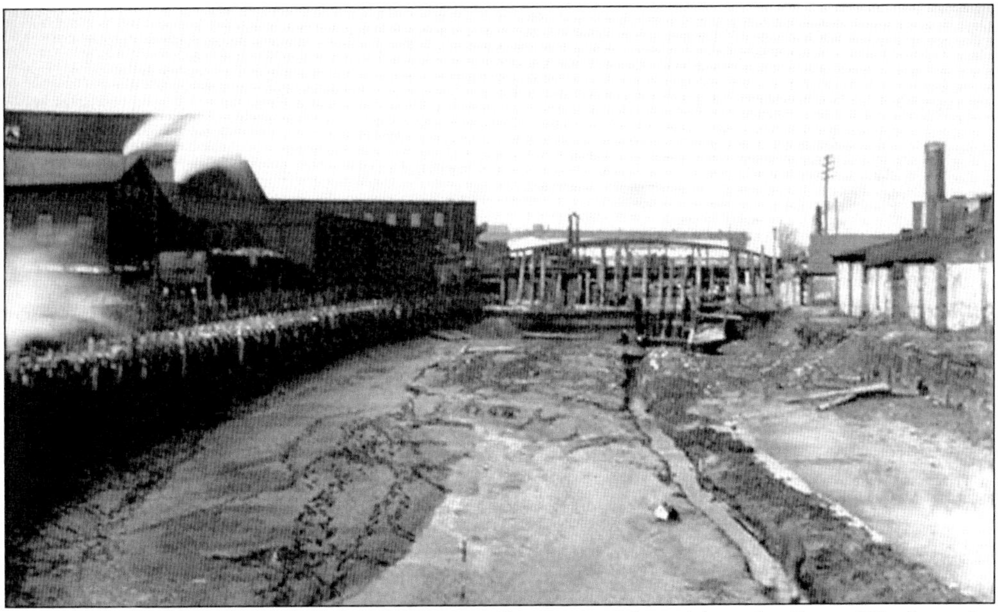

Because textile, fabric, and other industrial mills were so plentiful in the River Wards at the turn of the 20th century, the city planned to dig out the Aramingo Canal to enable better access from the mills to the ports on the Delaware River. Realizing the undertaking was not feasible, the city scrapped the plans. Before the project was cancelled, this section of the Aramingo Canal at York Street was pumped out.

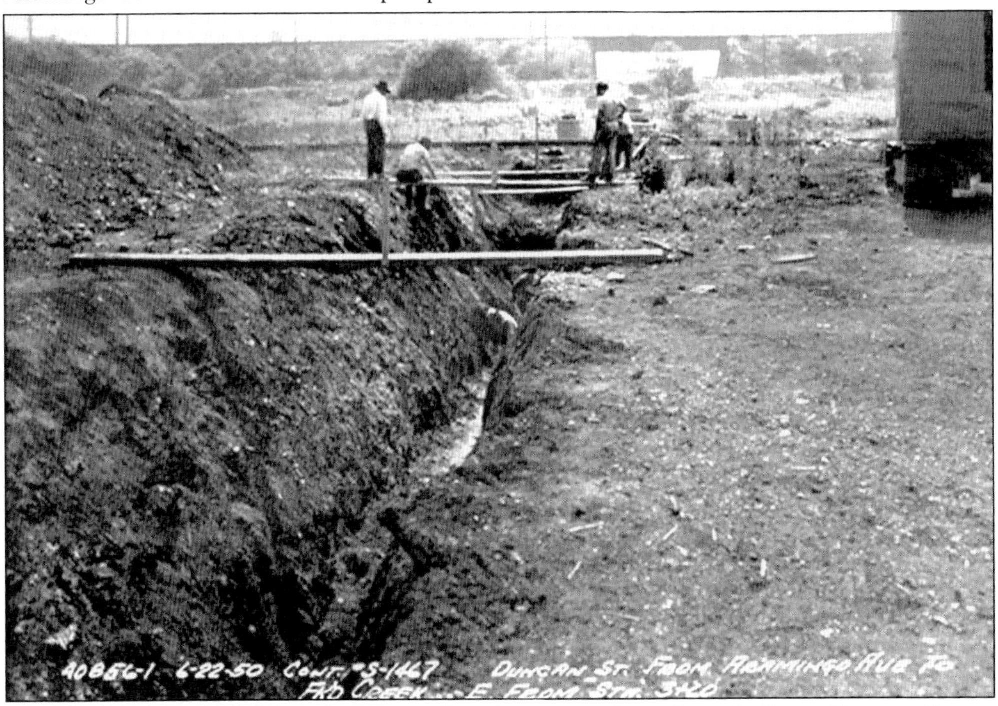

In 1950, the paving of the Aramingo Canal continued northward. From Duncan Street, looking south on Aramingo Avenue, the railroad bridge crosses overhead. This bridge is still used by Conrail and CSX.

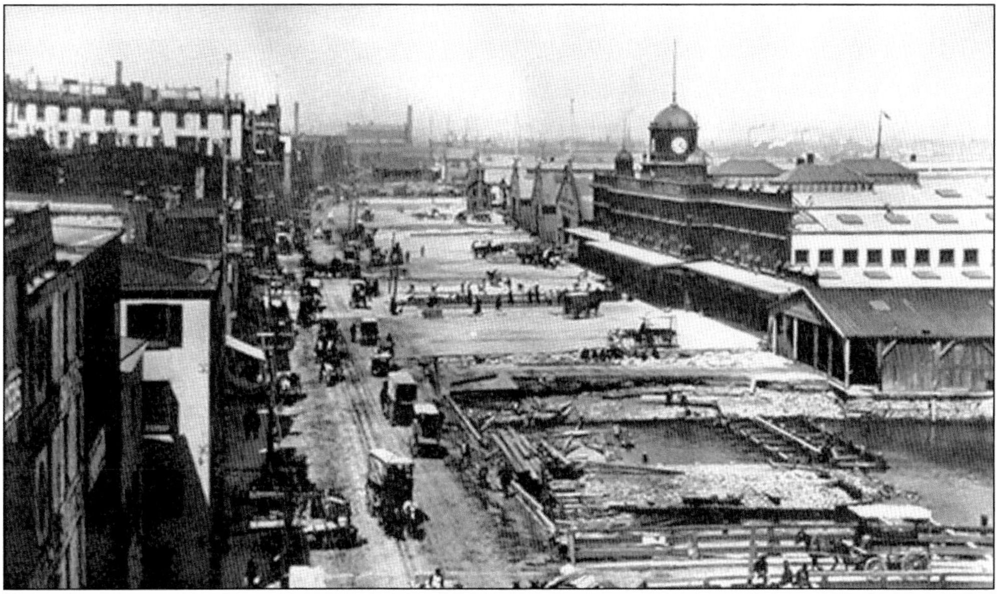

A rare aerial photograph of Delaware Avenue in Northern Liberties, taken in the 1800s, looks north toward Port Richmond. This area along the river was a bastion of the city's fruit-and-vegetable wholesale industry.

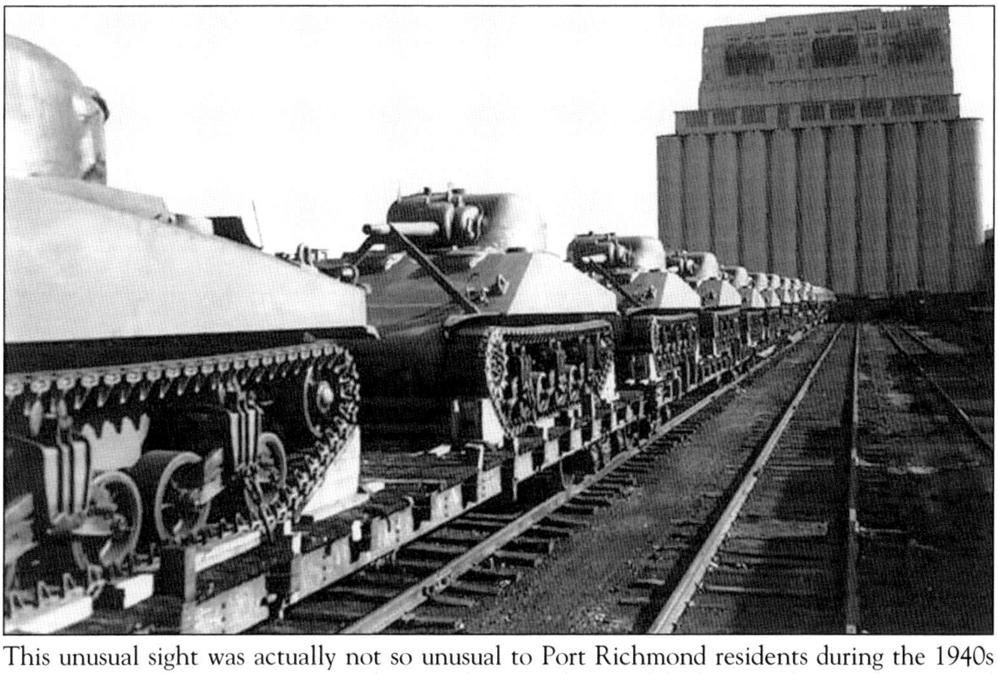

This unusual sight was actually not so unusual to Port Richmond residents during the 1940s through the late 1950s. Army tanks were built at the Frankford Arsenal in Bridesburg and were taken on flatbed trains to the Port Richmond shipping terminals for transport. In the rear of this photograph was the second of the large grain elevators that occupied this location on Allegheny Avenue. Until its recent implosion, the "Graino" was a neighborhood landmark.

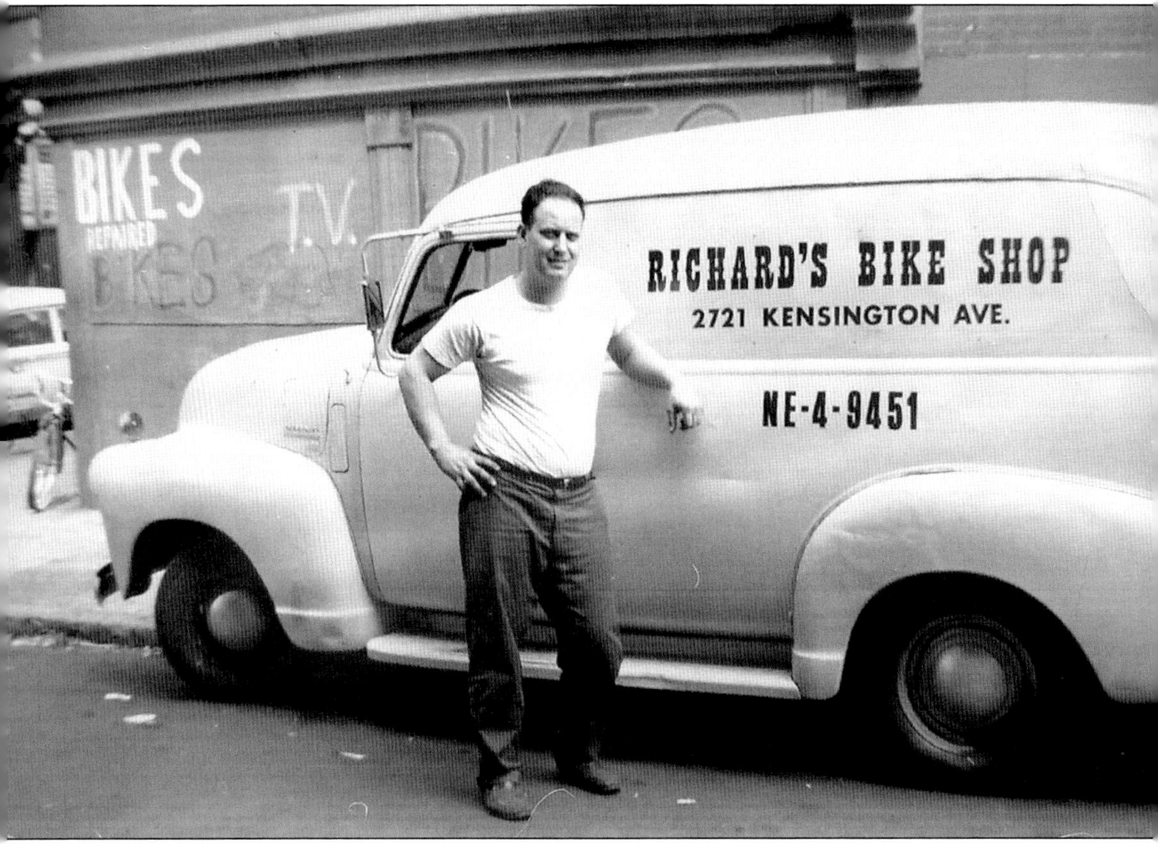

Small bicycle shops were a mainstay in the neighborhoods throughout the last century and some, such as Richard's Bike Shop at 2721 Kensington Avenue, are still in business. Owner Richard Cannon carries parts for and repairs many makes of bicycles, including some less-recognized brands.

Five

All Roads Lead to K&A

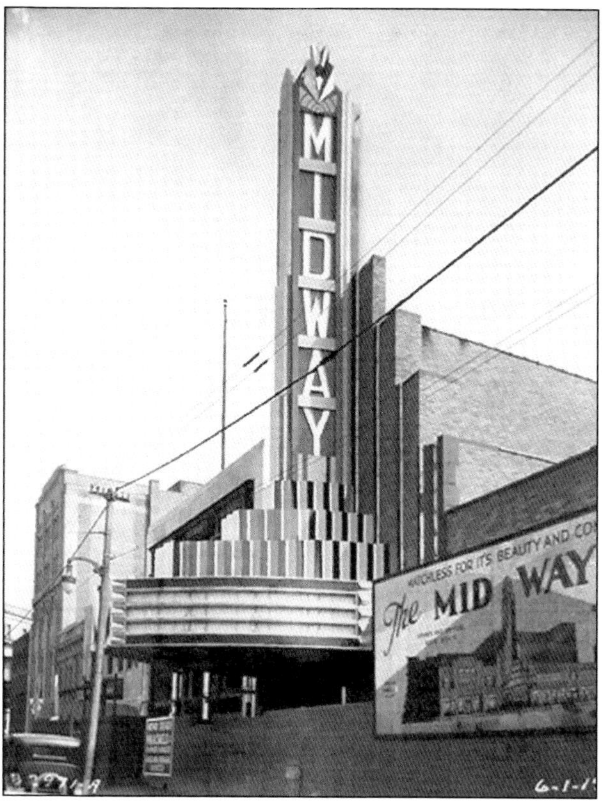

K&A, the intersection of Kensington and Allegheny Avenues, sits at the western end of the River Wards. From the 1950s through the 1970s, it was truly the hub of the River Wards, easily reached by many bus routes or the Frankford El. In addition to shopping, River Wards residents would travel to K&A to catch a movie at the architecturally beautiful Midway Theater, a mainstay of the area for many years.

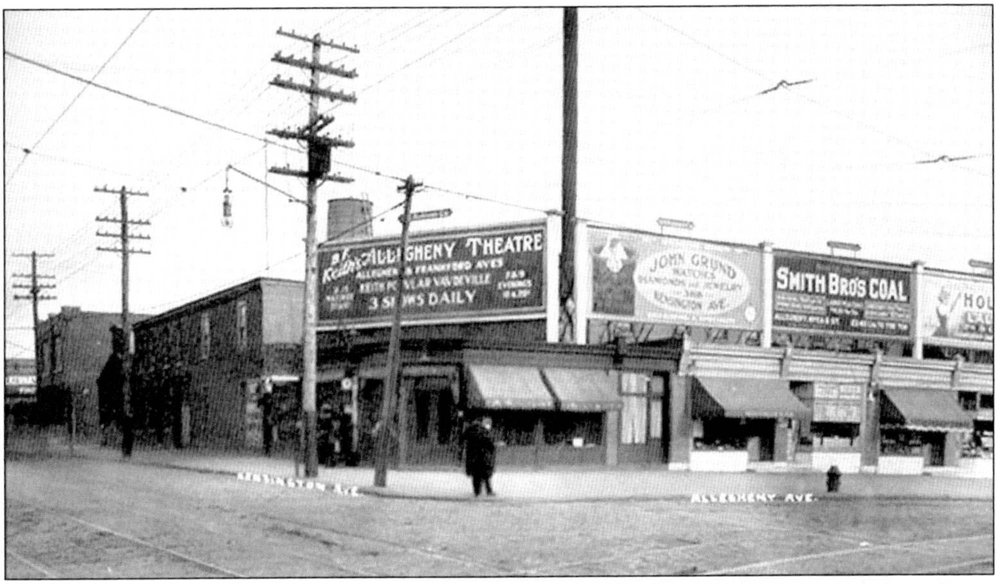

K&A is a major intersection that has undergone some change over the years. The northeast corner, shown here in 1911, became the site of the northbound El stop. Later, a Horn and Hardart's Automat restaurant catered to the shopping crowd and patrons of the Midway Theater, just a few buildings away. Today, a Philadelphia Electric Company office building and a Walgreen's drugstore occupy the site.

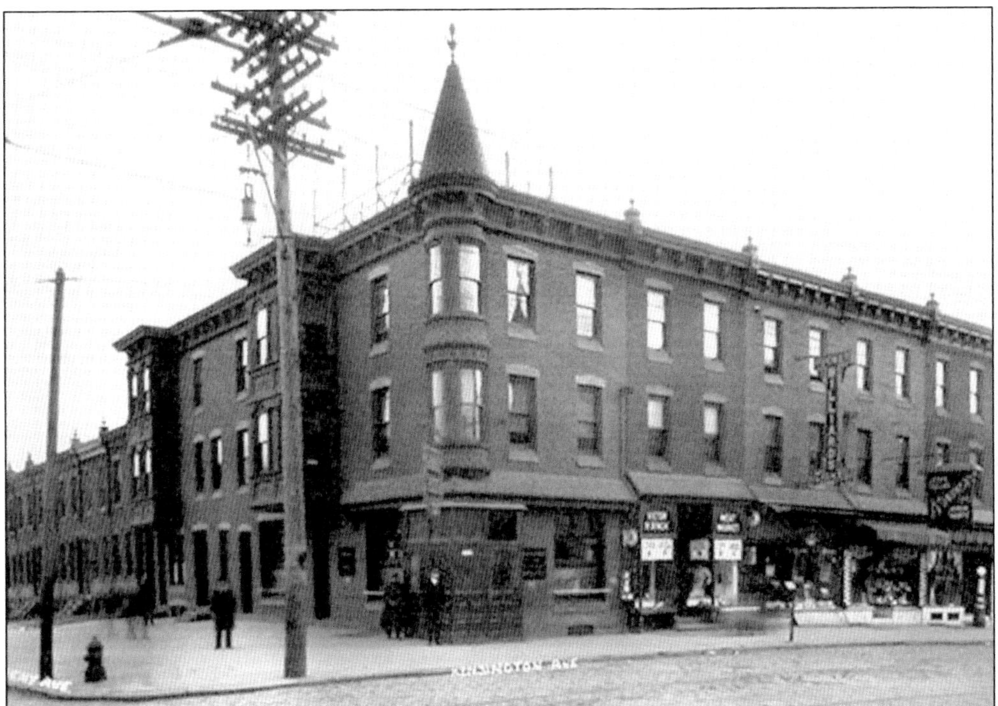

The southeast corner of the K&A intersection featured a saloon and billiard room in 1911. In the 1950s, Flagg Brothers Men's Shoe Store took over the corner. Today, a variety store stands there.

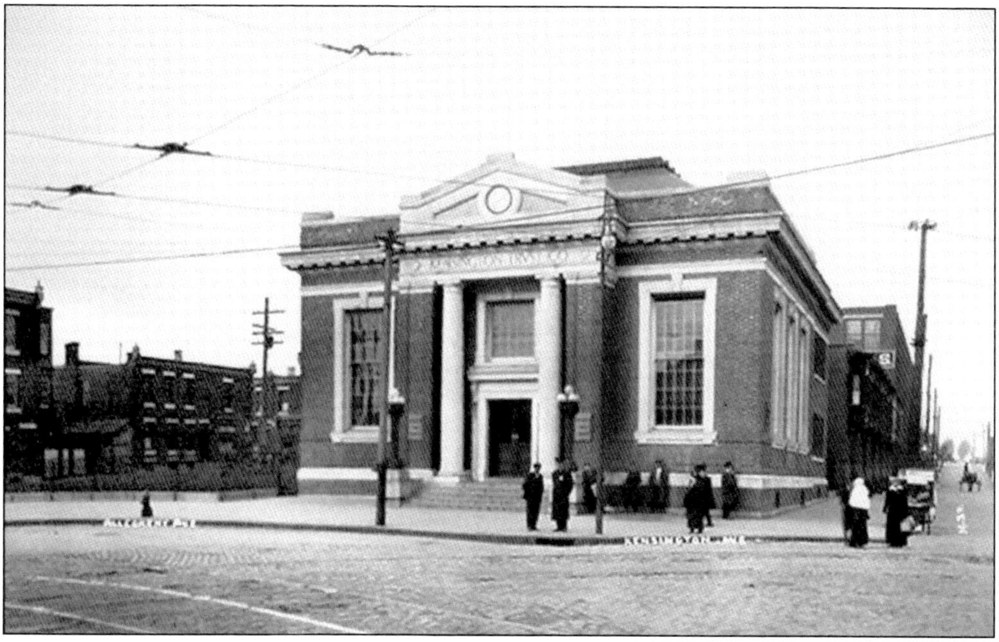

In 1911, the northeast corner of K&A was the home of the Kensington Trust Company. Since then, five banks have occupied this location. Today, it is the site of yet another bank. Interestingly, according to the original drawings by city planner Anthony Palmer, K&A is not in Kensington but in Harrowgate.

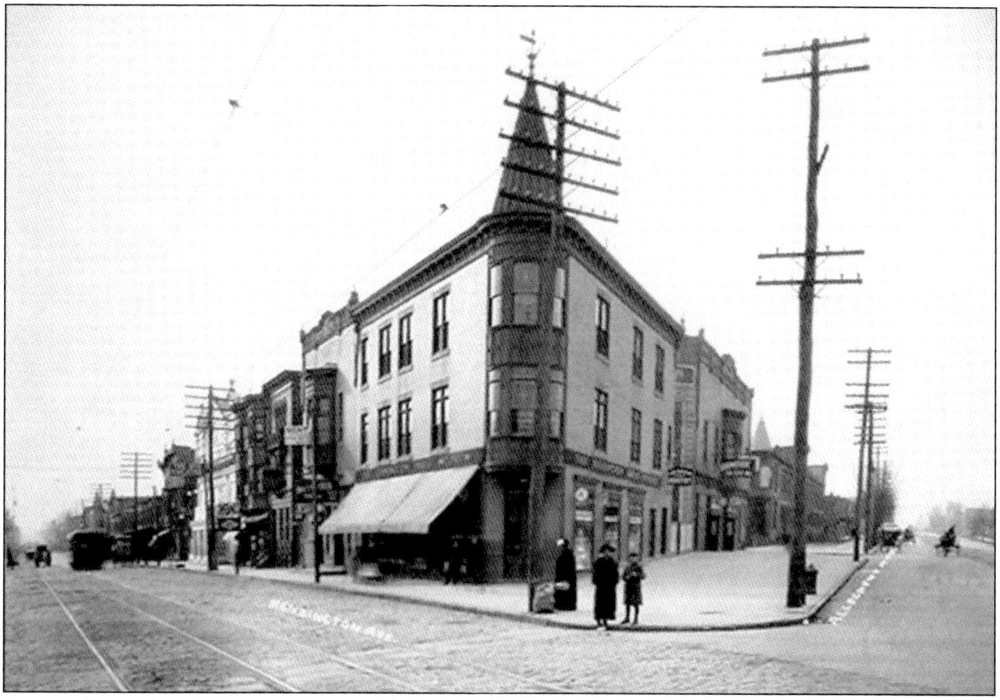

It is unclear what businesses occupied the southwest corner of K&A in 1911, but in its heyday, it was the site of Samit's Drugstore and Wimpy's Hamburgers. Today, the southbound El stop is on the corner with a Dunkin' Donuts nearby.

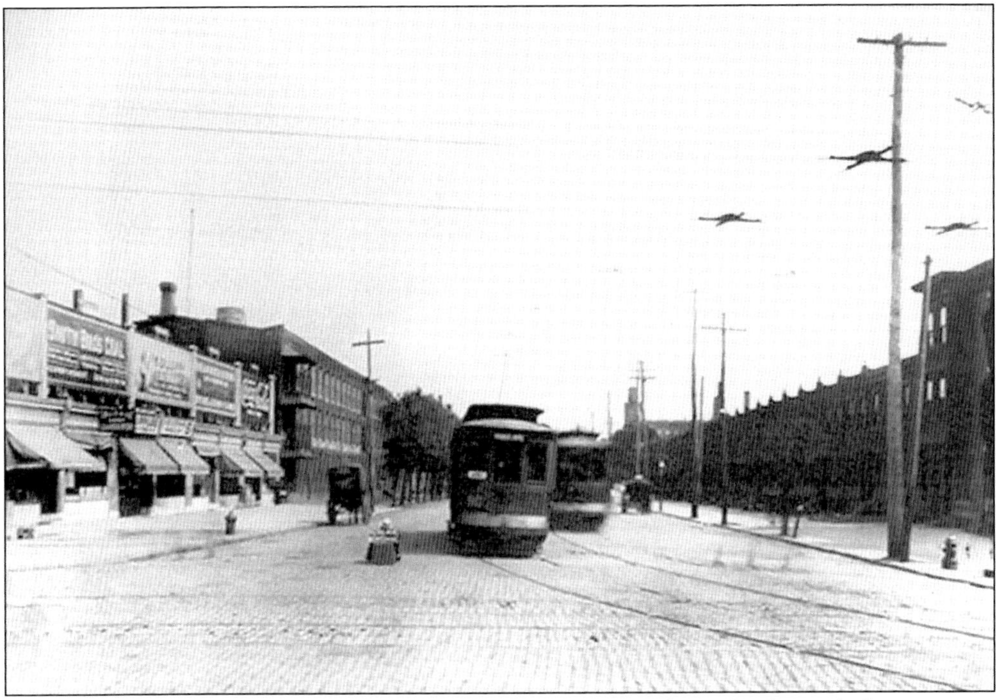

Looking east down Allegheny Avenue from Kensington toward Port Richmond, the avenue is lined with small stores, a large fertilizer company, and private homes.

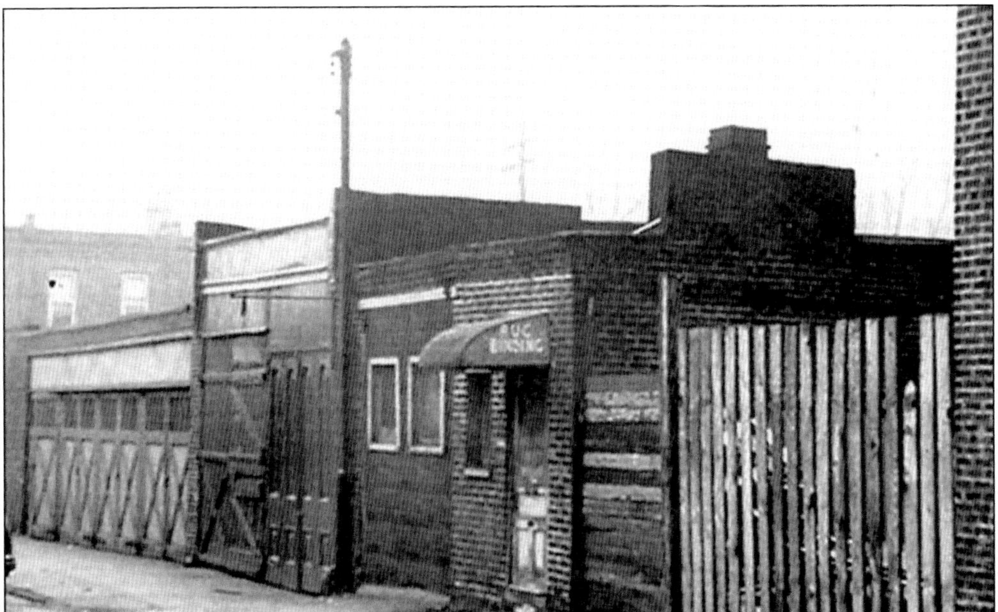

Long gone are the backyard businesses that cropped up behind the larger establishments on Kensington and Allegheny Avenues in the early 20th century. RUC Binding Company was one of those small businesses and was located on Hilton Street, behind the major intersection. The locally notorious Bubble Club was also located in the backyard area. Today, a large parking lot for Burger King and Blockbuster Video occupies the site.

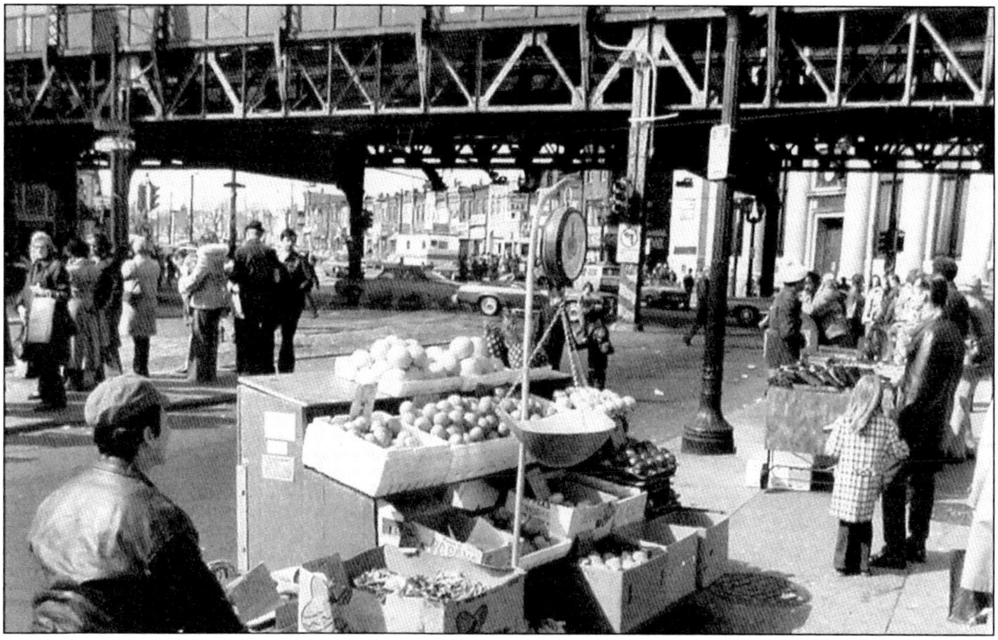

For a time in the mid-1970s, K&A was an outdoor market. The wide width of the avenue sidewalks and the heavy pedestrian traffic in the area made it an ideal location for vendors peddling everything from produce to leather goods. The enterprise came to a halt when local business owners complained of customers lost to these sidewalk vendors.

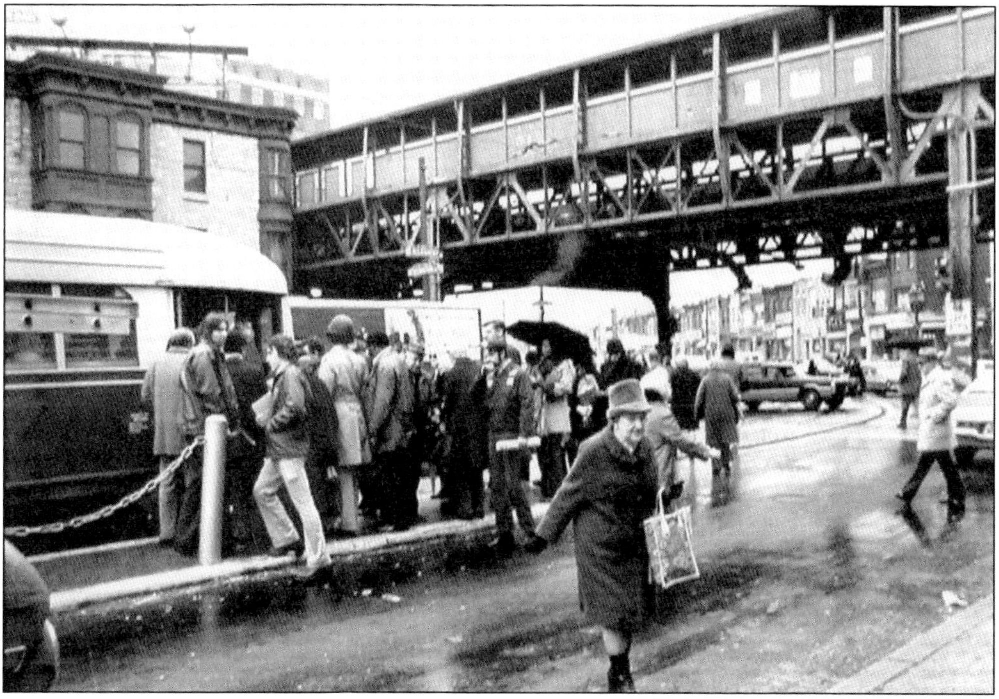

The busy K&A intersection of the 1970s has seen a lot of change over the years, but it still remains a vital area. Ethnic and economic changes are evident, but K&A still maintains some of what made it legendary.

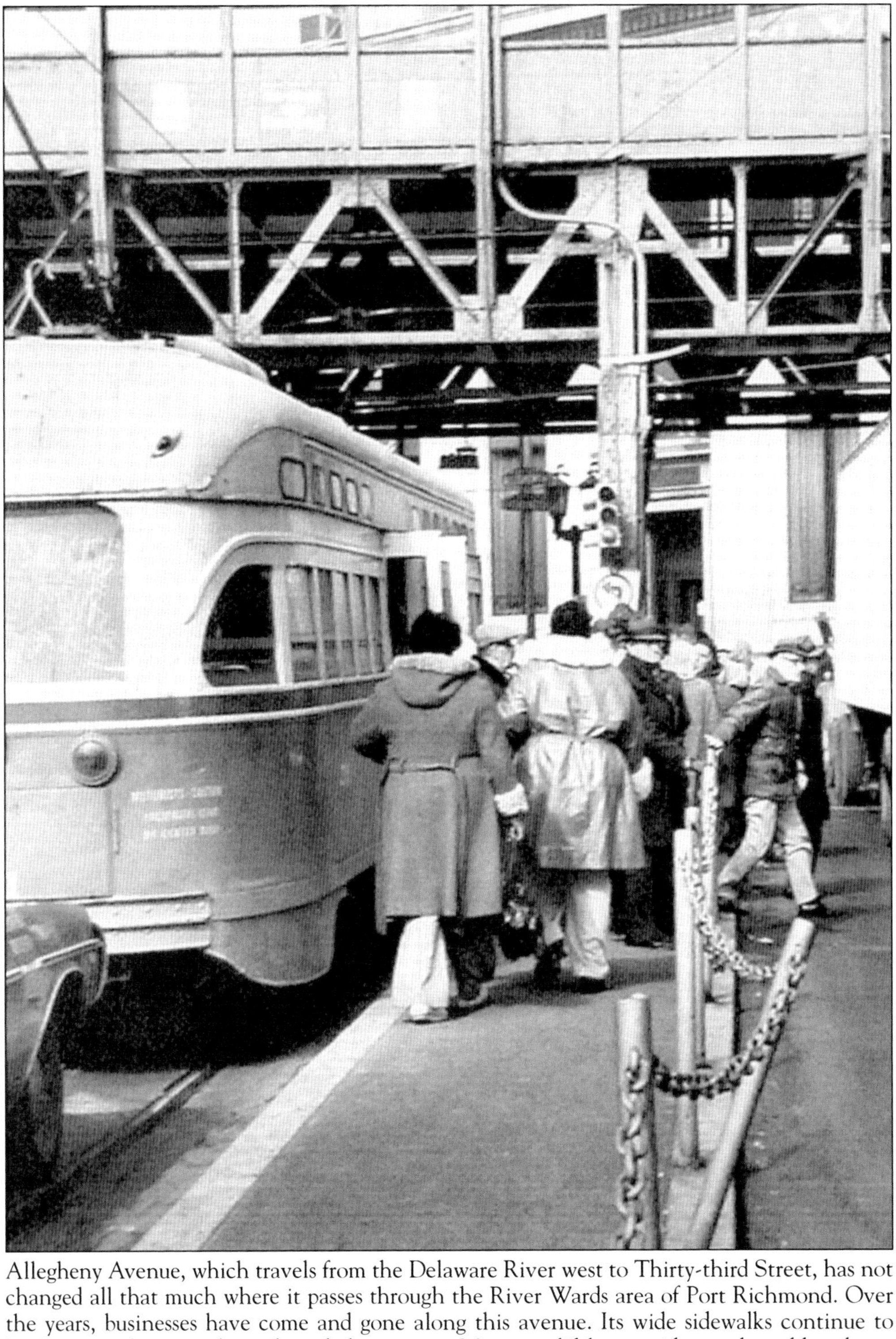

Allegheny Avenue, which travels from the Delaware River west to Thirty-third Street, has not changed all that much where it passes through the River Wards area of Port Richmond. Over the years, businesses have come and gone along this avenue. Its wide sidewalks continue to bustle as residents go about their daily routines. Many are lifelong residents who seldom leave the neighborhood where they can find everything they need and then some.

Six

"The Av" and the Ads

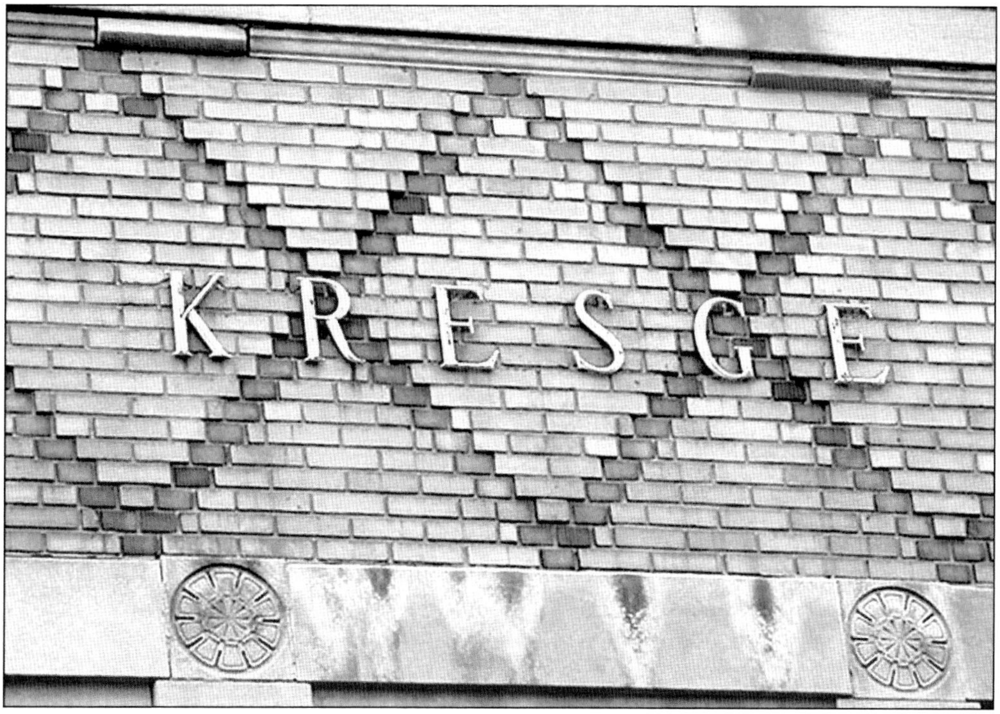

"The Av" was the nickname given to the stretch of stores on Kensington Avenue from Tioga Street to Somerset Street. In addition to the Av, many small shops of all varieties dotted the streets of the River Wards. Almost all of the stores advertised, mostly locally, in newspapers and church publications. Some of the stores had ornate signs like this one, made of solid yellow brass, that hung over Kresge's Five and Ten on Kensington Avenue. Although the store has been closed for some time, the sign still remains.

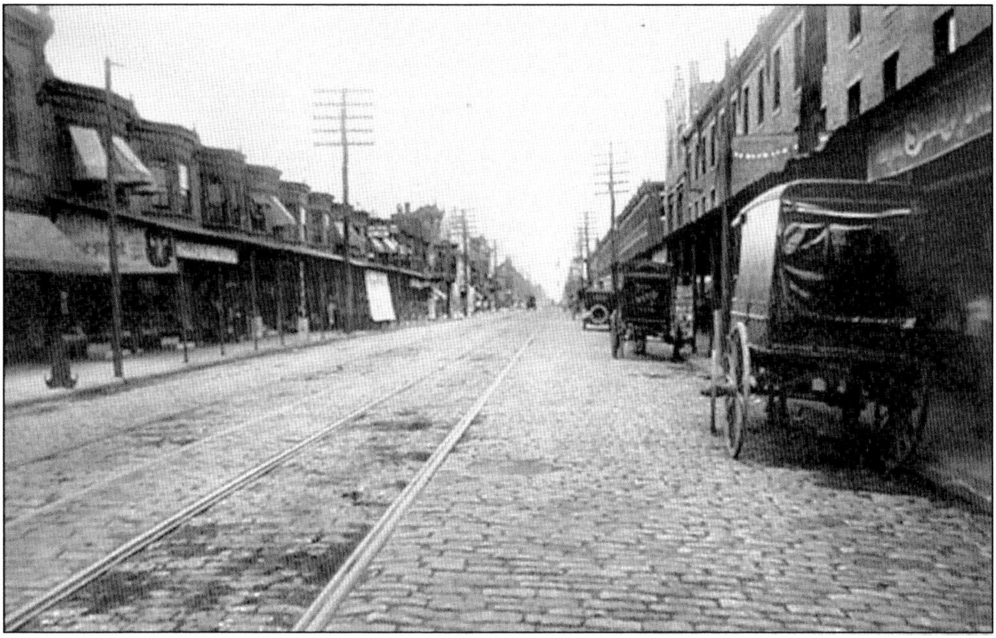

This late-1800s photograph of the 3100 block of Kensington Avenue is looking north to Allegheny Avenue from Clearfield Street. Even at this early date, many of these residences had businesses on their first floors.

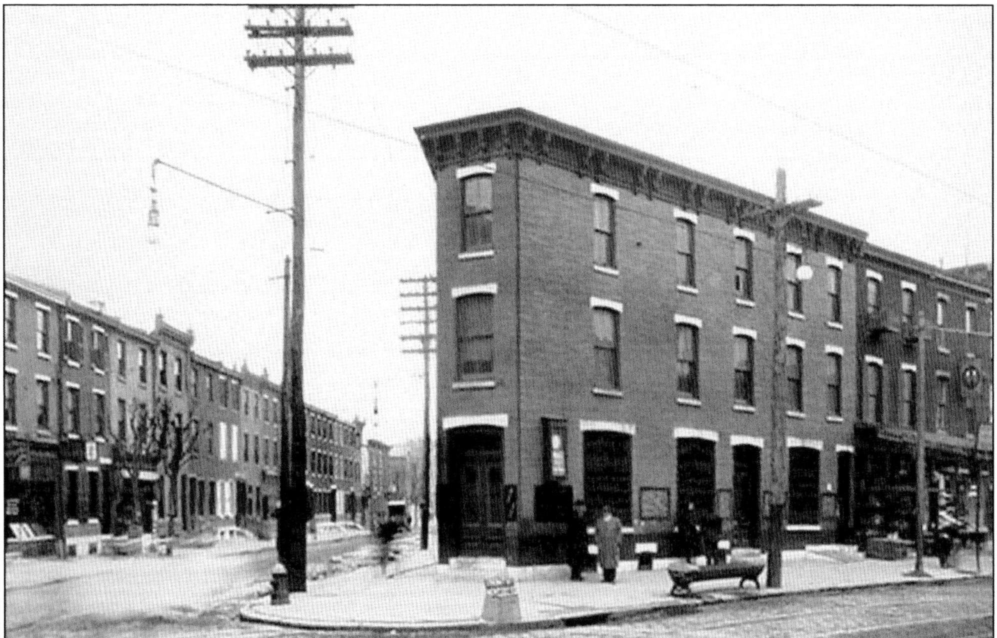

In the early 1940s, the west side corner of Kensington Avenue at Clearfield Street appeared to be residential. Before long, this intersection flourished as Uncle Miltie's, Stag Corner, and Chicken Galore took up residence. Today, a Chinese restaurant, an Asian variety store, and several jewelry stores are located here.

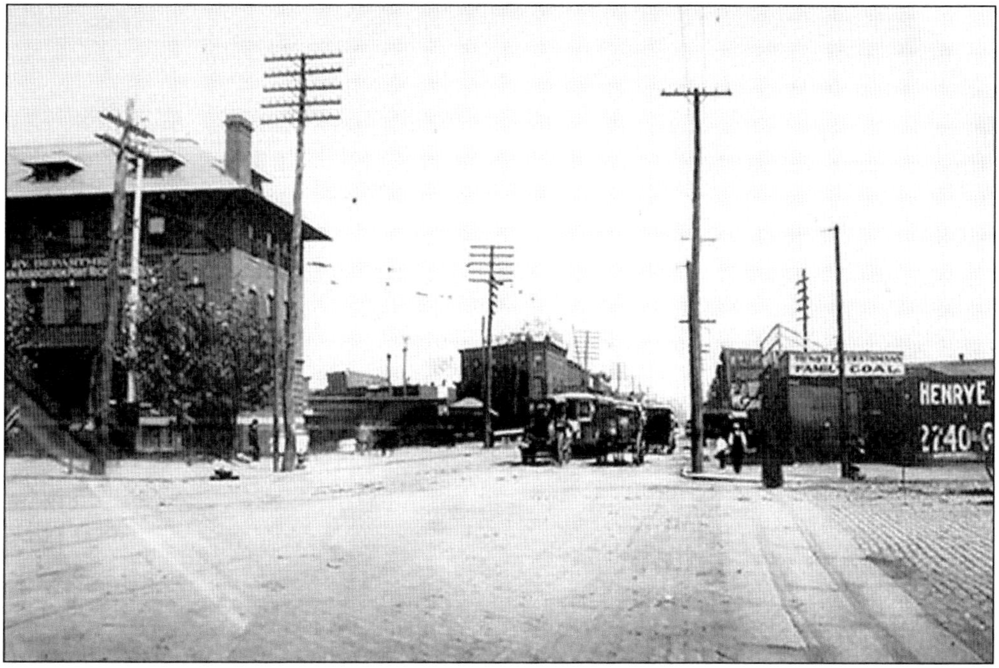

This photograph shows the intersection of Kensington and Lehigh Avenues in the early 1900s, before the city, for unknown reasons, excavated a three-square-city-block area. Note the coal company on the right.

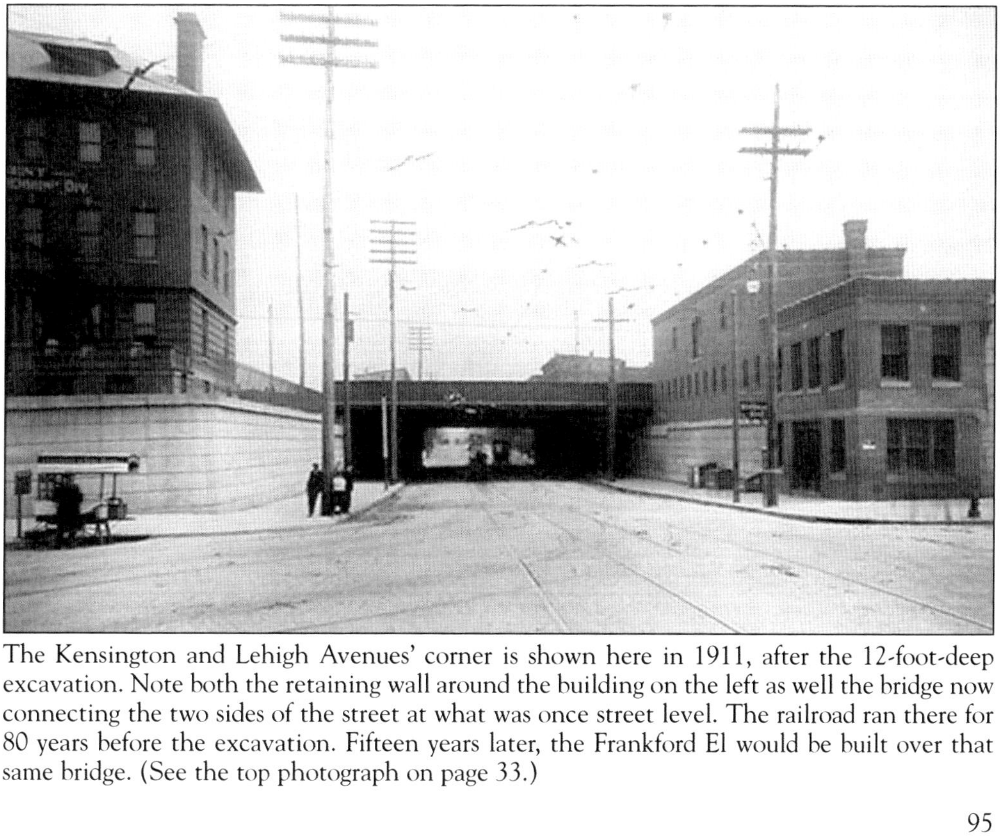

The Kensington and Lehigh Avenues' corner is shown here in 1911, after the 12-foot-deep excavation. Note both the retaining wall around the building on the left as well the bridge now connecting the two sides of the street at what was once street level. The railroad ran there for 80 years before the excavation. Fifteen years later, the Frankford El would be built over that same bridge. (See the top photograph on page 33.)

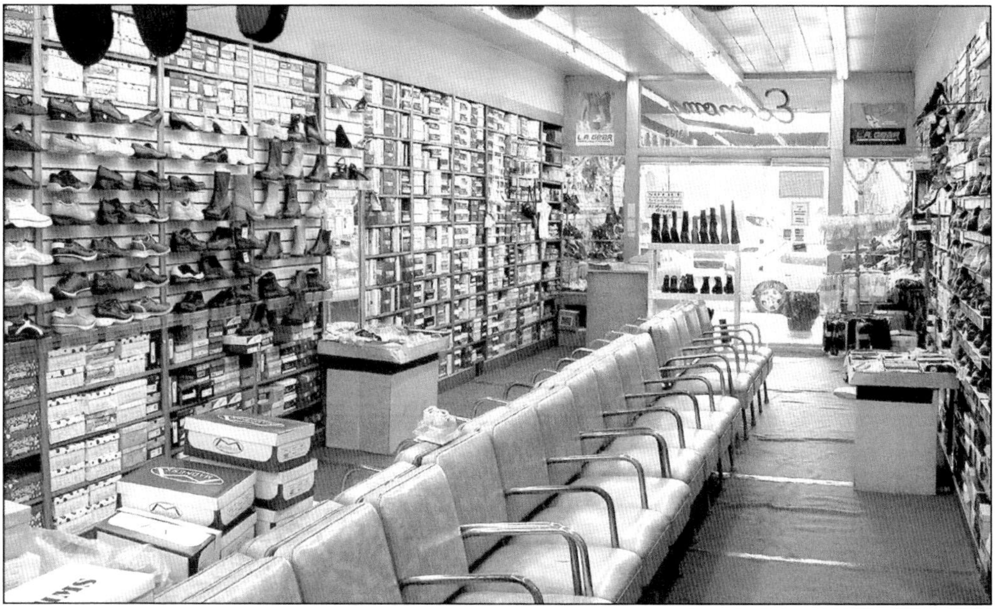

Paul Green, proprietor of the Economy Shoe Store, located on the Av, celebrated the store's 81st anniversary in 2002. Green, a former member of the Kensington Avenue Businessmen's Association, remembers all the stores that have come and gone on the avenue from Allegheny Avenue to Cambria Street. Changing little since the 1950s, the interior of the Economy Shoe Store appears frozen in time. Only the change in shoe styles suggests that this is a recent picture.

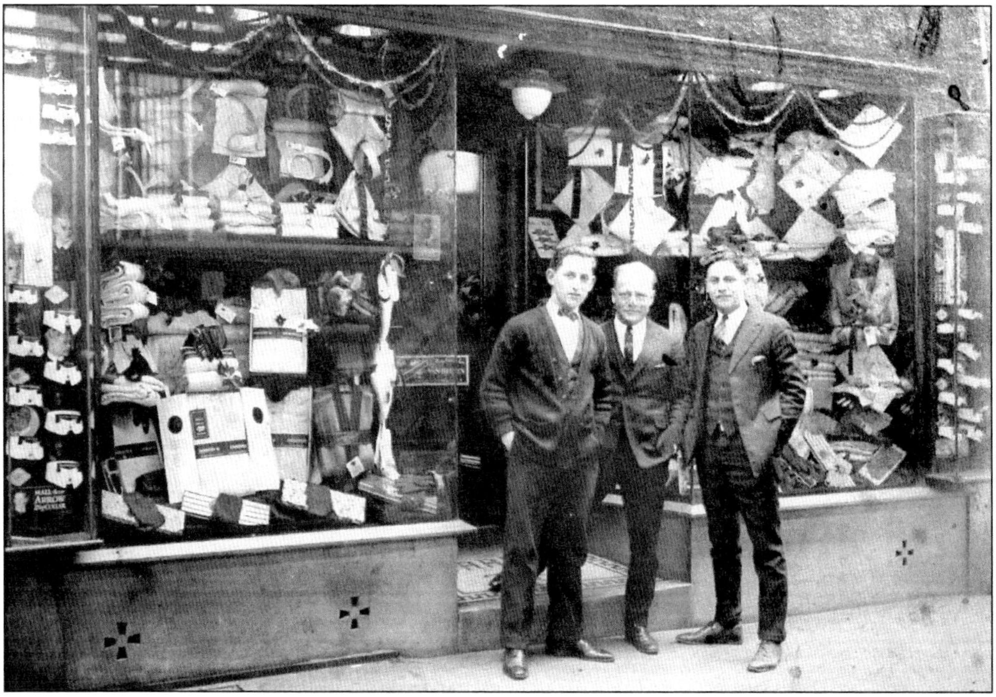

Harry's Men's Store was believed to have been opened for business for the first time by three brothers in the 1920s. Recently unearthed photographs, however, have convinced a family member that the store was opened before 1911.

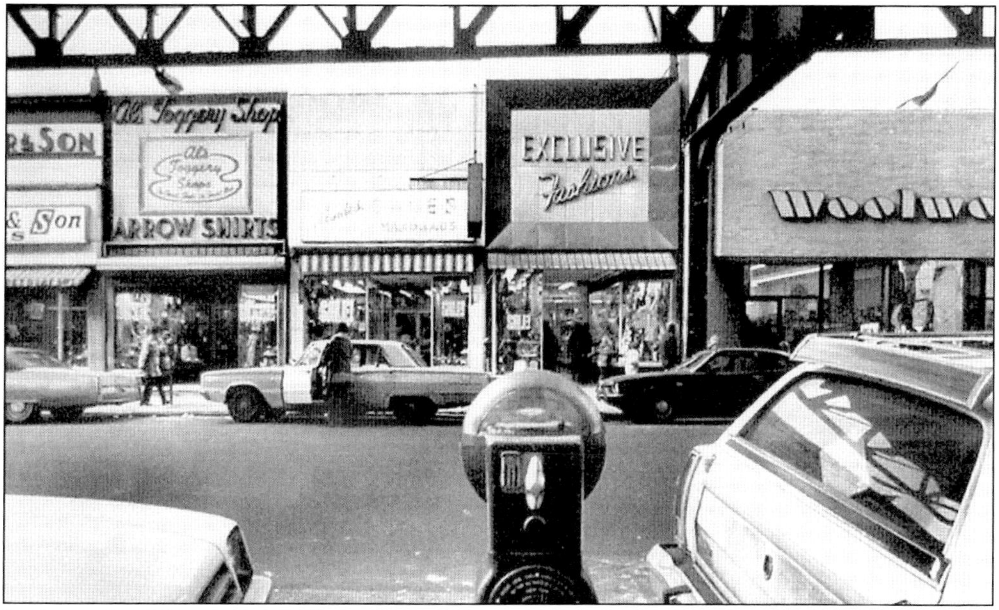

In the early 1950s, nickel parking meters were installed along Kensington Avenue in an effort to create revenue for the city. A nickel bought you an hour of shopping time. Today, a quarter buys 15 minutes. Pictured left to right are Father and Son's Shoe Store, Al's Toggery Shop, Landes Shoes and Handbags, Exclusive Fashions, and the original Woolworth's.

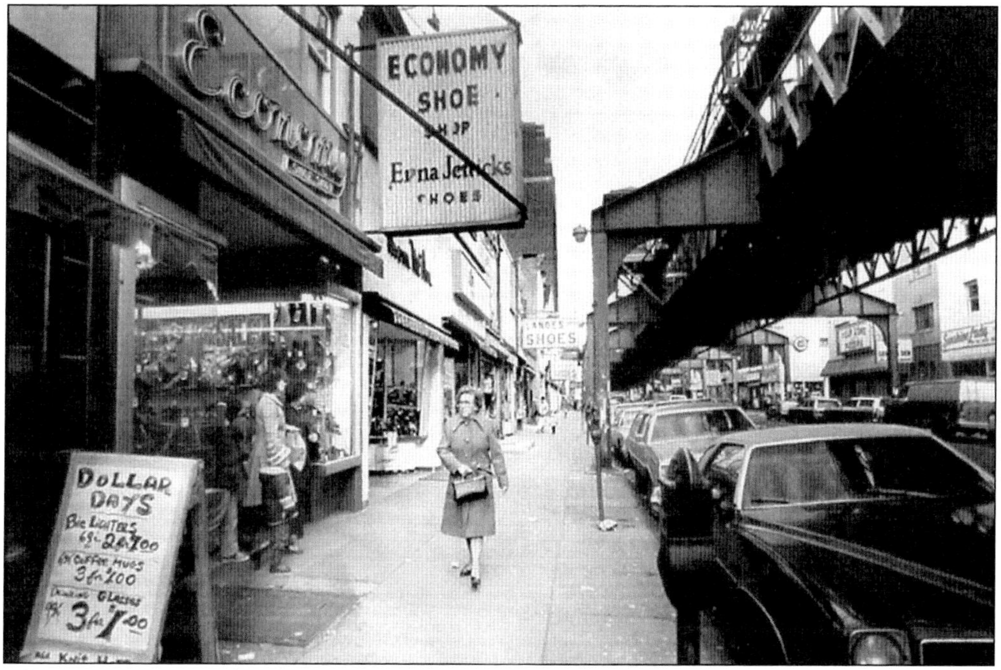

Like a giant centipede, the El drapes over both sides of Kensington Avenue. The ease in commuting to and from the northern and southern neighborhoods made the shopping strip a popular destination for many. This 1960s photograph depicts what appears to be a slow day on the Av, by 1960s standards.

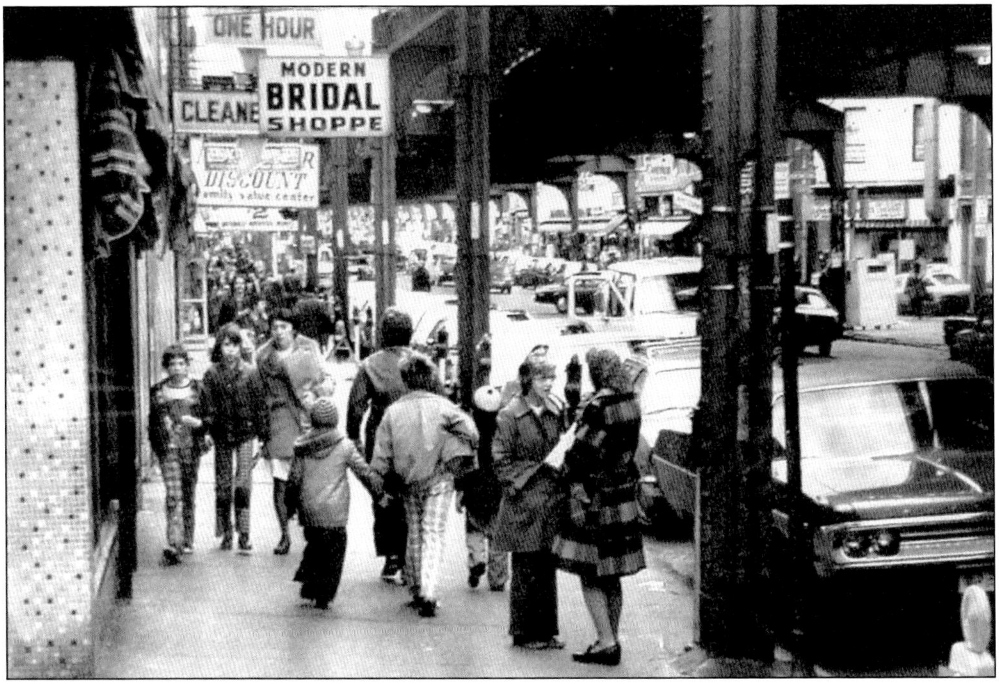

In the era before shopping malls, a trip to the Av was somewhat of a social event. In addition to running their errands, shoppers would stroll the strip, stopping for lunch at one of several restaurants or, perhaps, for an ice cream treat at the counter at the five and ten. This 1960s photograph of Kensington Avenue near Clearfield Street shows some of the many businesses in the area, such as Modern Bridal Shoppe, which furnished trousseaus for many River Wards brides, and the One-Hour Cleaners.

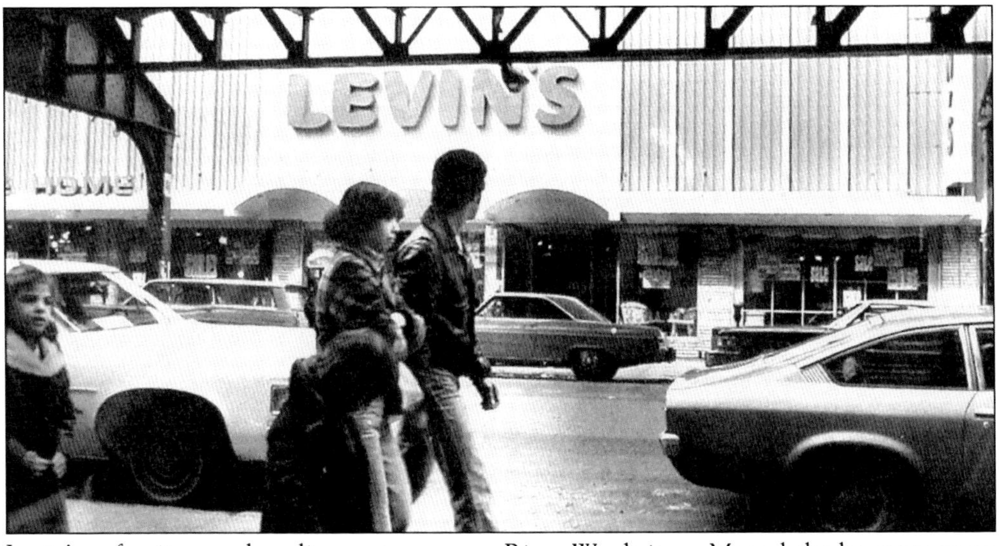

Levin's, a furniture and appliance store, was a River Wards icon. Many baby boomers, upon starting their first "real job" after graduating high school, would open up their first credit line at Levin's. The store sold just about everything, from alarm clocks to refrigerators. Every teen in the area knew Al, who ran the record department, which offered the latest in albums and 45s. The store also featured a television- and radio-repair shop.

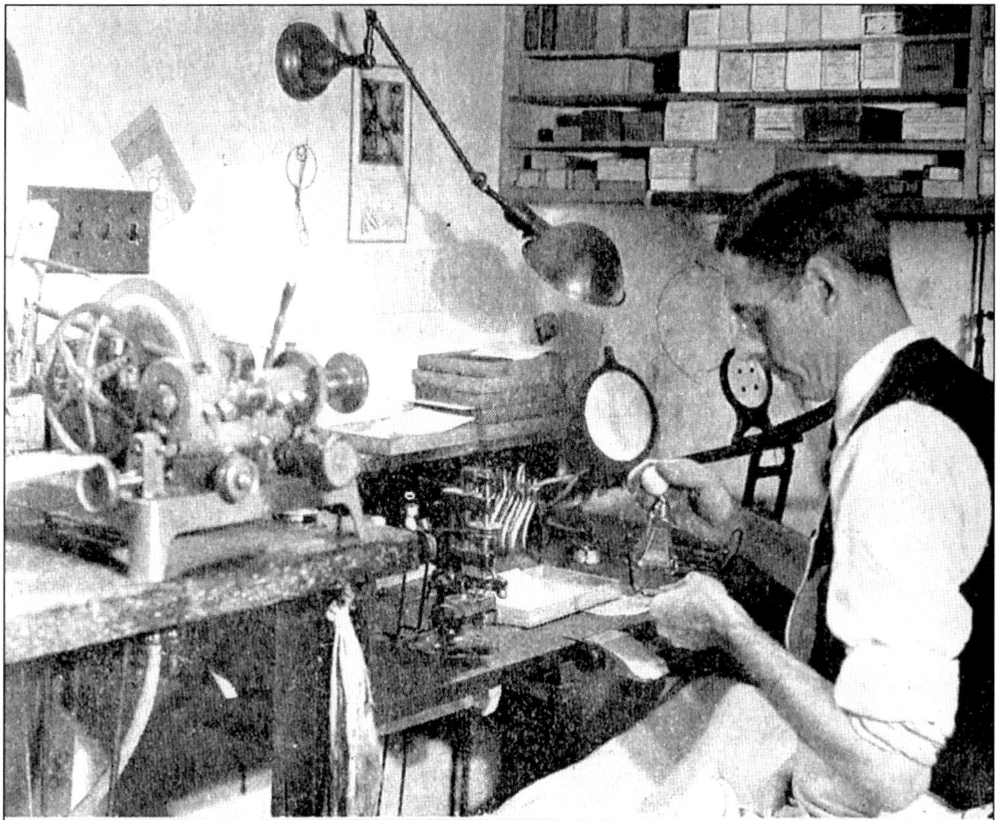

DR. WILLIAM R. CONLEY

OPTOMETRIST
and
DISPENSING OPTICIAN

REG. 228

855 E. ALLEGHENY AVENUE

Office Hours: Monday, Wednesday and Friday Evenings Until 8.30

This advertisement, featuring Dr. William R. Conley, a neighborhood optometrist with an office located at 855 East Allegheny Avenue, is one of hundreds of advertisements that appeared in the local newspapers, directories, and church bulletins. The following pages offer a series of advertisements that appealed to River Wards customers from 1890 to 1952.

Phone: REGent 2060

A. RZEPECKI
Hardware
3102-04 RICHMOND STREET

Compliments of
ST. JOSEPH'S HOUSE
for
INDUSTRIOUS BOYS
16th ST. & ALLEGHENY AVE.

CONNER
FUNERAL HOME
3056 & 3058 FRANKFORD AVENUE

GARfield 3225
RELIABLE SHOES
Priced Moderately
For the Little Tots and Grown-Ups
MULLER'S SHOE STORE
2321 E. CLEARFIELD STREET

MRS. M. FARRELL
Candies and Cigars
2362 EAST CLEARFIELD STREET
Do Your Christmas Shopping at
Farrell's

Bell Phone, Regent 3269
MAX L. SALEVSKY
City Dressed Meat Market
2328 EAST CLEARFIELD STREET
PHILADELPHIA, PA.
S. E. Corner Memphis and Clearfield Streets

LAFFERTY BROS.
Real Estate
F ST. and ALLEGHENY AVE.

AUGUSTIN & BAPTISTE
Caterers
255 SOUTH 15th STREET

Albert E. Dutrieuille
Caterer for All Occasions
40 SOUTH 19th STREET
PHONE: RIT. 9271

Bell Phone: Nebraska 3364-5
Estimates Given Without Charge
R. F. TORRE
2969-71--73 SALMON STREET
Philadelphia, Pa.
Auto Repairing, Bodies & Fenders Repaired, Hy-Grade Auto Painting, Cars to Hire for Funerals and All Occasions.

JOHN A. McVEIGH
Plumbing & Heating
1823 RIDGE AVENUE

WILLIAM FRANK
Grain—Hay—Straw
Also Accessories
3300 GAUL STREET
NEB. 6671

CLASS RINGS AND PINS
P. J. FRIEDEL
Manufacturing Jewelers
733 WALNUT STREET
2nd Floor
WAL. 5041
REPAIRING A SPECIALTY

DANIEL J. KEATING
Plumbing & Heating
613 SOUTH 24th STREET

These advertisements, taken from a book published in 1929, show an interesting mix of neighborhood businesses.

Phone, Regent 0288

FRANCIS X. RILEY
(Registered)
PLUMBING AND HEATING
2967 Belgrade Street
Estimates Furnished

Bell, Regent 4702

LOUGHRIN BROS.
WHOLESALE CONFECTIONERS
2724 E. CLEARFIELD STREET
Agents for SAMOSET and DAGGETT'S CHOCOLATES
Keystone: East 8085

Dr. Charles J. Shannon
Dental Surgeon
2864 FRANKFORD AVENUE

As Good as the Best, as Low as the Lowest
John P. Gallagher & Son
Funeral Director and Embalmer
Main Office
2154 N. BROAD STREET, PHILA., PA.
Phones—Freemont 1122 Freemont 4341
Branch Office
2439 GERMANTOWN AVE., PHILA., PA.
Phones, Regent 8824 Nebraska 6356

M. R. SOMERS

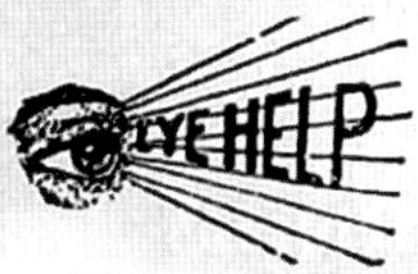

BELL PHONE

DR. J. E. STRECKER
OPTOMETRIST AND OPTICIAN
763 E. ALLEGHENY AVENUE

COMPLIMENTS OF
Immaculate Conception Convent
39TH AND PINE STREETS

Bell Phone, Garfield 2053 Keystone, East 8717

A. W. PETERS
Hardware, House Furnishings, Painters', Plumbers' Electrical and Radio Supplies, Glass, Keys, etc.
2323 EAST CLEARFIELD STREET

COMPLIMENTS OF
RALPH DE FREHN
3123 FRANKFORD AVENUE

Phones: Regent 2276 Park 3295

KANE'S FLORAL SHOP
"SAY IT WITH FLOWERS"
2550 NORTH FRONT STREET
Funeral Work a Specialty
Wm. Bannon, Prop.

HESS IRON WORKS, Inc.
E. WESTMORELAND AT GAUL STREETS
Builders Iron Work, Sheet Metal Work, Fire Escape, Repairs, of all Descriptions
Boiler and Stack Repairs
Regent 4213

HOLT CIGAR CO.
CITY HALL SQUARE (WEST)
EVERY DAY A BARGAIN DAY

Compliments of the
RICHMOND GROCERY CO.

ATLAS CASKET CO.
3207 CEDAR STREET

The Holt Cigar Company is still in business and recently requested a copy of this rare advertisement.

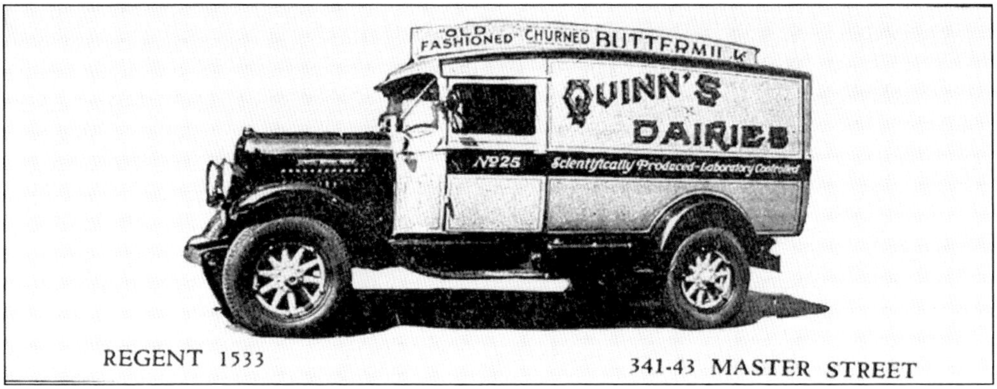

Quinn's Dairies, a mom-and-pop company in the late 1800s, did not last long. Larger, consolidated companies, such as Harbison's and Abbott's, soon took over its business.

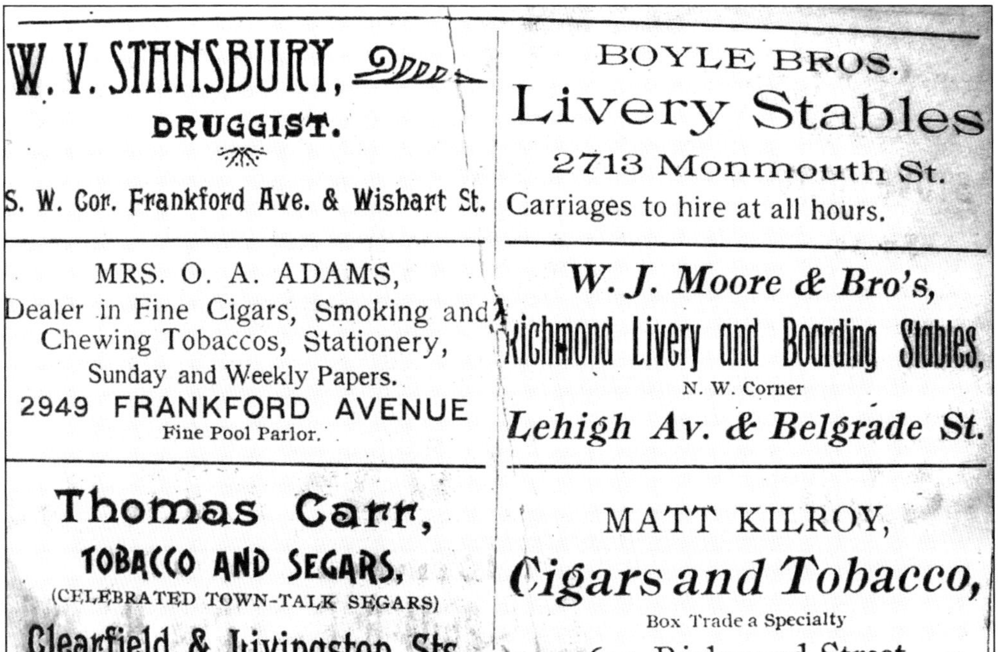
W. V. STANSBURY,
DRUGGIST.
S. W. Cor. Frankford Ave. & Wishart St.

BOYLE BROS.
Livery Stables
2713 Monmouth St.
Carriages to hire at all hours.

MRS. O. A. ADAMS,
Dealer in Fine Cigars, Smoking and
Chewing Tobaccos, Stationery,
Sunday and Weekly Papers.
2949 FRANKFORD AVENUE
Fine Pool Parlor.

W. J. Moore & Bro's,
Richmond Livery and Boarding Stables,
N. W. Corner
Lehigh Av. & Belgrade St.

Thomas Carr,
TOBACCO AND SEGARS,
(CELEBRATED TOWN-TALK SEGARS)
Clearfield & Livingston Sts.

MATT KILROY,
Cigars and Tobacco,
Box Trade a Specialty
2654 Richmond Street.

The sale of tobacco products was apparently a profitable venture in the River Wards in the late 1800s.

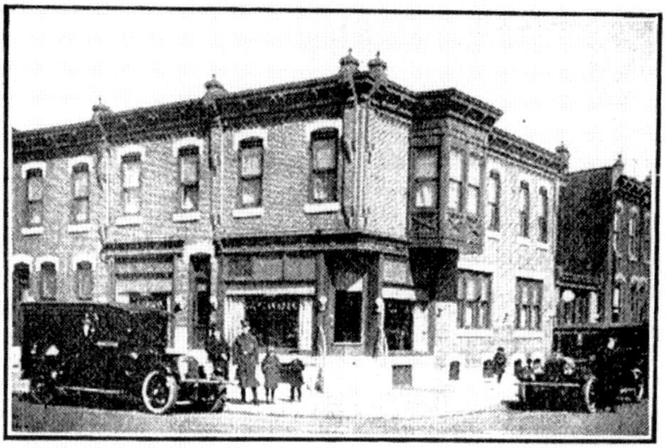

FRANCIS J. FLANAGAN

UNDERTAKER and EMBALMER

Cor. of E. CLEARFIELD & BELGRADE ST.

Still in operation, Flanagan's Funeral Home has been a Port Richmond fixture for decades.

Telephone: Regent 9150
Keystone: East 8686

Kindly Service Wins High Regards

During the trying hours of sorrow, close friends and relations should be relieved of every responsibility connected with the funeral. It is at this hour that the funeral director steps in and smoothly and quietly attends to all the many details connected with the arrangement of the funeral.

When our services are required, it is a real satisfaction to know that everything may be entrusted to us, and that it will be done completely and satisfactorily.

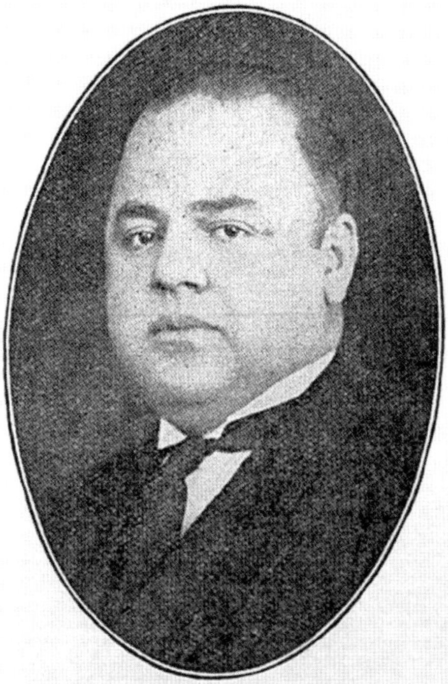

ANTONIO J. ERRICHETTI

UNDERTAKER

2956 SALMON STREET

Errichetti Funeral Home provided burial services for the Italian parishioners of Mother of Divine Grace Church in Port Richmond.

WASHABLE and SUN TESTED PAPERS——WORK GUARANTEED

E. A. JARVIS 2900 GAUL STREET

PAPERHANGER

RE 9-9628 ESTIMATES CHEERFULLY GIVEN

LUMBER
MILLWORK

WALL BOARDS
STAIRWORK
MOULDINGS

LIME
SAND
CEMENT

PLASTER
FLUE PIPE
PLASTER LATH

Richmond Lumber Co.

NE 4-1386-7 3318 RICHMOND ST., PHILA., PA.

SKI'S BAKERY

3128 BELGRADE STREET

FINE BAKED GOODS

Bread - Cake - Pies - Buns

NE 4-6261

THOMAS C. SMITH

BOOKS and STATIONERY

2927 KENSINGTON AVENUE

SCHOOL SUPPLIES Telephone: RE 9-8851

W. A. McCauley

DRUGS

ENJOY WHITMAN'S CANDY

Deliciously Fresh From Our Refrigerated Candy Cabinet

NE 4-9872 3122 RICHMOND STREET

GREETING and RELIGIOUS CARDS -:- WRAPPINGS

Candy - Toys - Smokers' Needs - Religious Articles

YEAKEL'S GIFT SHOPPE

2500 EAST ALLEGHENY AVENUE

TELEVISION and FACSIMILE, Inc.

TELEVISION SERVICE — INSTALLATION

2418 N. NINTH STREET

Convert your present set to a larger screen at little cost

SHOW THIS TO OUR SERVICE MEN AND SAVE $1.00

Another mix of neighborhood advertisements features Yeakel's Gift Shoppe, a family-run enterprise that operated on the corner of Gaul Street and Allegheny Avenue throughout most of the 20th century. The store's founder was known in the area as "Mommy Yeakel."

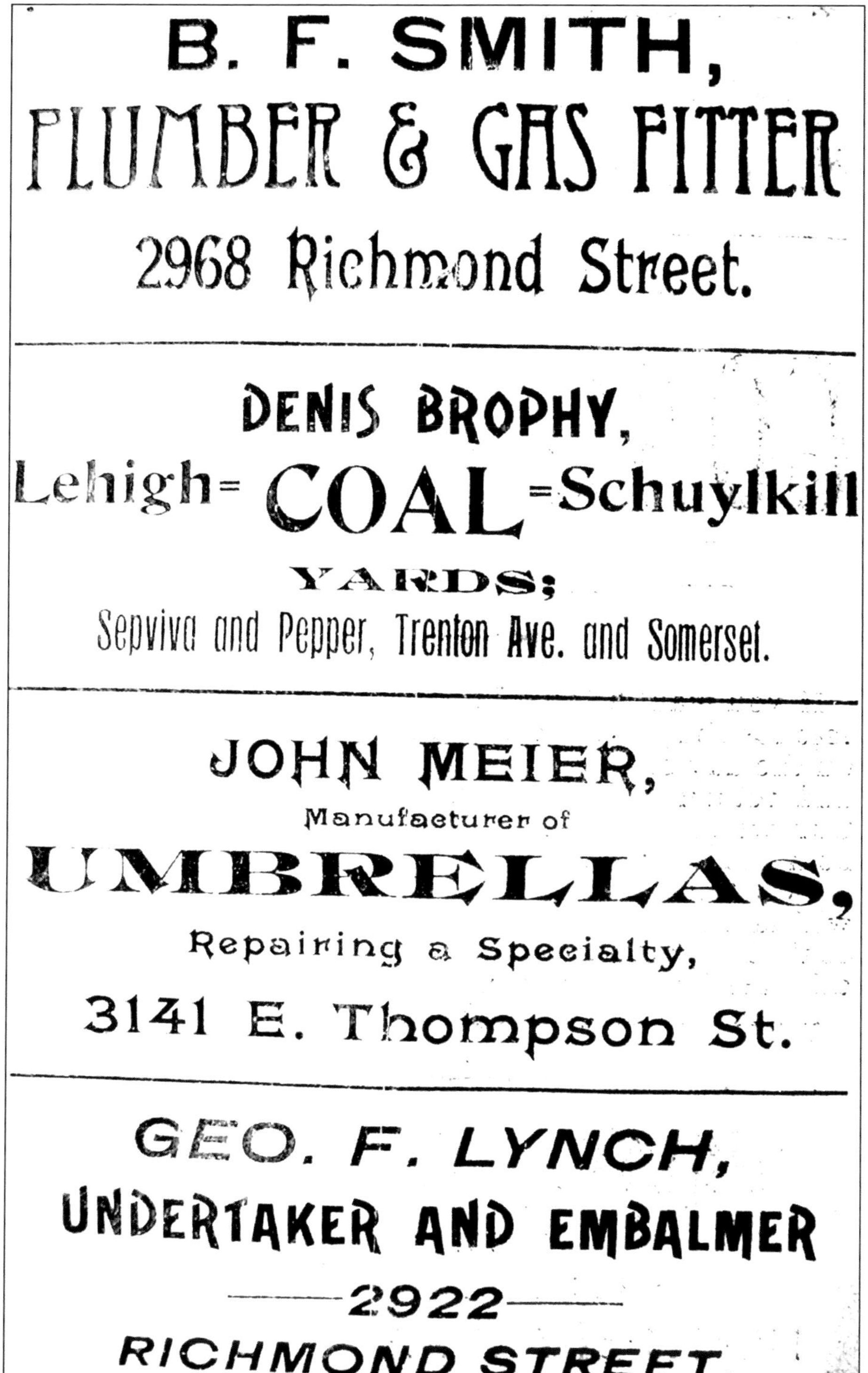

This 1891 advertisement, taken from the original printer's plate, shows not only an interesting variety of advertisements but also an unusual mixture of print types.

CURRANS—Gas and Accessories
CANDY, CIGARS and ICE CREAM
3101 RICHMOND STREET
Nebraska 9023

DR. S. J. KRYGIER
DENTIST
3161 RICHMOND STREET
Garfield 2999

Ackley's Music Store
Everything Musical
Victrolas and Records
CROSLEY and FEDERAL RADIOS
3161 FRANKFORD AVENUE

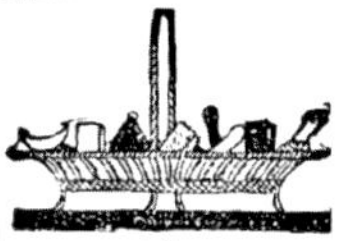

GEISLER'S
FANCY CAKES and ICE CREAM
Wedding and Birthday Cakes
2600 E. ALLEGHENY AVENUE
Garfield 3033

GEORGE J. KAIB
CEDAR and CLEARFIELD STREETS
DELICATESSEN and
FANCY GROCERIES
LUNCH MEATS

Joseph J. Sankowski
Merchant Tailoring

Many of the businesses in the Port Richmond area at the end of the 19th century were of the mom-and-pop variety. In many cases, the operations remained family-owned for generations.

...inski's CELEBRATED ICE CREAM
2738 E. Allegheny Avenue.
(Opposite Car Depot)

JOHN J. BYRNES,
Carpets, Oilcloths, Lignums,
Linoleums, Rugs, Window Shades,
37 S. SECOND STREET,
Below Market East Side

DR. E. C. WILEY,
DENTAL ROOMS,
S.E. Cor. Allegheny Ave. & Thompson St.
DENTISTRY IN ALL BRANCHES.
SPECIALIST IN GOLD WORK.
Nitrous Oxide Gas Administered.

JOHN H. NUGENT,
UNDERTAKER,
3082 Frankford Avenue

H. L. KILNER & CO.,
Catholic Publishers, Booksellers and Importers,
103 S. ELEVENTH ST.
(near Chestnut.)
RELIGIOUS ARTICLES OF ALL KINDS.

H. BURNS,
GROCERIES,
EMERALD & ALLEGHENY AVE
Hungarian Flour a Specialty.

From Northern Liberties north to Frankford, the River Wards was dotted with small businesses of every kind. Over the years, groceries, meat markets, hardware stores, furniture stores, and dry-good shops gradually gave way to chain-store conglomerates. Today, a few corner stores still conduct profitable business in the neighborhoods, providing personalized service within steps of River Wards residents' homes.

Seven

THE RIVERFRONT

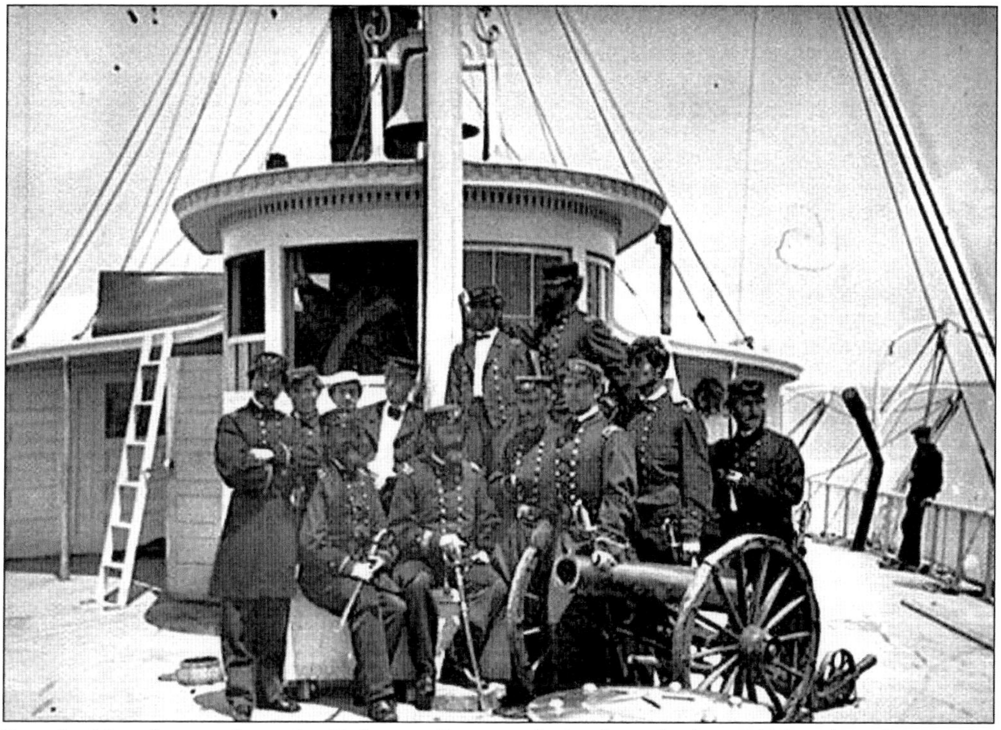

Boat building began along the Delaware River as far back as the late 1600s, when the Swedes carved out small boats for shad fishing. Eventually, more sophisticated boatyards evolved and grew as commerce increased. During the Civil War, Union soldiers were often seen along the Delaware River waterfront.

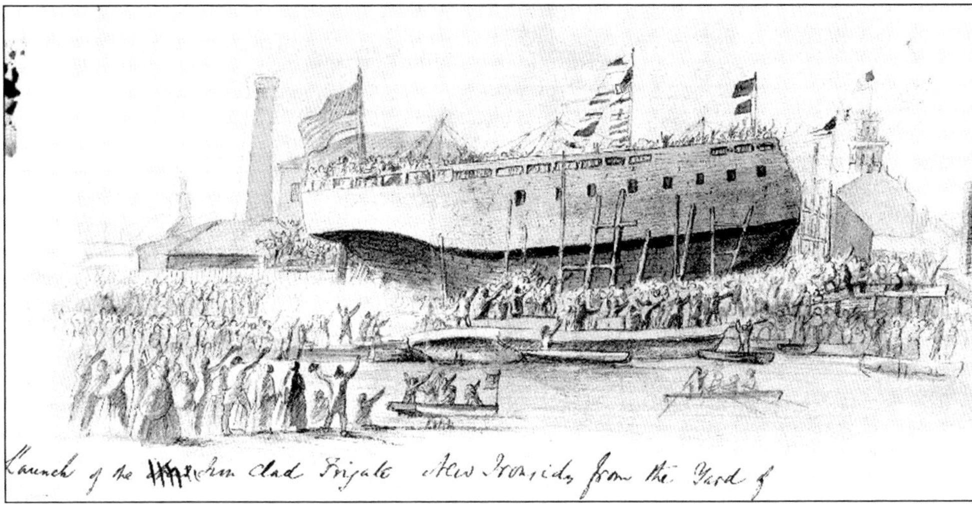

This pencil drawing is believed to have been created somewhere in the River Wards before or during the American Revolution. The sketch identifies the ship as an ironclad frigate, but its name is not discernable. It appears it was built without a dry dock, and it is not known how or from where it was launched.

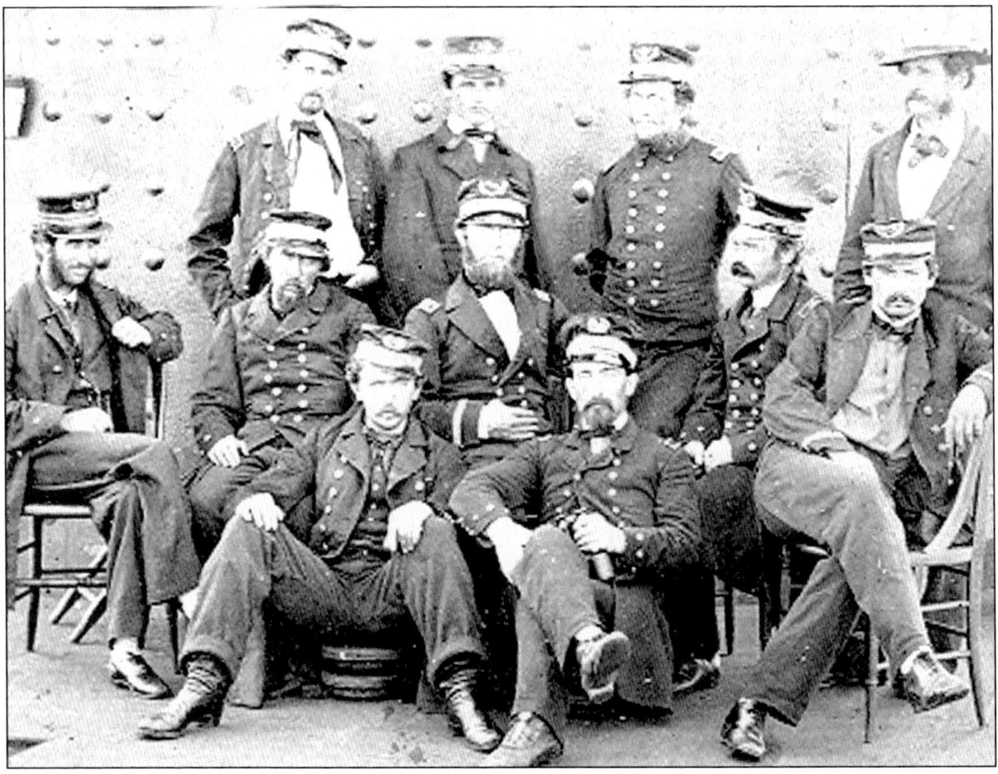

Philadelphia saw many of her young men march off to battle during the Civil War. A large number of them sailed off down the Delaware River to meet the Confederate army as it approached the North. At one of the many wharfs that lined the banks of the Delaware in the River Wards, a group of Union sailors and civilians posed in front of a heavily riveted ship—a true ironclad.

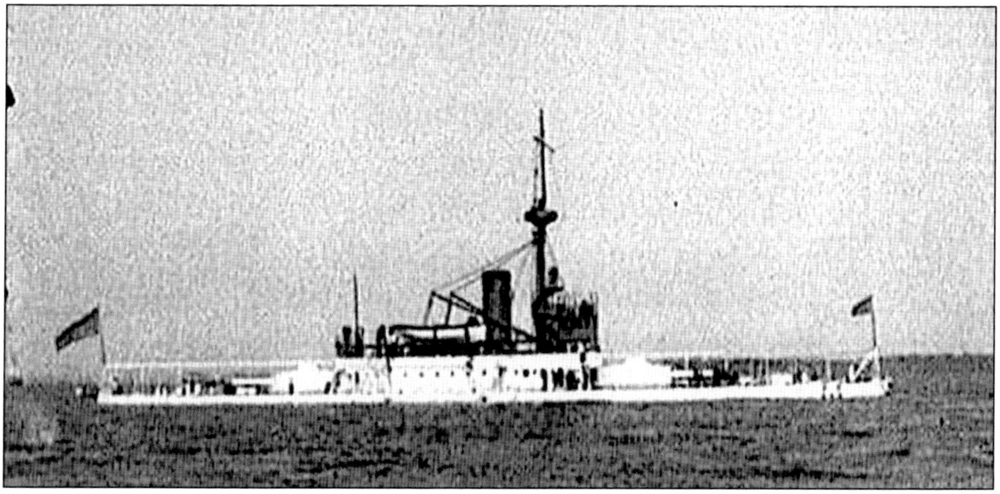

The *Alabama* was built in the late 19th century at Cramp Shipyard, a major shipbuilding company founded by William Cramp in 1830, in Kensington. Cramp Shipyard remained an integral part of the riverfront industry throughout the 1950s. As an interesting aside, shipyard employee Robert James was developing an antivibration device for the U.S. Navy in 1943, when he accidentally invented the Slinky. James first demonstrated the toy in Gimbel's Department Store in downtown Philadelphia and sold over 400 Slinkys in 90 minutes.

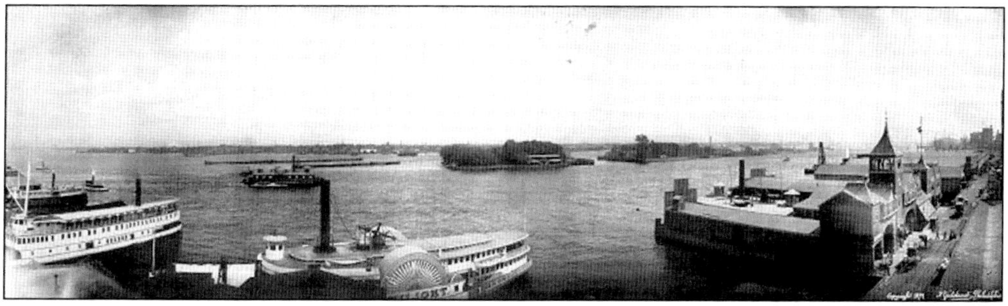

This rare photograph shows the boon along the riverfront in the River Wards just after the Civil War. These boats are pleasure steamboats that docked along the Northern Liberties section. This image is another indication of just how much the riverfront was used for leisure activities.

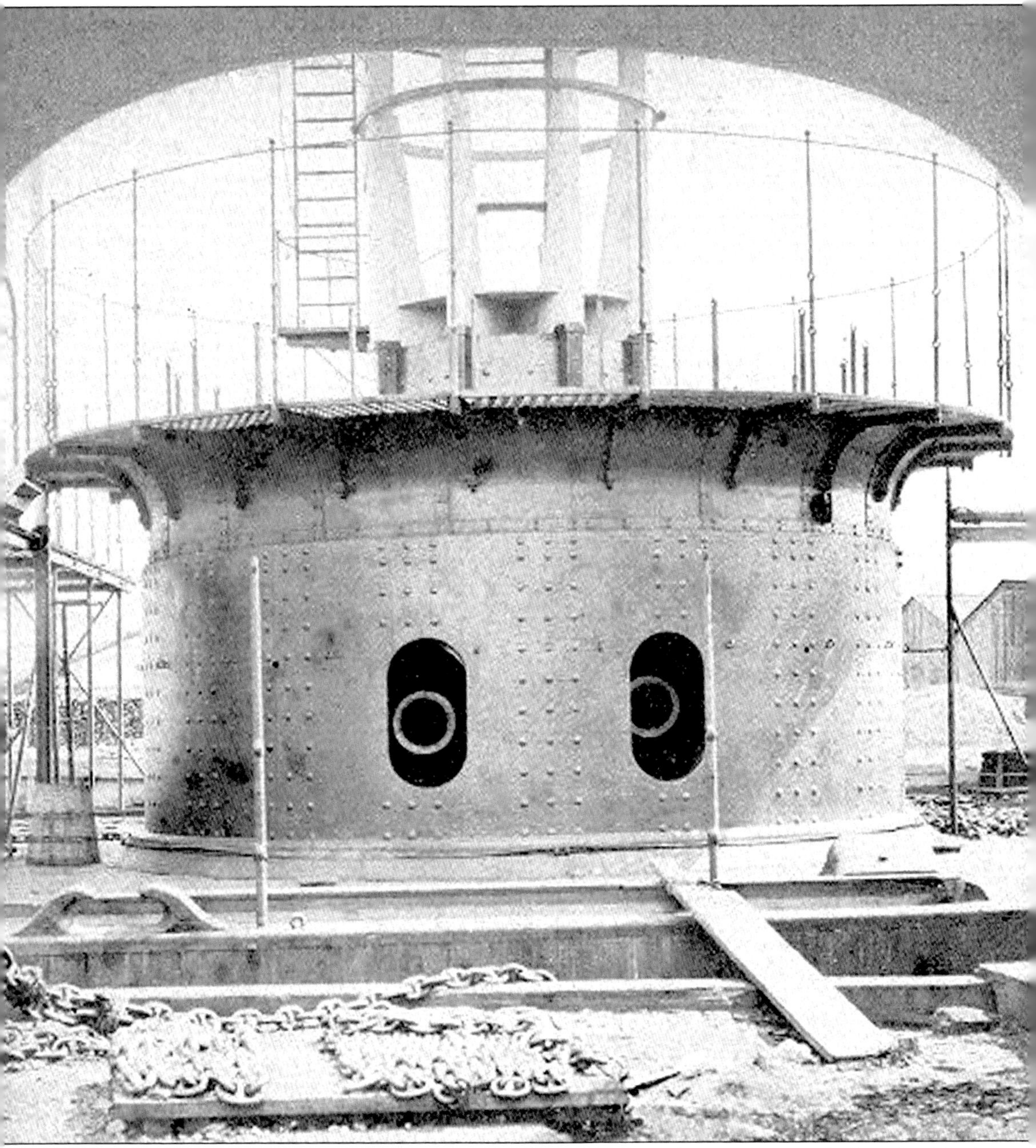

A closeup of the turret on the monitor ship *Terror*, built at Cramp Shipyard after the Civil War, shows how the metal housing enclosed and protected its long-range gun and operator. The photograph is part of a stereoscope, a viewing system in which two photographs of the same subject, taken at slightly different angles, are set behind two lenses. When seen through the lenses, the two images become one with added depth and dimension. Although many stereoscopes were made, they are extremely rare today.

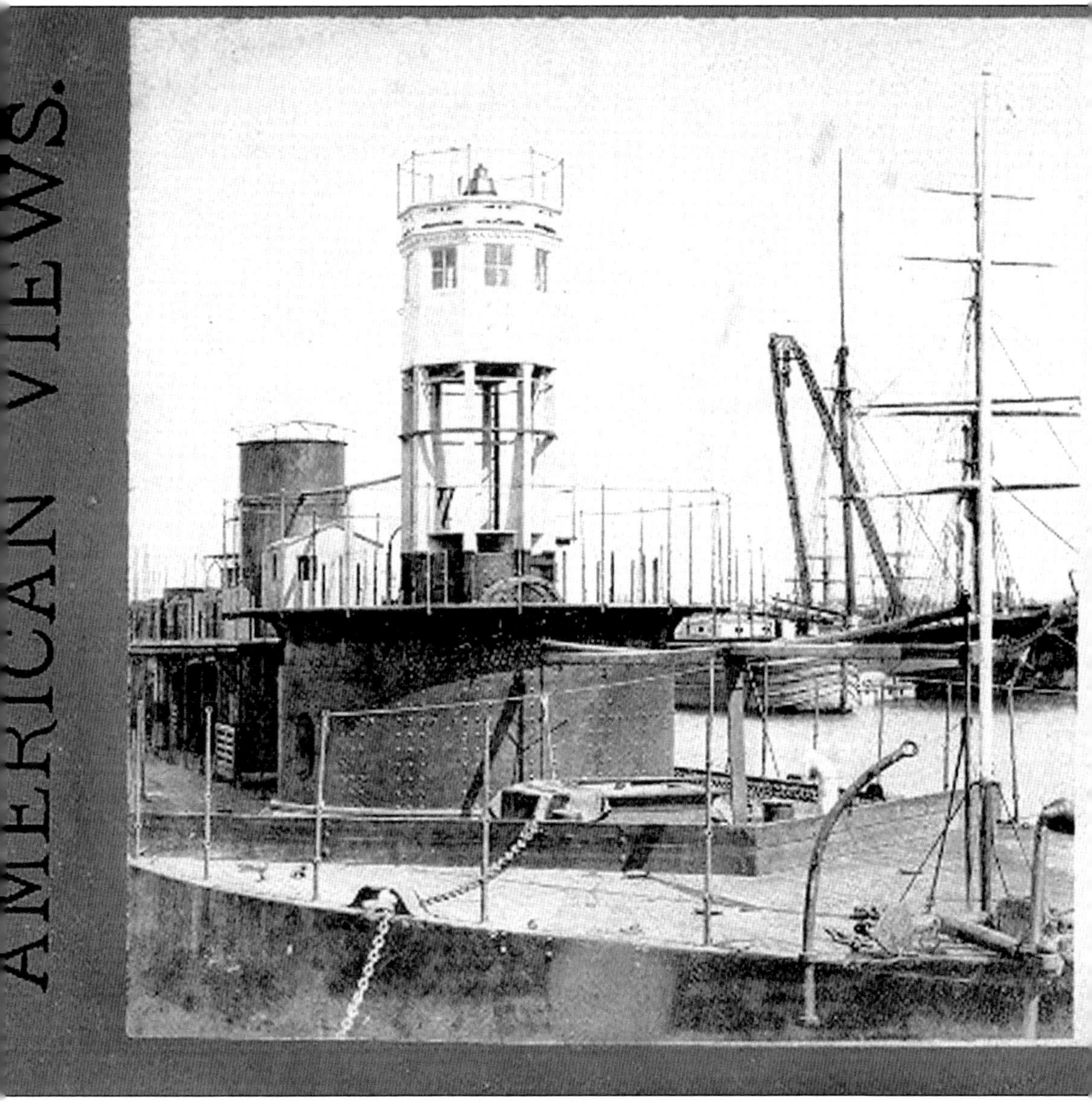

Another stereoscope of the *Terror* shows the ship at a much wider angle. Monitors were ships that sat very low in the water, only exposing the turret and on-deck guns. The monitors were used in the defense of America from the late 1800s to the very early 1900s. During World War I, monitors were determined to be ineffective and too slow for travel to Europe. This led to a new hull design that also facilitated the introduction of torpedoes.

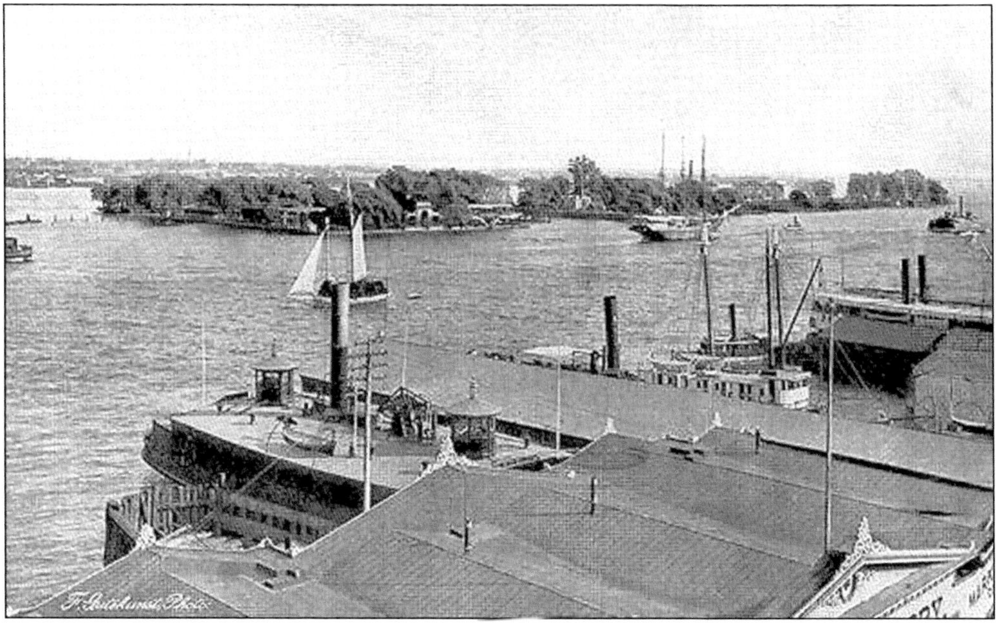

Windmill Island was an arguably useless piece of property located just a few yards off the banks of the Delaware River near Northern Liberties. The island hampered almost every proposed development. The Army Corps of Engineers finally removed it in the early 1900s.

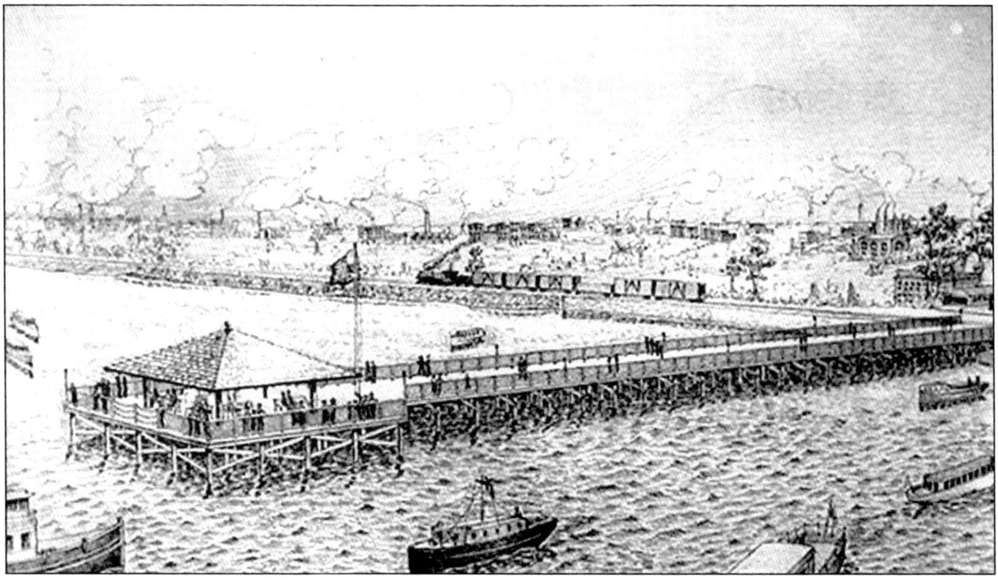

This early sketch was presented to the city of Philadelphia for consideration in the 1920s, when the city was planning to build leisure piers and public docks in the River Wards. This design was rejected, and the city agreed to a simpler plan. Once built, the piers enjoyed great popularity into the 1940s.

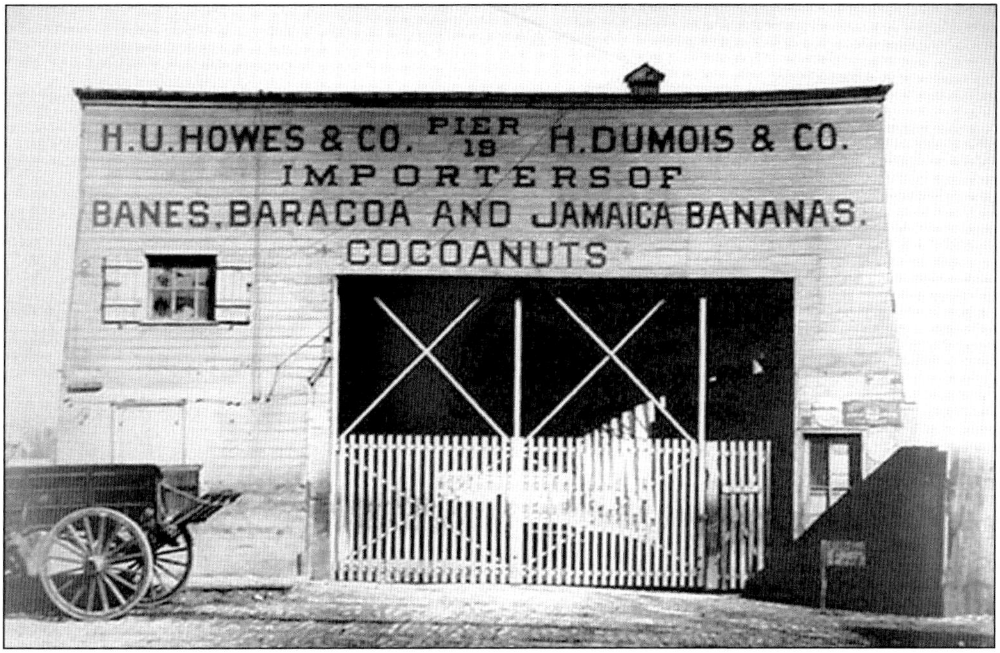

The commercial docks along Delaware Avenue in Northern Liberties were where fruit and vegetables were brought in from the tropics. In the 1700s, produce from the Caribbean was also known as Colonial Goods.

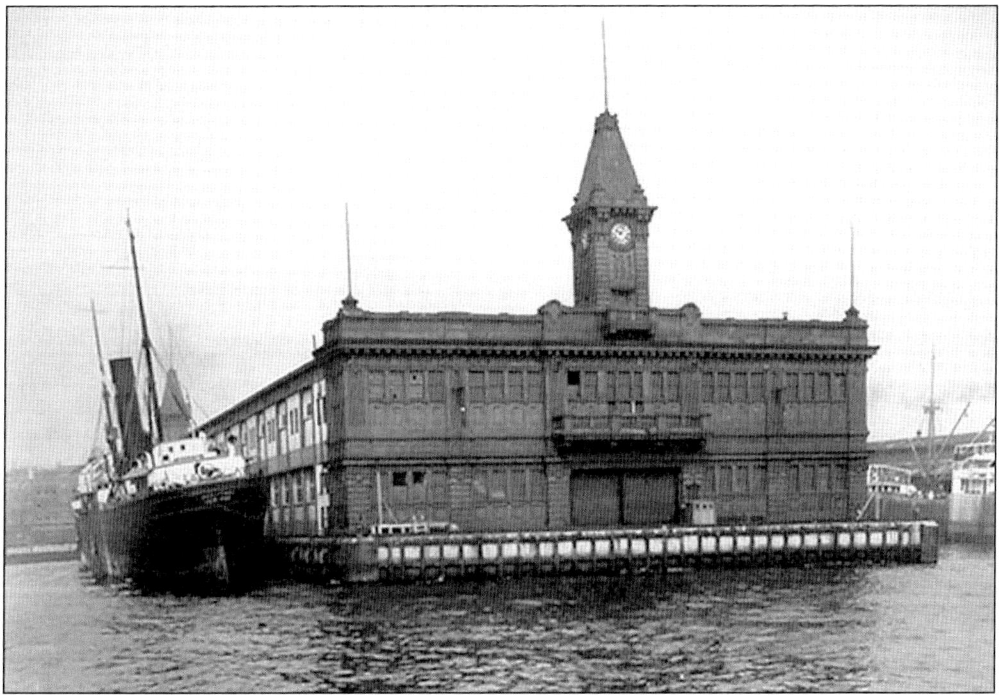

As the years passed, more elaborate piers were built. The ports of Philadelphia were soon able to handle large ships from around the world. The River Wards ports became major import terminals. These newer docks all along the Delaware River became known as Municipal Piers.

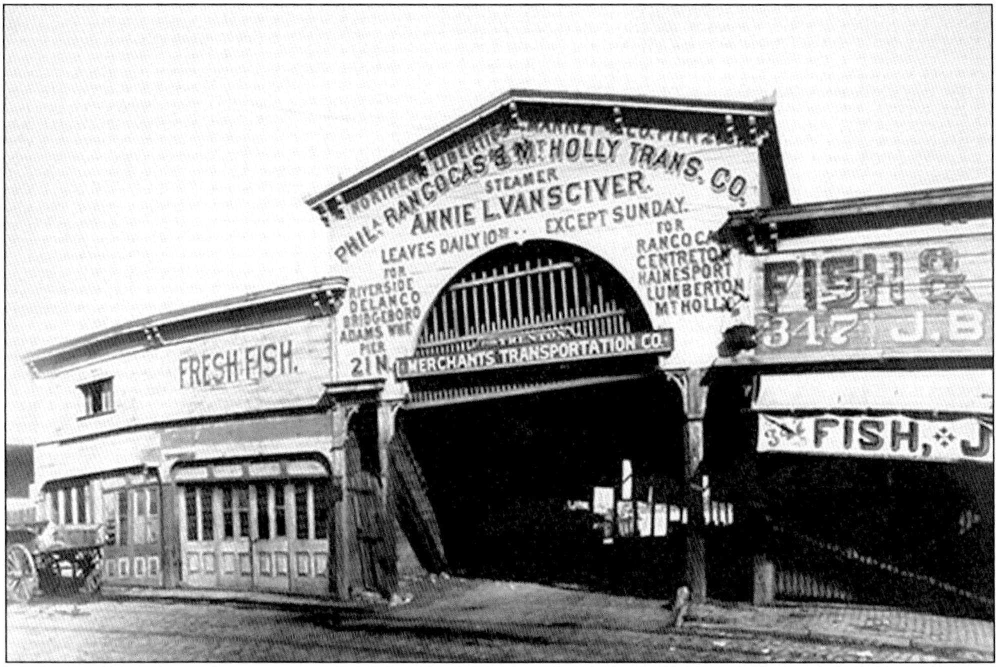

Produce and product piers incorporated with local steamship lines that handled transportation to the neighboring township of northern New Jersey. The steamer *Annie L. Van Sciver* would leave its Northern Liberties dock for a daily run. This form of transportation ceased operation when the train lines and large suspension bridges were built over the Delaware River.

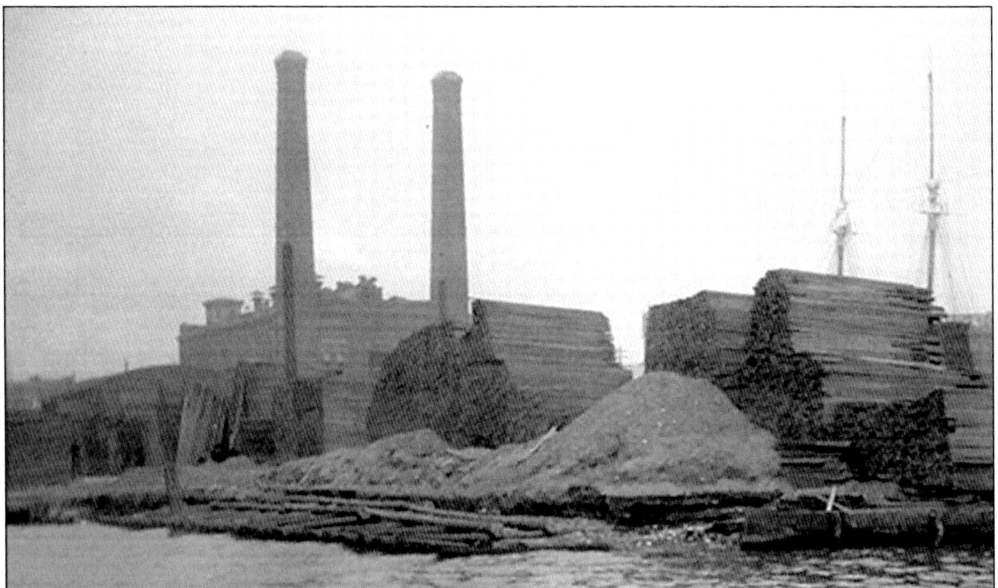

As the population of the River Wards grew, a need arose for large power plants to supply energy to homes and industry. A system was also developed for collecting rubbish throughout the neighborhoods for transport to a centrally located incinerator. As supply met demand, the face of the riverfront was drastically altered.

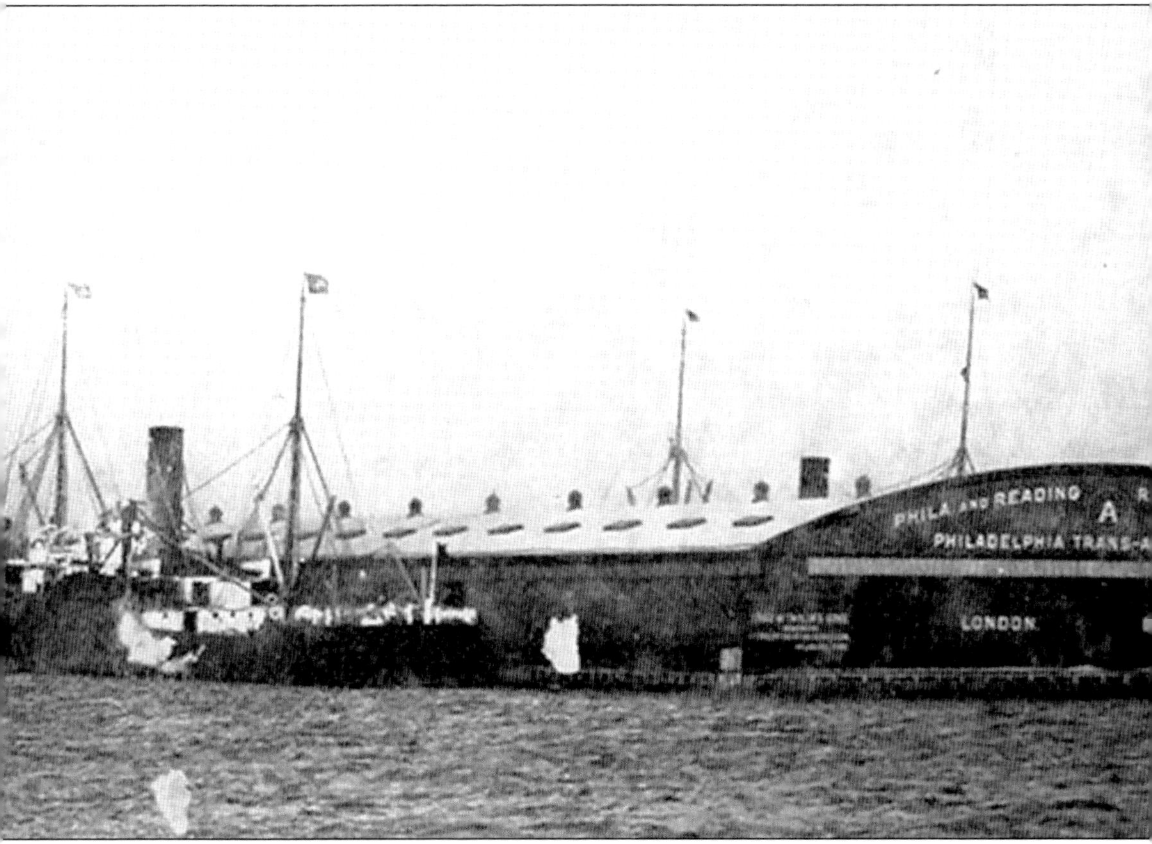

Before advances in aviation made long-distance flight possible, steamships were the only means of travel between the United States and Europe. The Philadelphia Trans-Atlantic Terminal in Northern Liberties provided transportation to and from London, England.

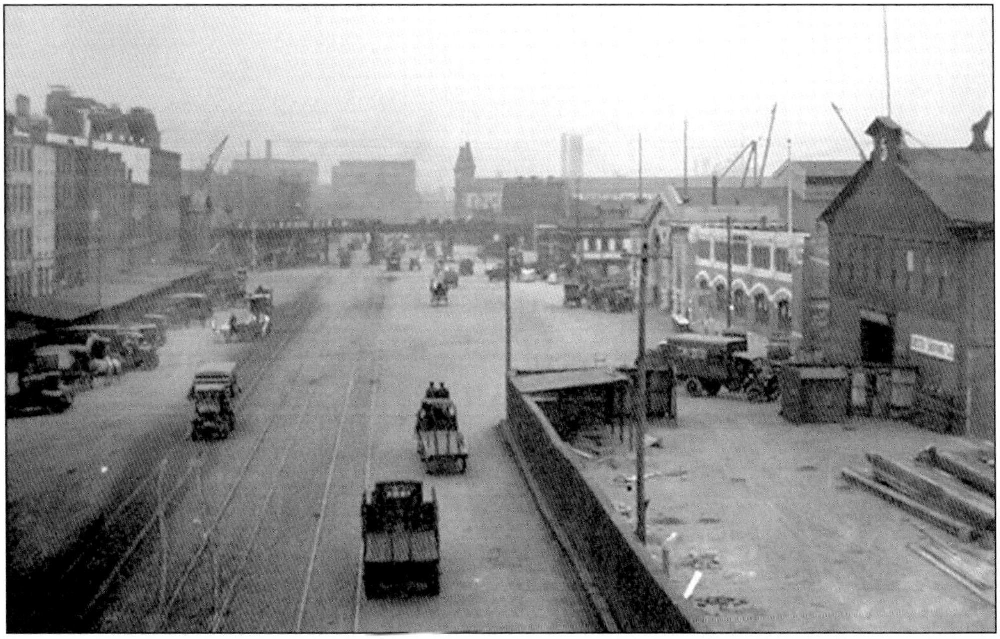

This photograph from the 1920s is believed to be of the edge of Philadelphia proper in Northern Liberties looking north. The rail tracks shown along Delaware Avenue are not train tracks but may have been used by horse-drawn trolleys and wagons. Interestingly, the bridge shown in the distance could not be found in any records.

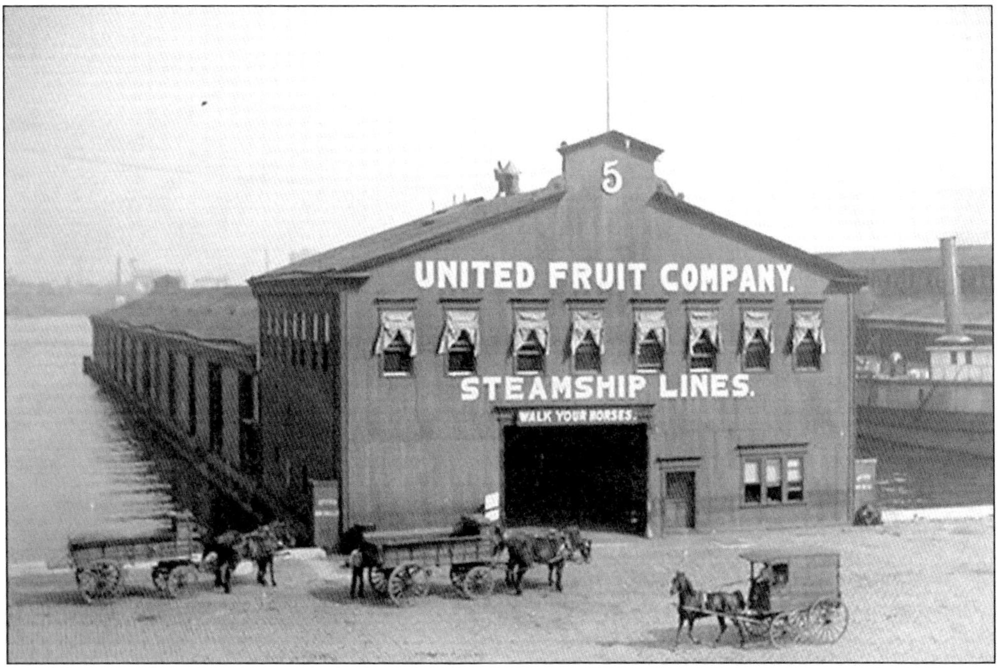

This late-19th-century photograph, taken from a rooftop on the opposite side of Delaware Avenue, shows one of the old wooden piers. The legend over the entrance instructs drivers to walk their horses, which was standard practice along the waterfront. Driving horse-drawn wagons in enclosed spaces was apparently dangerous.

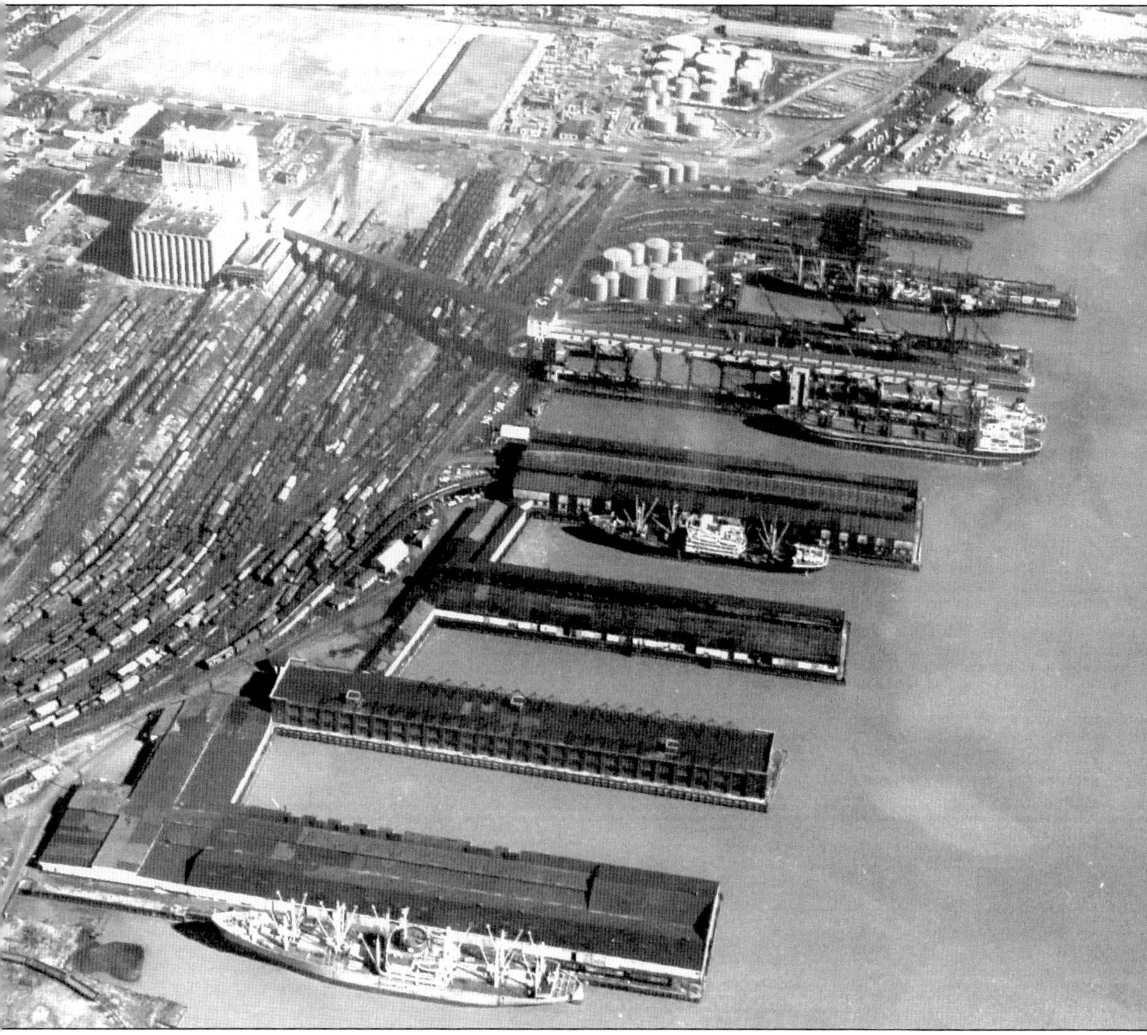

This aerial view of the Delaware River and Allegheny Avenue Reading Terminal area was taken in the 1950s, at a time when the terminal was operating 24 hours a day. This view clearly shows the Grain Elevated near the upper left. The large structure stood out as landmark for aviators, who could see it from miles away and used it as a point of orientation.

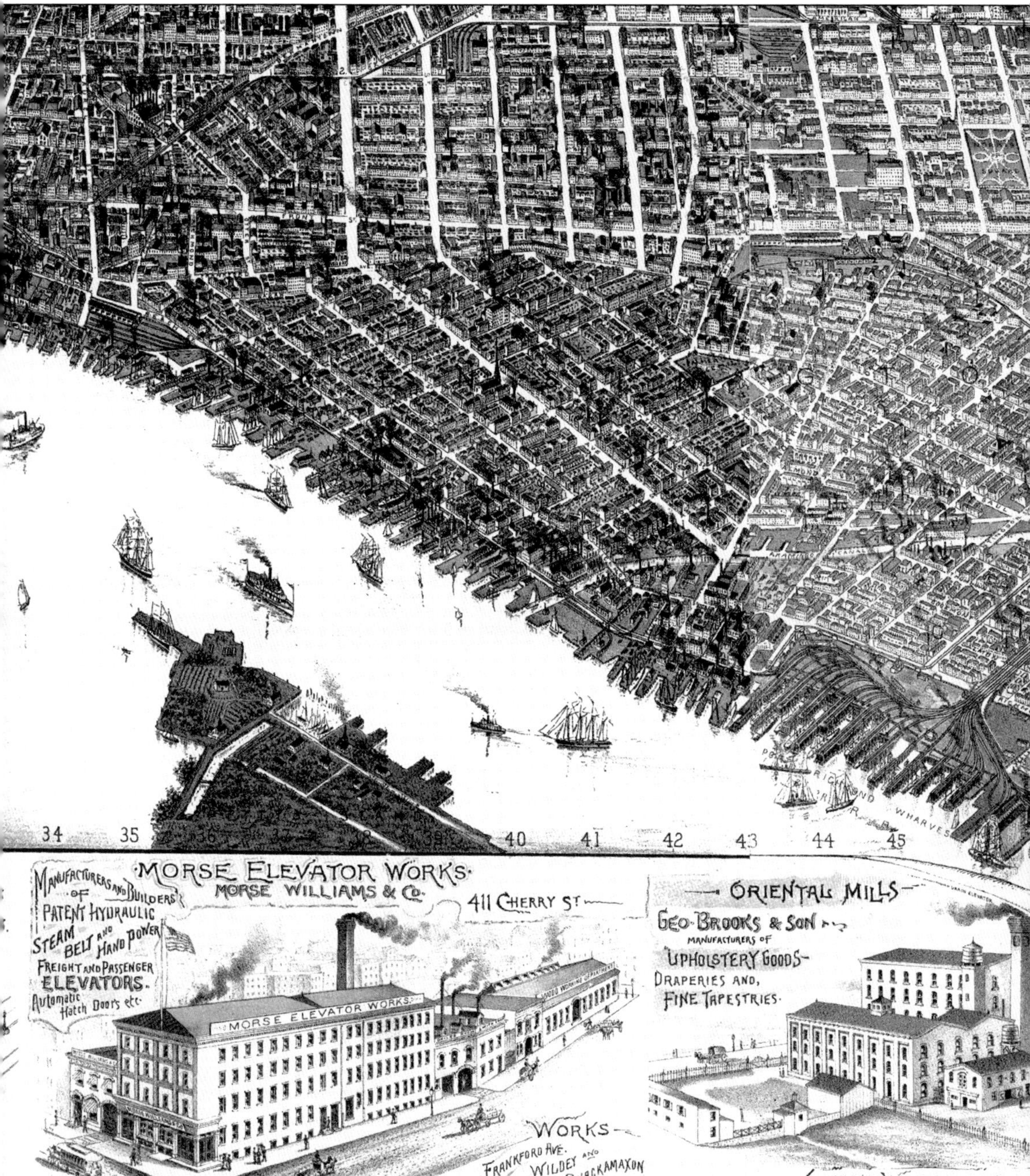

Within this two-page spread is a tiny section of a map that is actually 15 feet across by 9 feet high. After the Civil War, Union soldiers were lifted high in the air by hot air balloons. These army engineers would hand draw an bird's-eye view of the city. This section of the map is the River Wards of Philadelphia, drawn in 1883. Real estate developers, as well as city planners and private businesses, used the map. In what is probably the first truly accurate map of the area, you can see the way the River Wards follow the shape of the river. William Penn had his surveyor, Thomas Holme, design the city squarely, with all streets running north, south, east, and west.

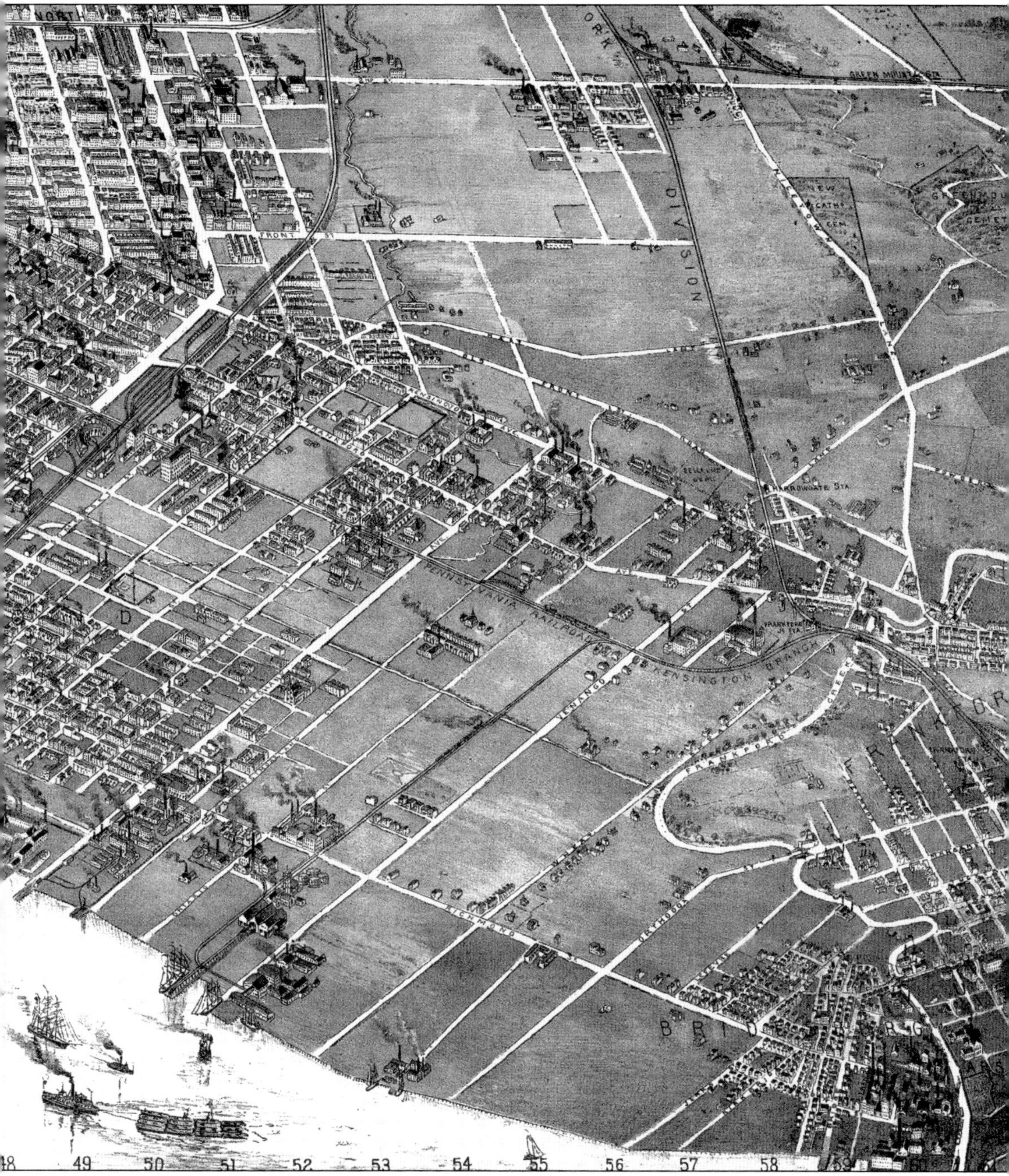

As the city grew and consumed the townships north, it became impossible to keep to the plan. As Front Street went north from the city proper, streets were built from Front Street to the river, veering away from true east and west. Cross streets caused the north and south streets to also run off course. This is clearly depicted on the map. Local industry and private companies sponsored the drawing of the map and in return had their businesses beautifully illustrated and displayed on its borders, as seen here. Large companies would have much smaller versions of the map printed and given out as advertisement handouts.

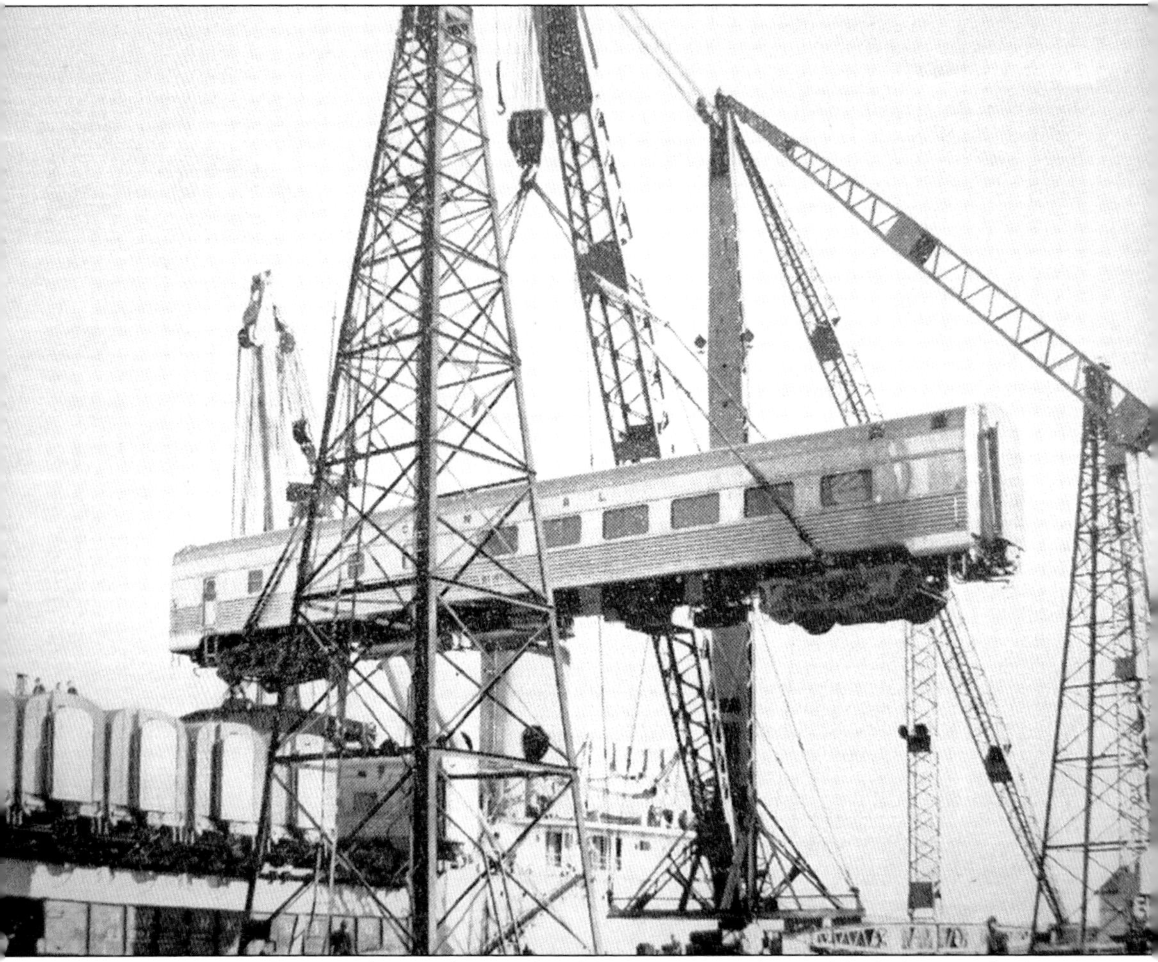

In the 1940s and 1950s, the Reading Railroad line in Port Richmond laid claim to the largest privately owned railroad tidewater terminal in the world. This photograph shows a passenger car, built at the Budd Company in Philadelphia, being loaded on a ship headed to South America. The derrick being used here was the largest privately owned derrick on the East Coast.

Eight

LEFTOVERS

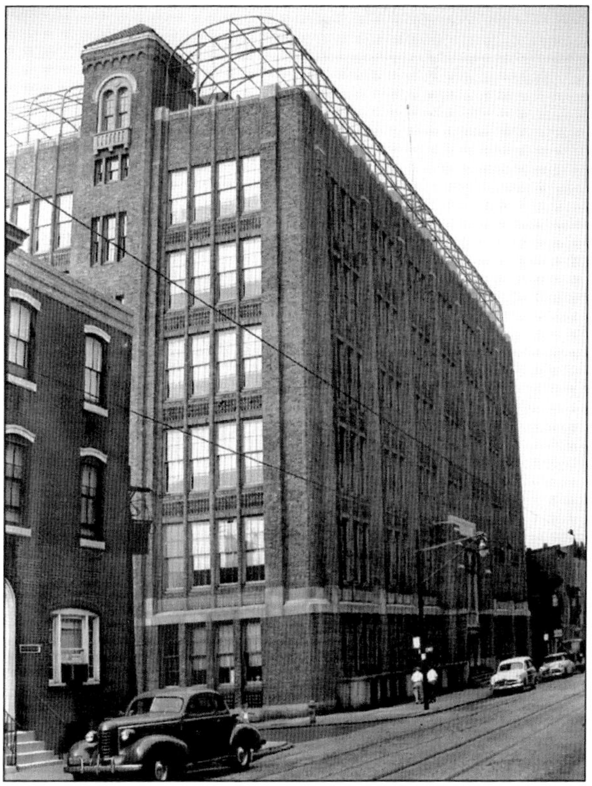

When it comes to the River Wards section of Philadelphia, volumes could be filled with photographs and illustrations. If a picture is worth a thousand words, this book helps capture the rich history of the River Wards and the integrity of its people, past and present.

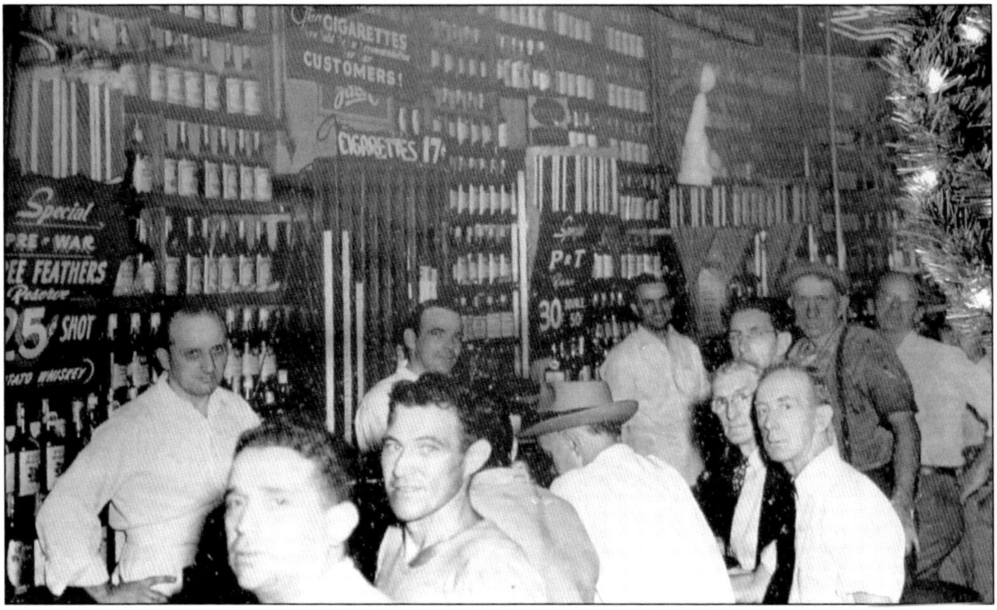

Jack's Famous Bar located at K&A, dates back to World War I and is still open for business. This photograph, taken in 1946, shows some neighborhood folks enjoying a few drinks. Note the signs offering cigarettes for 17¢ and a shot of whiskey for 25¢. Today, the shelves are lined with bottles of whiskey from the 1920s. Old, faded, whiskey-bottle labels make interesting conversation pieces for patrons.

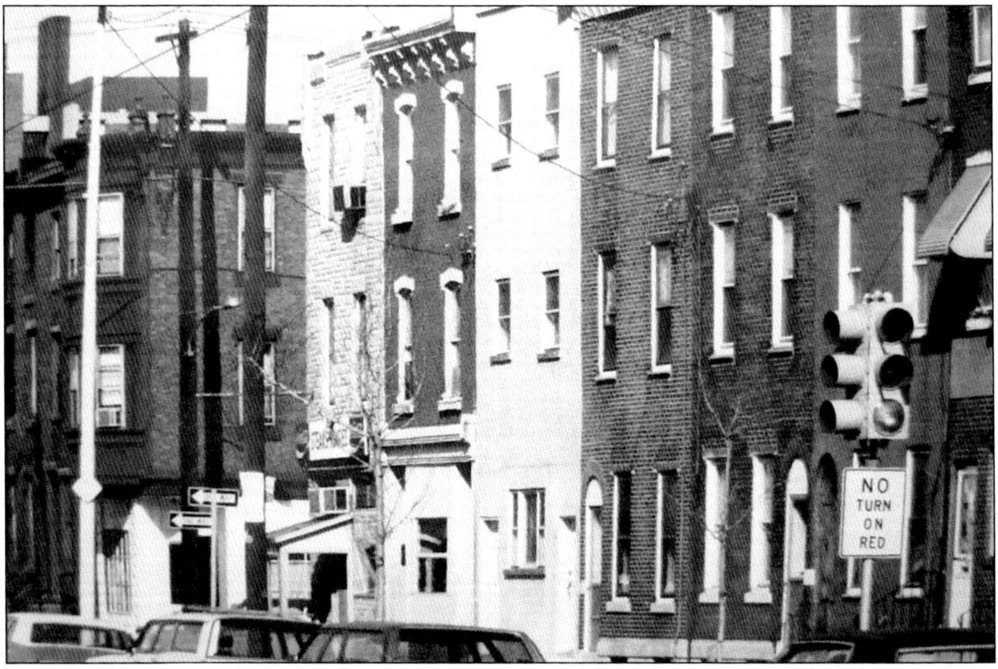

Baby boomers in Port Richmond will remember Tom's Luncheonette, located on the northeast corner of Chatham Street and Allegheny Avenue. Tom's was a favorite neighborhood spot to enjoy a quick burger and a Coke in the early 1960s. Outside the luncheonette, the unpaved sidewalk is inlaid with red brick.

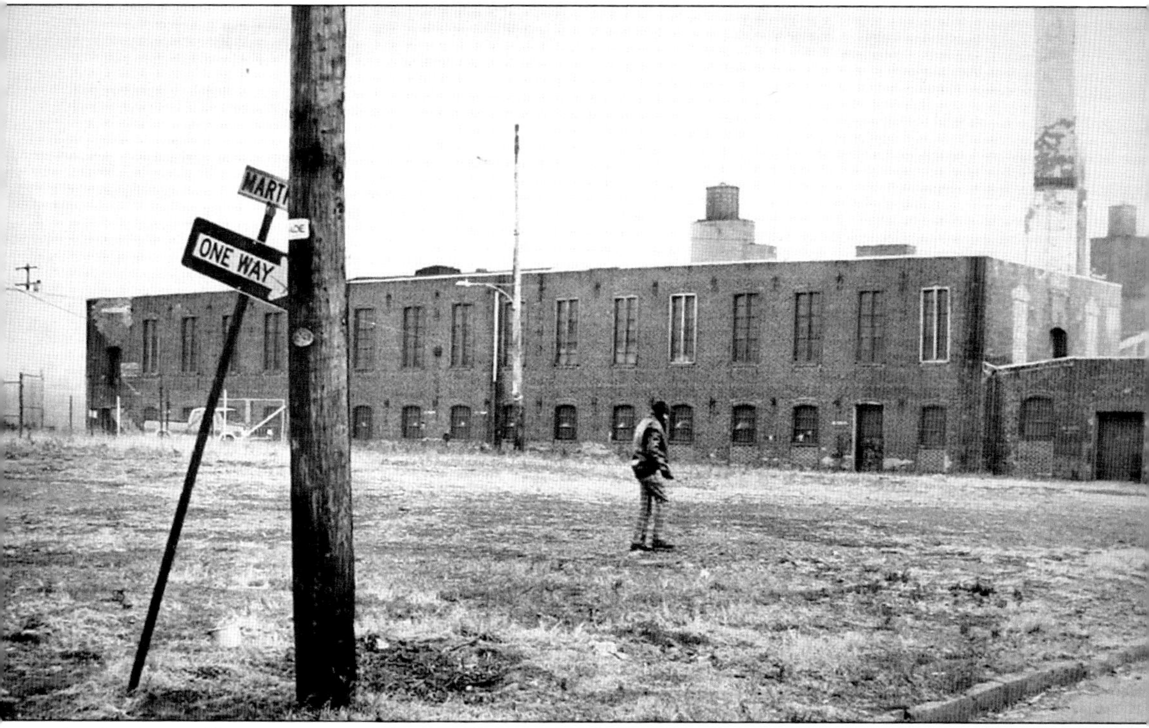

At the foot of Lippincott and Amber Streets stood the old "Shoey," a four-story shoe factory that seemed to employ nearly every woman in the neighborhood at one time or another in the 1950s. The factory manufactured all sorts of footwear, as well as combat boots for the military. Other companies that employed many people in the neighborhoods during the early to mid-20th century included Star Metal, at Ann Street and Trenton Avenue; Goldman Paper Company, at Weikel Street and Allegheny Avenue; Wilson Homes, at Frankford Avenue and Westmoreland Street; Penn Slaughterhouse, at Aramingo Avenue and Ontario Street; and Technitrol Electronics Company, at Allegheny Avenue and Jasper Street.

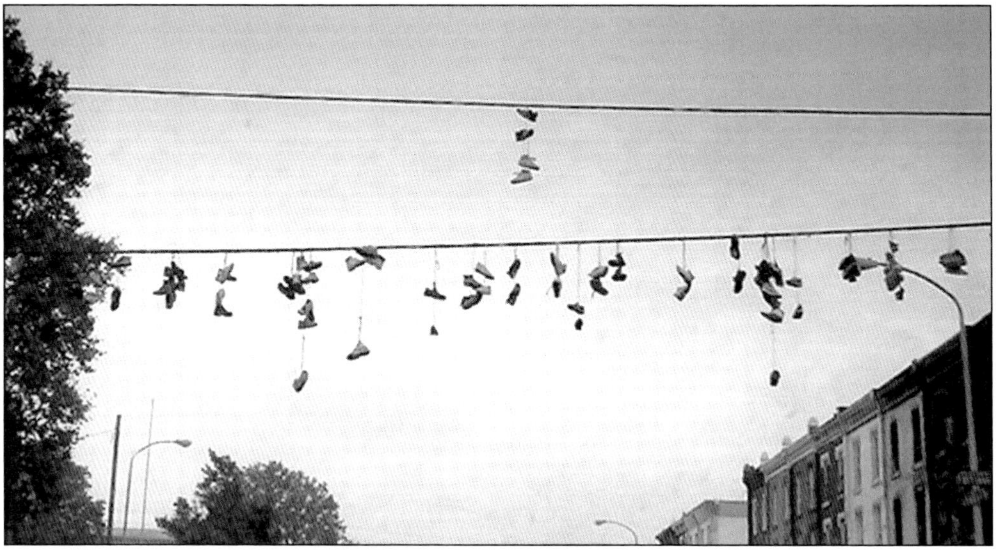

The Chuck Taylor Converse was the sneaker of choice for every boy in the River Wards in the late 1950s and early 1960s. For $4.98 a pair, "Chucks" in black or white, high-top or low, could be purchased at Uncle Miltie's or Dennery's Sporting Goods on Kensington Avenue. When money was tight, "bobos," a far less-popular shoe, would have to do for about half the price of the Chucks. Whatever your choice of footwear, when you could not put anymore cardboard in them to cover the holes in the sole, your sneakers took their place of honor on the telephone wires.

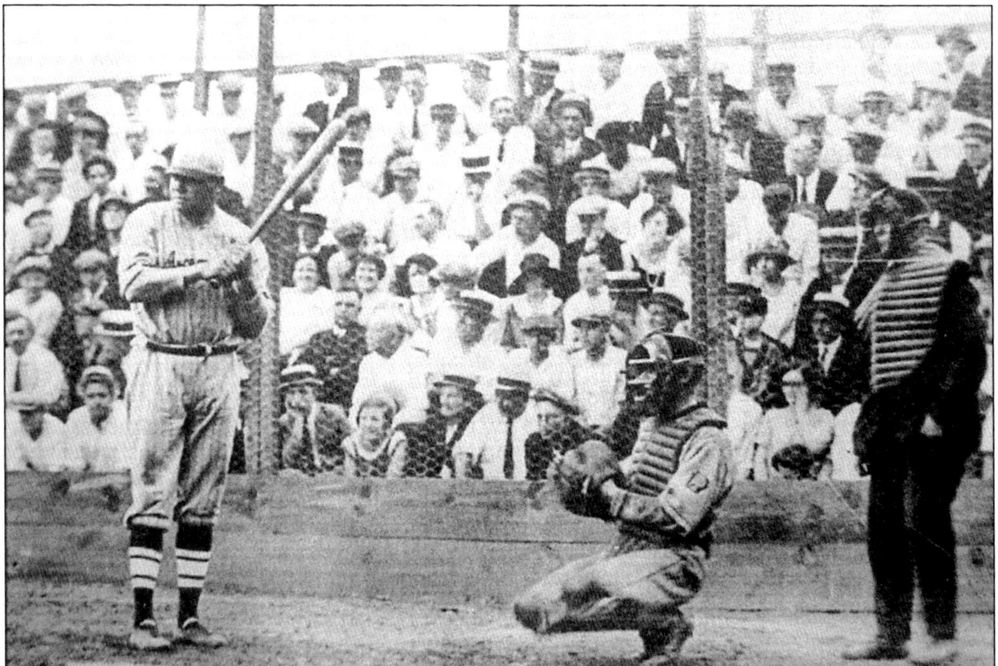

This photograph of Babe Ruth appeared in a commemorative booklet marking the 100th anniversary of Ascension of Our Lord Church in Harrowgate. The photograph carries the caption " 'The Babe' at bat for the Ascension Team."

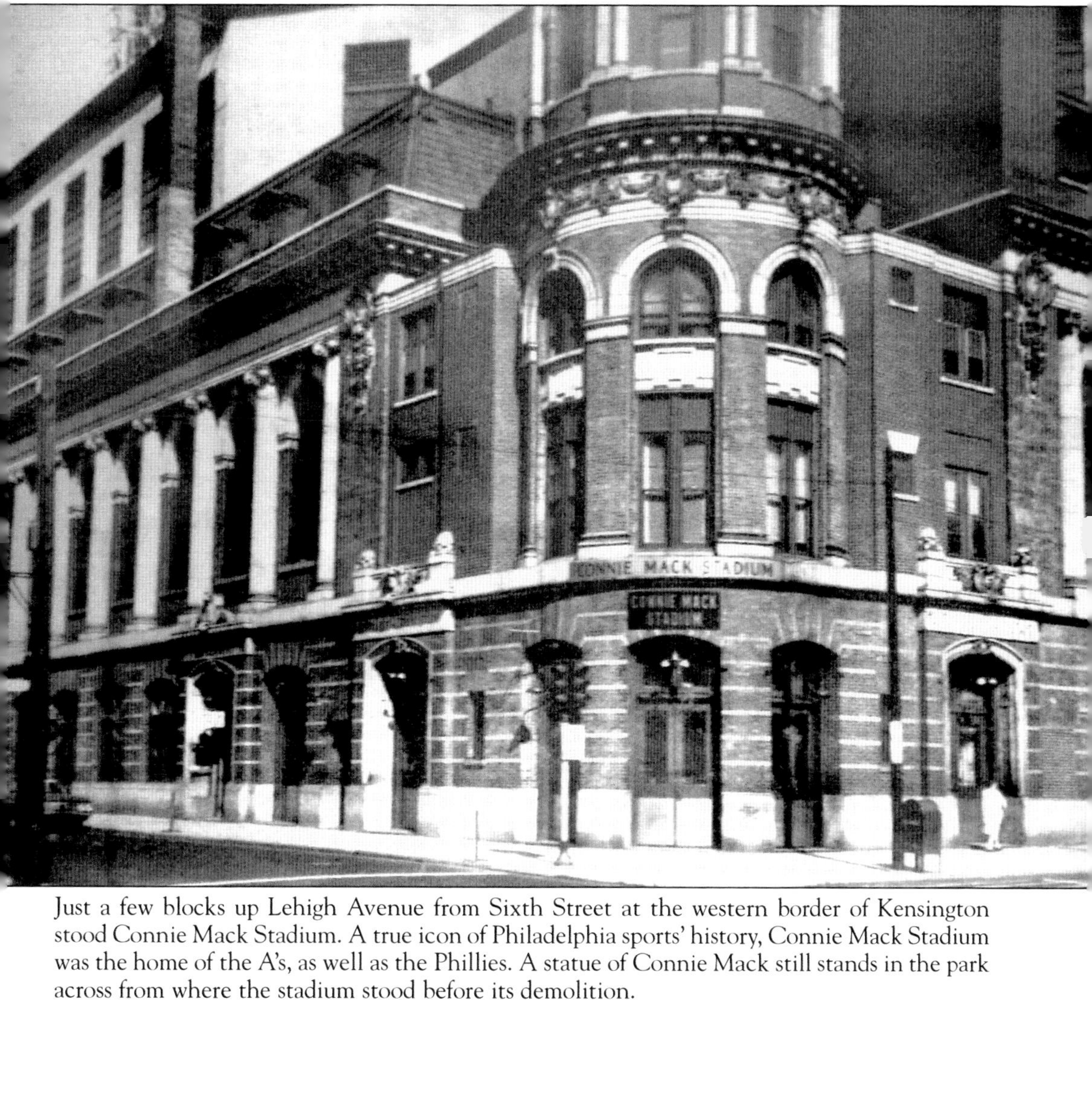

Just a few blocks up Lehigh Avenue from Sixth Street at the western border of Kensington stood Connie Mack Stadium. A true icon of Philadelphia sports' history, Connie Mack Stadium was the home of the A's, as well as the Phillies. A statue of Connie Mack still stands in the park across from where the stadium stood before its demolition.

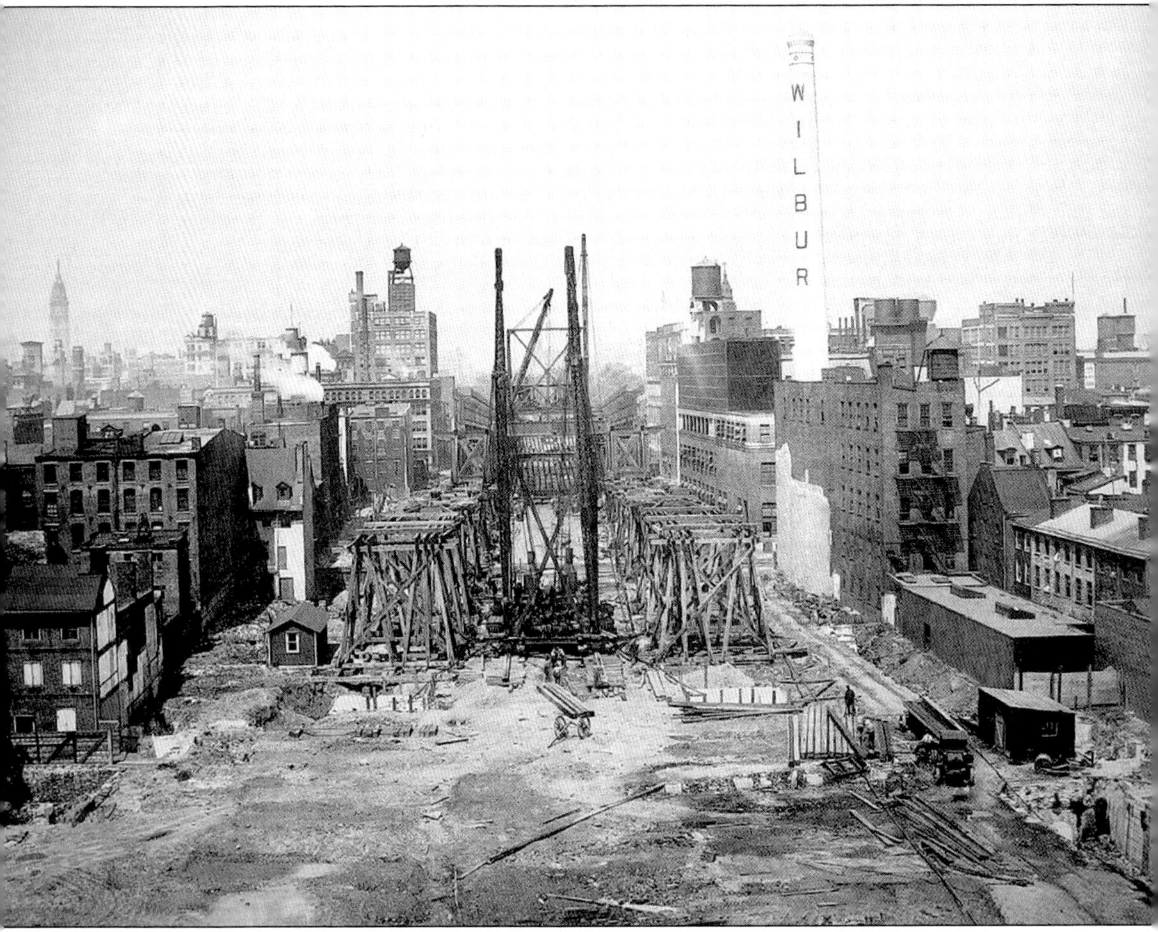

Another structural marvel of the River Wards is the Benjamin Franklin Bridge built in 1925, the longest suspension bridge of its time. It took 1,300 men to build the bridge, and thirteen of those men lost their lives in the course of construction. The bridge continues to be a major crossover, connecting Philadelphia and Camden, New Jersey. This amazing photograph of an early point in the bridge's construction shows Philadelphia's City Hall looming in the background at the left, with William Penn looking down from the clock tower.

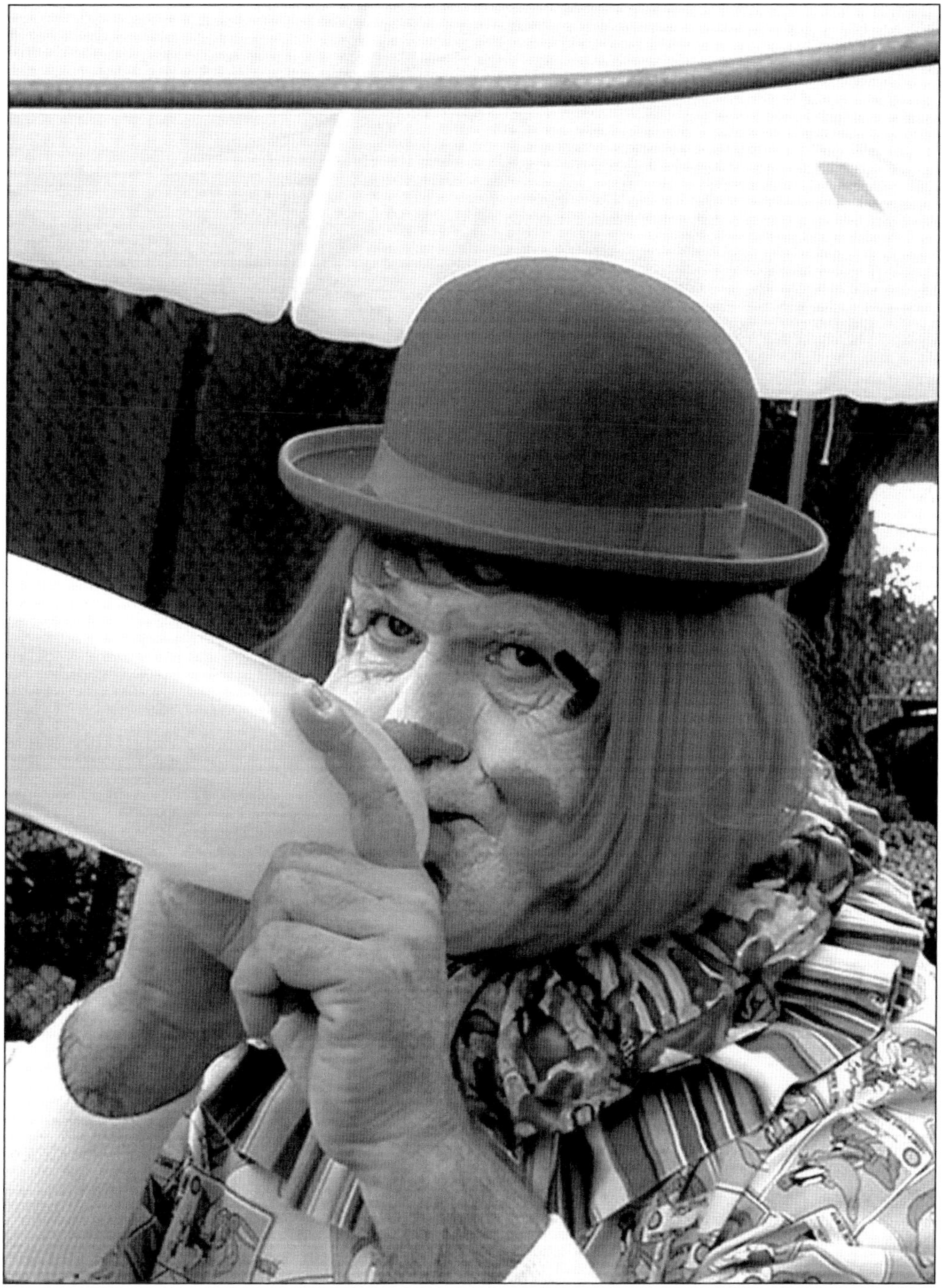

Port Richmond native Charles Grohn is every River Wards child's favorite clown. For over 30 years, Chollie the Clown has entertained the neighborhood residents at block parties, birthdays, church functions, and just about any kind of festive gathering. Chollie's specialty is balloon animals, which he gives out to the crowds. One of Chollie's old tricks was to put a transistor radio inside a balloon. When the balloon was inflated the radio would be playing inside it.

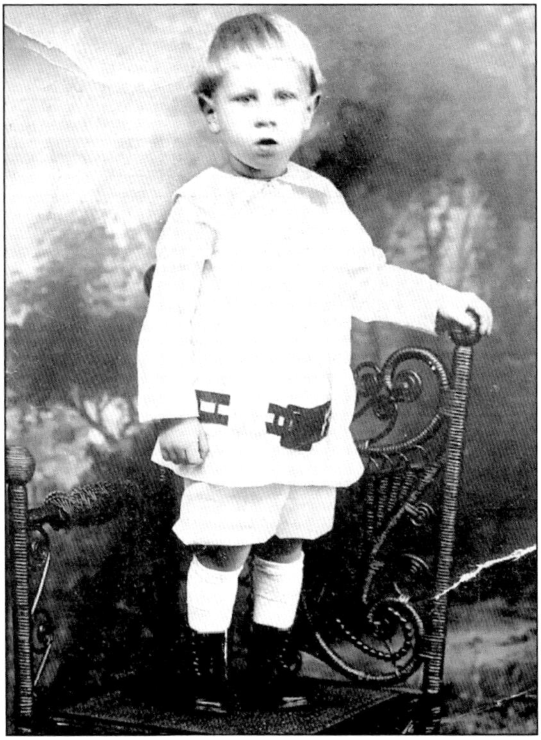

Peter D. Holmes, father of the author, was probably not too happy to be dressed up for this c. 1915 photograph.

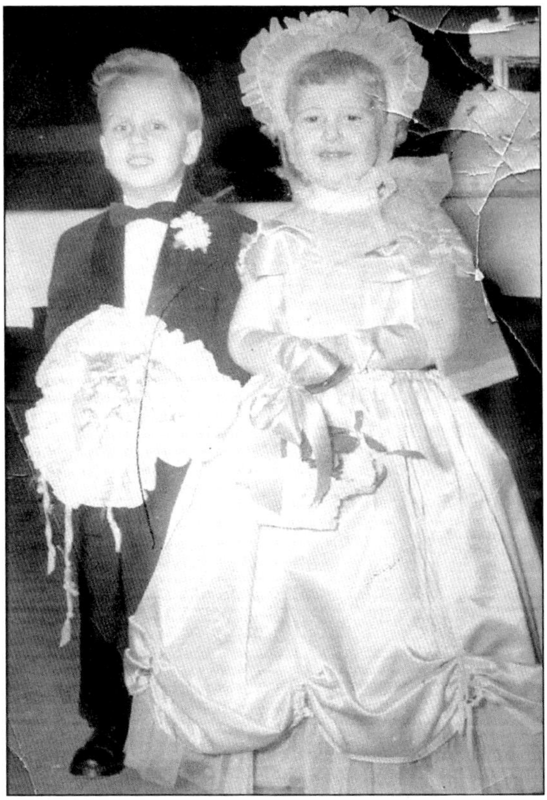

The author shares his father's sentiments as he prepares to take part in a neighbor's wedding over 40 years later. To add insult to injury, he had to walk down the aisle with a girl—Stella Street neighbor Gail Dirsch.